ATTACK OF THE KILLER FACTS!

1,001 TERRIFYING TRUTHS

ABOUT LITTLE GREEN MEN, GOVERNMENT MIND-CONTROL, FLESH-EATING BACTERIA, AND GOAT-SUCKING VAMPIRES

ERIC GRZYMKOWSKI

Aadamsmedia
Avon, Massachusetts

D0668502

Published by
Adams Media, a division of F+W Media, Inc.
57 Littlefield Street, Avon, MA 02322. U.S.A.
www.adamsmedia.com

ISBN 10: 1-4405-1196-9
ISBN 13: 978-1-4405-1196-7
eISBN 10: 1-4405-2539-0
eISBN 13: 978-1-4405-2539-1

Printed in the United States of America.

10   9   8   7   6   5   4   3   2   1

Library of Congress Cataloging-in-Publication Data
is available from the publisher.

This publication is designed to provide accurate and authoritative information with regard to
the subject matter covered. It is sold with the understanding that the publisher is not engaged
in rendering legal, accounting, or other professional advice. If legal advice or other expert
assistance is required, the services of a competent professional person should be sought.

—From a *Declaration of Principles* jointly adopted by a Committee of the
American Bar Association and a Committee of Publishers and Associations

Many of the designations used by manufacturers and sellers to distinguish their product are
claimed as trademarks. Where those designations appear in this book and Adams Media was
aware of a trademark claim, the designations have been printed with initial capital letters.

Certain sections of this book deal with activities and devices that would be in violation of various federal, state, and local laws if actually carried out or constructed. We do not advocate the
breaking of any law. This information is for entertainment purposes only. We recommend
that you contact your local law enforcement officials before undertaking any project based
upon any information obtained from this book. We are not responsible for, nor do we assume
any liability for, damages resulting from the use of any information in this book.

Interior illustrations:
Line art © Clipart.com; Silhouettes © Neubau Welt; Pg. 87 prince istockphoto/art12321;
Pg. 101 Lung istockphoto/linearcurves; Pg. 112 poop istockphoto/simonox; Pg. 103, 115
zombie istockphoto/fajean; Pg. 116 sheep istockphoto/bubaone; Pg. 127 robot istockphoto/
Aaltazar; Pg. 129 pills istockphoto/tokhiti; Pg. 159 spaghetti monster istockphoto/PowerChild;
Pg. 184 sea turtle istockphoto/hypergon; Pg. 194 ship istockphoto/filo.

This book is available at quantity discounts for bulk purchases.
For information, please call 1-800-289-0963.

CONTENTS

INTRODUCTION

If you are one of the enlightened few who has partied with a bearded lady, spotted the chupacabras, or been abducted by aliens, then you already know that incredibly freaky things are happening all around us. Unfortunately, not everyone can be so lucky.

The rest of us are skeptical. We need cold, hard evidence that Never Never Land is a real place (it is), that the University of Tennessee keeps a garden of decomposing bodies (they do), or that Bigfoot vacations on Mars (he might). There's nothing wrong with skepticism, but the world of the weird is so saturated with misinformation and wild speculation that sorting fact from fiction is a monumental task, one that no sane individual would ever undertake.

But sanity is overrated, so I dove headfirst into the underground world of ghosts, aliens, wild men, circus freaks, monsters, dangerous animals, serial killers, and microscopic angels of death and filtered out the wild fallacies so you don't have to. Instead of hearsay and unconfirmed myths, you can rest assured that all 1,001 facts contained in these pages are 100 percent probably true. Maybe.

But once I'd dipped my toes into the paranormal waters, I discovered one undeniable fact about the world of the oddball. It can be scary at times, but above all else, it is freaking hilarious. At various times in history all of the following have happened: a guy heated a lava lamp on his stove to see what would happen and it exploded and killed him, women swallowed tapeworms to lose weight, a guy ate an entire airplane, and doctors blew smoke up the rectums of drowning victims to resuscitate them.

Each fact was more ludicrous than the one before it, and I found myself thinking about the levels of idiocy and general creepiness exhibited by those around us. I wanted to weigh in on the true nature of the Loch Ness Monster or the possibility that aliens disguise themselves as Men in Black and terrorize humanity. So I did just that—more than 1,000 times.

Be forewarned, there are plenty of facts in here that might shock or offend. And the commentary will no doubt shock and offend. Like my assertion that it is okay to eat sausage made out of humans, as long as it is cheap. It is perfectly acceptable to get offended while you comb through these pages, but keep in mind that it's all in good fun. And be thankful that it wasn't you who thought of it.

And if you end up laughing out loud at the truly deplorable suggestions and comments throughout the book, go for it. Nobody's watching. In all likelihood you are perfectly safe, sitting on the commode with nobody around to judge or reprimand you. Don't like what I've written? Bring a Sharpie into the bathroom and add your own. It's your book now, so do what you want with it. But please, above all else, enjoy it.

MICROSCOPIC MAYHEM

GERMS, BACTERIA, AND MICROSCOPIC ORGANISMS SURE TO RUIN YOUR DAY

FACT ATTACK: Nuclear attack wipes out humanity, bacteria inherit earth! The *Deinococcus radiodurans* bacterium can survive a 15,000, gray dose of radiation. Ten grays is enough to kill a human, and 1,000 enough to kill a cockroach. *The Guinness Book of World Records* lists it as the world's toughest bacterium. *But think, if you swallowed a million of them you'd be invincible!*

❯ "Extremophiles: World's Weirdest Life," Live Science, *www.livescience.com.*

FACT ATTACK: Scientists discover world's laziest bacteria! The *Thermococcus* bacteria can survive on less energy than scientists once assumed necessary to sustain life. *They also thought a man could not live on Hot Pockets and Red Bull alone. They were wrong.*

❯ "Extremophiles: World's Weirdest Life," Live Science, *www.livescience.com.*

FACT ATTACK: Millions taken down by malaria! Approximately 300 million people around the world are affected by malaria. Every year between 1 and 1.5 million individuals die from the disease. *But they are mostly the weak ones.*

❯ "Malaria," microbiology bytes.com, *www.micro biologybytes.com.*

FACT ATTACK: Beware female skeeters that suck blood! Only female mosquitoes can transmit malaria to humans, as the males feed on plant liquid instead of human blood. *Best to swat indiscriminately, just to be safe.*

❯ "Malaria," microbiology bytes.com, *www.micro biologybytes.com.*

FACT ATTACK: **Little germ factories out to make you sick!** The flu begins to be contagious about one day before the patient exhibits symptoms and continues to be contagious for five to seven days in adults. For children the contagious period can last up to two weeks. *Which is why you should never hug a child.*

❯ Julia Layton, "Are Colds and the Flu Most Contagious Before or After You Start Showing Symptoms?" Howstuff works.*com*, *http://health .howstuffworks.com.*

FACT ATTACK: **Cannibalism causes world's rarest disease!** The rarest disease in the world only affects a tribe of cannibals in New Guinea. It is called Kuru, or laughing sickness, and scientists believe they contract it by eating contaminated human brains. *But that's the best part!*

❯ Sanjeev Garg, *501 Astonishing Facts* (Pustak Mahal, 2010).

FACT ATTACK: **Deadly virus kills millions!** Human immunodeficiency virus (HIV), a disease that attacks the immune system, has killed more than 26 million people since 1981. *We can joke about it now though.* South Park *said so.*

❯ "Factsheets: CDC HIV/AIDS," Centers for Disease Control and Prevention, *www.cdc.gov.*

❯ "Global HIV/AIDS Estimates, End of 2008," Avert, *www.avert.org.*

FACT ATTACK: **AIDS: the silent killer!** One in five individuals living with HIV are unaware they are infected. *At least the other deadly diseases have the courtesy to let you know they intend to end your life.*

❯ "Factsheets: CDC HIV/AIDS," Centers for Disease Control and Prevention, *www.cdc.gov.*

FACT ATTACK: It's raining bacteria! Scientists believe that some species of bacteria that reside in clouds evolved the ability to induce rain showers to spread themselves over the earth. *The bacterial invasion has already begun.*

> Christine Dell'Amore, "Rain-making Bacteria Ride Clouds to 'Colonize' Earth?" National Geographic News, January 12, 2009, *http://news.national geographic.com.*

FACT ATTACK: **Parasites cheaper than salon dye job!** An infestation of hookworms can cause the hair of the host to change color. The host's fingernails may also change shape or even cave in. *At least you know what to look out for now.*

> Eric Elfman, *Almanac of the Gross, Disgusting, & Totally Repulsive: A Compendium of Fulsome Facts* (RGA Publishing Group, Inc., 1994), 22.

FACT ATTACK: Poop holds hundreds of eggs! During a hookworm infestation, a single gram of human feces can contain as many as 400 eggs. *My condolences to the guy who had to measure.*

> Eric Elfman, *Almanac of the Gross, Disgusting, & Totally Repulsive: A Compendium of Fulsome Facts* (RGA Publishing Group, Inc., 1994), 22.

FACT ATTACK: **Warts are tough to avoid!**

More than 100 different viruses cause warts. *You keep those suckers forever too. Like luggage.*

❯ The Sanders Family, *Gross News: Gross (but Clean) Stories from Around the World* (Andrews McMeel Publishing, 2006).

FACT ATTACK: **Ladies' rooms more vile than men's rooms!** Germs that can make you ill are twice as common in the women's room as the men's. *Your dirty little secret is out, ladies.*

❯ The Sanders Family, *Gross News: Gross (but Clean) Stories from Around the World* (Andrews McMeel Publishing, 2006).

FACT ATTACK: **Beware projectile vomit!** If an individual suffering from food poisoning vomits in your immediate vicinity, it is possible to inhale the now airborne bacteria and get sick yourself. *So no, I won't hold your hair back.*

❯ The Sanders Family, *Gross News: Gross (but Clean) Stories from Around the World* (Andrews McMeel Publishing, 2006).

FACT ATTACK: **Yellowstone hot springs a virtual petri dish!** Scientists have found members of the *Aquifex* genus of bacteria living in the hot springs of Yellowstone National Park which reach temperatures up to 205 degrees Fahrenheit. *Not so much "living" as "not dying."*

❯ "Extremophiles: World's Weirdest Life," Live Science, *www.livescience.com.*

FACT ATTACK: **Bacteria survive vacuum of space!**

Streptococcus mitis, a bacterium that infects the nose and throat, hitched a ride on the *Surveyor* 3 probe in 1966. The bacteria were still alive when *Apollo* 12 astronauts retrieved the probe's camera two and a half years later. *We have met the enemy, and we are sorely outmatched.*

❯ Jason Stahl, "20 Things You Didn't Know About . . . Aliens," *Discover* magazine, January 2007, *www.discovermagazine .com.*

FACT ATTACK: **Cats cause birth defects!** Many felines

carry *Toxoplasma gondii,* a parasite that causes birth defects and miscarriages in humans. For this reason, doctors generally advise expectant mothers to steer clear of felines. *If anyone can think of a credible argument against rounding up all the world's cats and throwing them into a volcano, I'm all ears.*

❯ Anahad O'Connor, *Never Shower in a Thunderstorm: Surprising Facts and Misleading Myths About Our Health and the World We Live In* (Times Books, 2007).

FACT ATTACK: **Bacteria in the bathroom will find a toothbrush!** When you flush the toilet, microscopic

droplets of water laden with bacteria can float into the air. They can land on anything in the immediate vicinity, including your toothbrush. *Which would explain why my razor smells like poop.*

❯ Anahad O'Connor, *Never Shower in a Thunderstorm: Surprising Facts and Misleading Myths About Our Health and the World We Live In* (Times Books, 2007).

FACT ATTACK: **Giant lizard not as unhygienic as we thought!** Scientists once believed that the mouth

of the Komodo dragon was so infested with bacteria that a single bite would cause blood poisoning in a matter of days. They now know that the lizard actually injects a deadly venom with its bite that ultimately kills its victim. *Summary: Komodo dragons, still terrifying, but for a different reason.*

❯ Carolyn Barry, "Komodo Dragons Kill with Venom, Researchers Find," National Geographic News, May 18, 2009, *http://news.national geographic.com.*

FACT ATTACK: **Bones have a seven-year expiration date!** Every seven years, the cells in your skeletal system completely replace themselves. *If you break them, they grow back stronger. Try it.*

❯ Barbara Seuling, *Your Skin Weighs More Than Your Brain: and Other Freaky Facts About Your Skin, Skeleton, and Other Body Parts* (Picture Window Books, 2007).

FACT ATTACK: **Most deadly substance on earth discovered!** Botulinum, the virus that causes botulism, is the most dangerous substance known to man. With less than 1/10,000th of a milligram proving fatal to humans, it is 6 million times more deadly than rattlesnake venom. *Does how deadly something is really matter? Example: Is falling out of a plane onto a bed of spikes more deadly than having your head chopped off?*

❯ Carole Marsh, *The Official Guide to Germs* (Gallopade International, 2003).

FACT ATTACK: **Surgeons routinely inject patients with deadly virus!** Plastic surgeons inject a form of botulinum when performing Botox surgery to eliminate wrinkles. There are some risks, but the procedure is rarely life threatening. *Except when you go in a couple hundred times.*

❯ Carole Marsh, *The Official Guide to Germs* (Gallopade International, 2003).

FACT ATTACK: **Tuberculosis back from the dead!**
With the discovery of drugs to treat tuberculosis in the 1940s, cases of the disease dropped dramatically. Due to increases in population and the rise of HIV—which weakens the immune system—cases are back on the rise. Today, about 8 million new cases of tuberculosis occur every year. *HIV: the disease that keeps on taking.*

> "Tuberculosis," Directors of Health Promotion and Education, *www.dhpe.org.*

FACT ATTACK: **Skanky college kids reduce visits to health center!** Psychologists from Wilkes University in Pennsylvania discovered that college students who had sexual intercourse once a week, but not more than that, were better able to fight off colds and flu. *Not worth it to skip round two.*

> Carole Marsh, *The Official Guide to Germs* (Gallopade International, 2003).

FACT ATTACK: **Worm longer than a six-story building!** The largest recorded tapeworm was more than sixty feet long. *The host must have been more worm than human by that point.*

> "Parasites: 10 Frightening Facts," UKTV.co, *www.uktv.co.uk.*

FACT ATTACK: **Indestructible parasite survives outside of host!** The parasite that causes Giardiasis has a protective outer shell that allows it to survive outside of a host for months. *Great, where am I supposed to find a microscopic shell cracker?*

> "Parasite Quick Facts," Discovery, *Monster Inside Me.* *http://press.discovery.com/ekits/monsters-inside-me.*

FACT ATTACK: Government sniffs out bio-terrorism!
In 2003, the U.S. government installed high-tech sensors in major cities to detect the outbreak of smallpox, anthrax, and other deadly diseases in the event of a biological terrorist attack. The CDC also monitors visits to doctors' offices and emergency rooms searching for signs of an epidemic. *And now the terrorists know that. Assuming they read bathroom books.*

❯ Carole Marsh, *The Official Guide to Germs* (Gallopade International, 2003).

FACT ATTACK: Parasites love men! Men are twice as likely to die from a parasite-induced illness than women. *Ya, but we still get paid more.*

❯ "Parasites: 10 Frightening Facts," UKTV.co, *www.uktv.co.uk.*

FACT ATTACK: Anthrax deadlier than bubonic plague! NATO keeps a list of the top thirty-one infectious agents terrorists might use as biological weapons. The top four are anthrax, smallpox, bubonic plague, and botulism. *Somebody got paid to inform NATO that anthrax and smallpox are dangerous.*

❯ Carole Marsh, *The Official Guide to Germs* (Gallopade International, 2003).

FACT ATTACK: Global warming could unleash smallpox! Although the parasites that cause smallpox were eliminated from the wild through a worldwide vaccination effort, some still lie dormant in the ice of Greenland. Many scientists worry they could be released by global warming. *One vaccine, please.*

❯ "Parasites: 10 Frightening Facts," UKTV.co, *www.uktv.co.uk.*

FACT ATTACK: Morning sickness good for mommy and baby! Some scientists speculate that morning sickness evolved as a way to protect mother and child from parasites. *Or as punishment for listening to that snake in the Garden of Eden.*

> "Parasites: 10 Frightening Facts," UKTV.co, *www.uktv.co.uk*.

FACT ATTACK: OCD keeps you well! People who wash their hands seven times a day are 75 percent less likely to catch a cold. *People who don't are 100 percent more likely to run the faucet and pretend to wash their hands to avoid public ridicule.*

> "Germ Warfare: How to Protect Yourself," *The Today Show*, January 2, 2008.

FACT ATTACK: Bacteria makes you flex yourself to death! *Clostridium tetani*, the bacteria that causes tetanus, resides in soil and infiltrates the body through open wounds. The bacteria releases a neurotoxin that causes spasms so violent they can tear muscles and split bones. *Still afraid of needles?*

> Joy Masoff, *Oh Yuck! The Encyclopedia of Everything Nasty* (Workman Publishing Company, January 2000).

FACT ATTACK: Parasitic worm number-one cause of grasshopper suicide! The horsehair worm is a microscopic organism that invades the bodies of grasshoppers and steals their nourishment. Once it matures, it takes over the grasshopper's mind, compelling it to jump into a body of water so the fully-developed worm can escape and reproduce. *Thankfully it has an extremely shortsighted view of its mind-control powers.*

> Matthew Hayden, "The 7 Most Horrifying Parasites on the Planet," Cracked.com, March 30, 2009, *www.cracked.com*.

FACT ATTACK: Plague wipes out most of Europe! The bubonic plague is considered one of the most deadly diseases known to man. Researchers estimate the total death toll at around 75 million individuals, with anywhere from one- to two-thirds of Europeans succumbing to the epidemic in the 1300s. *Suddenly, polio's not looking so bad.*

❯ "Top 10 Worst Diseases," Listverse.com, November 15, 2007, *www.listverse.com.*

FACT ATTACK: World's worst disease still creeping around! Most people associate the bubonic plague with the Middle Ages, but the disease still infects people today. Thirty-one individuals contracted the disease during an outbreak in Peru in 2010. *We may not have eradicated bubonic plague, but at least grandpa can take a pill and get an erection. Way to go, doctors.*

❯ AP, "Peru Bubonic Plague Outbreak Infects 31," CBS News, August 3, 2010, *www.cbsnews.com.*

FACT ATTACK: Smallpox completely eliminated from earth (almost)! Janet Parker, a medical photographer in Britain, is believed to be the last smallpox fatality in the modern world. She died in 1978 after a researcher at her laboratory accidentally released some of the virus into the air ten months after the disease was eradicated in the wild. *"And here it is folks, the very last smallpox speci . . . oops."*

❯ Colette Flight, "Smallpox: Eradicating the Scourge," BBC, November 5, 2009, *www.bbc.co.uk.*

FACT ATTACK: Science 1; Nature 5346! Smallpox is the only infectious disease affecting humans to have been completely eradicated from the wild. *<sarcasm>Good thing we still keep stockpiles of that stuff in labs. </sarcasm>*

❯ "Top 10 Worst Diseases," Listverse.*com*, November 15, 2007, *www.listverse.com.*

FACT ATTACK: Cattle-killing virus bites the dust! In 2010, scientists confirmed that they had completely eliminated rinderpest, a disease that affects cattle, from the wild. When the disease arrived in Africa at the end of the nineteenth century it killed off between 80 and 90 percent of cattle on the continent. *Suck it, smallpox.*

❯ Pallab Ghosh, "Rinderpest Virus Has Been Wiped Out, Scientists Say," BBC, October 14, 2010, *www.bbc.co.uk.*

FACT ATTACK: Deadly disease kills in hours! In severe cases, cholera is one of the most rapidly fatal illnesses known to man. After the onset of symptoms, a healthy person can become hypotensive within an hour, resulting in death within three hours if left untreated. *As a side note, it's hard to ford the river and shoot buffalo by yourself when your cousin dies of it on the Oregon Trail.*

❯ "Top 10 Worst Diseases," Listverse.*com*, November 15, 2007, *www.listverse.com.*

FACT ATTACK: Water keeps rabid animals at bay!
Both humans and animals suffering from rabies
are often terrified by the sight of water. Scientists
believe this is related to the excruciating pain experienced by sufferers when consuming liquids. *I finally
have an excuse to kill my roommate's cat. Clearly she's rabid.*

> "Rabies," Health Encyclope-
dia, *www.healthscout.com.*

FACT ATTACK: Rabies, deadly but rare! In
2008, there were only two reported cases
of human rabies infections. *Since the only
"cure" is execution, it's understandable why so few
people reported it.*

> Ker Than, "Zombie Virus"
Possible via Rabies-Flu Hybrid?"
National Geographic News,
October 27, 2010, *http://news
.nationalgeographic.com.*

FACT ATTACK: # Your mouth is a cesspool!

There are about 1 billion bacteria in the human mouth.

And to them, you are a god!

> National Geographic, *Weird But True: 300 Outrageous Facts* (National Geographic Children's Books, 2009).

**FACT ATTACK: Public drinking water not fit for
consumption!** In 2010, the *Toronto Star* newspaper
conducted a test of twenty public fountains and
free-standing coolers around the city to determine
bacteria levels. The analysis revealed that half the
samples contained more than 300 colony-forming
units per milliliter. *Which we must assume is a lot.*

> Diana Zlomislic, "*Investiga-
tion Finds Filthy Spouts on
Public Drinking Fountains,*" The
Toronto Star, August 28, 2010.
www.thestar.com.

FACT ATTACK: Fountain contains more bacteria than dog dish! Of the water samples tested by the *Star*, the cleanest resided outside of a local coffee shop— inside a dog bowl. *Solution: Let your dog use the fountain first.*

❭ Diana Zlomislic, "*Investigation Finds Filthy Spouts on Public Drinking Fountains,*" *The Toronto Star*, August 28, 2010. *www.thestar.com.*

FACT ATTACK: **Earth weighed down by microbes!** Microbes account for about 60 percent of the earth's biomass. *Let's hope a leader never arises.*

❭ "Fun Facts about Microbes," U.S. Department of Energy. *http://microbialgenomics.energy.gov.*

FACT ATTACK: So many microbes, so little time! Scientists have classified less than half a percent of the estimated 2 to 3 billion microbial species. *But by the year 2215 they should be all set.*

❭ "Fun Facts about Microbes," U.S. Department of Energy. *http://microbialgenomics .energy.gov.*

FACT ATTACK: Bacteria can be good for you! Scientists recently discovered that the bacteria found in yogurt could help fight tooth decay by preventing harmful bacteria from attaching to teeth. They plan to incorporate the helpful strain into gum and toothpaste. *Good, because I'll be damned if I'm eating yogurt.*

❭ "Bacteria Added to Gum, Toothpaste, and Deodorant," Live Science, August 21, 2006, *www.livescience.com.*

FACT ATTACK: **Oil-eating bacteria save Gulf Coast!**

Following the Deepwater Horizon oil spill in the spring of 2010, blooms of oil-eating bacteria were found in huge concentrations around the area of the leak. Within a few months of the spill, the microbes had removed as much as 16 percent of the 205.8 million gallons of oil from the gulf. *Nature really needs to stop bailing us out.*

❭ Lea Winerman, "Almost 75% of Oil in Gulf Now Accounted For, Government Says," PBS, August 4, 2010. *www.pbs.org.*

❭ Lea Winerman, "Study: Oil-Eating Microbes Plentiful in Gulf Oil Spill," PBS, August 24, 2010. *www.pbs.org.*

FACT ATTACK: **Majority of germs harmless!**

Only 1 to 2 percent of the 60,000 known germs are harmful to healthy humans with normal immune systems. *Tell that to the Tree Man.*

❭ Joseph Brownstein and Radha Chitale, "10 Germy Surfaces You Touch Every Day," ABC News, September 5, 2008. *http://abcnews.go.com/health.*

FACT ATTACK: **Superbug overcomes antibiotics!**

Methicillin-resistant *Staphylococcus aureus* (MRSA) is a superbug resistant to many forms of antibiotics. MRSA can cause vomiting, internal bleeding, high fever, and can eventually lead to complete organ failure. *How many of your organs were you using anyway?*

❭ Jessica Snyder Sachs, "The Superbugs Are Here," Prevention.com. *www.prevention.com.*

❭ "The Killer in the Locker Room," *Men's Health. www.menshealth.com.*

❭ Victor Epstein, "Texas Football Succumbs to Virulent Staph Infection From Turf," Bloomberg.com, December 21, 2007. *www.bloomberg.com.*

FACT ATTACK: Superbug attacks athletes! One study showed that football players were sixteen times more likely to contract a MRSA infection than the average person. No one is certain why athletes are more at risk. *Clearly the nerds are up to something.*

> "The Killer in the Locker Room," *Mens' Health.* www.menshealth.com.

FACT ATTACK: Cave formations actually piles of poop! In 2009 scientists discovered that colorful cave formations found in Hawaii once believed to be mineral deposits were actually mounds of excrement produced by microbes found inside the cave. *The scientific equivalent of discovering Santa is actually your mom and dad.*

> Richard A. Lovett, "Lava Cave Minerals Actually Microbe Poop," National Geographic News, November 20, 2009. *http://news.national geographic.com.*

FACT ATTACK: Bacteria invade stomach, crave chocolate! A 2007 study found that cravings for chocolate could be linked to different bacterial colonies living in the stomachs of certain individuals. Scientists took blood and urine samples of eleven men who never ate chocolate and compared them to those of daily chocolate eaters. Levels of various substances different in the two groups suggested the men contained different types of bacteria in their stomachs, which could be causing the cravings. *My stomach microbes crave Guinness and buffalo wings.*

> Seth Borenstein, "Urge for Chocolate Could Be Gut Feeling," Associated Press, October 12, 2007. *www.usatoday.com.*

FACT ATTACK: Worms invading your ass! Nearly all humans experience pinworms, a parasite that causes itching around the anus, at some point in their lives. To determine if you have an infestation, have a partner gently touch around your anus with tape while you sleep, when the worms are most active. They will stick to the tape and should be visible. *Some things are better left unconfirmed.*

> "Even More Gross Facts You May Have Never Wanted to Know," Associated Content, June 11, 2007, *www.associatedcontent.com.*

FACT ATTACK: Doctors working while sick! A study appearing in the *Journal of the American Medical Association* found that more than half of doctors surveyed admitted to coming into work while sick. More than 30 percent claimed to have done so more than once in the previous year. *Ever see a doctor smoking? Now that shit's confusing.*

❯ Associated Press, "Working While Sick? Study Finds Even Doctors Do It," NPR, September 14, 2010. *www.npr.org.*

FACT ATTACK: Picnic tables crawling with germs! In general, a picnic table contains more germs than a Porta-Potty. *But only if the Porta-Potty has never been used.*

❯ Jeanie Lerche Davis, "Germs: They're Everywhere," WebMD, June 23, 2004, *www.webmd.com.*

FACT ATTACK: **Keep your hands to yourself!** Seventeen percent of Americans disinfect after shaking hands. *The rest of us aren't crazy.*

❯ Jeanie Lerche Davis," Germs: They're Everywhere," WebMD, June 23, 2004, *www.webmd.com.*

FACT ATTACK: Just let it ring! In the office, phone receivers harbor more germs and bacteria than any other surface. *People still use phones at work?*

❯ Jeanie Lerche Davis, "Germs: They're Everywhere," WebMD, June 23, 2004, *www.webmd.com.*

FACT ATTACK: Your body has more bacteria than cells! The average human's digestive system contains ten times more bacteria than there are cells in the entire body. This amounts to approximately two pounds of bacteria. *And that's just the average human.*

❯ "Fascinating Facts," Microbiology Online. *www.microbiologyonline.org.uk.*

FACT ATTACK: Child donates deadly organs! In late 2009 four individuals who received several organs from a deceased four-year-old boy experienced spasms, seizures, and visual disturbances. The culprit was *Balamuthia mandrillaris*, a rare species of amoeba that killed the little boy and passed on through his organs. *If I ever need an organ, please check it for deadly parasites before you shove it in me.*

❯ Maryn Mckenna, "Brain Amoebas. Organ Transplants. Brrr," Wired.com, September 17, 2010. *www.wired.com.*

❯ "*Balamuthia Mandrillaris* Transmitted Through Organ Transplantation," Centers for Disease Control and Prevention, December 14, 2009. *www.cdc.gov.*

FACT ATTACK: Dangerous amoeba delightfully rare! There have been only 200 recorded cases of *Balamuthia mandrillaris* in humans since its discovery in 1990. *If you are one of those 200 people, knowing that fact makes it infinitely worse.*

❯ Maryn Mckenna, "Brain Amoebas. Organ Transplants. Brrr," Wired.com, September 17, 2010. *www.wired.com.*

❯ "*Balamuthia Mandrillaris* Transmitted Through Organ Transplantation," Centers for Disease Control and Prevention, December 14, 2009. *www.cdc.gov.*

FACT ATTACK: Bacteria more deadly in space! The vacuum of space can increase the potency of many deadly bacteria. One study found just eighty-three hours in space was enough to increase the deadliness of salmonella threefold. *Reason 342 to never travel in space.*

❯ Barry E. DiGregorio, "Deadly Microbes from Outer Space," *Discover* magazine, February 1, 2008. *www.discovermagazine.com.*

FACT ATTACK: Weaponized car spews deadly bacteria! If you use tap water instead of windshield washer fluid, you are essentially turning your car into a biological weapon. The warm, stagnant water is an ideal climate for the proliferation of the *Legionella* bacterium, which can cause Legionnaires' disease when inhaled. *Or you could just fill it with anthrax and cut out the middleman.*

❯ Emma Wilkinson, "Windscreen Water Infection Risk," BBC, June 13, 2010. *www.bbc.co.uk.*

FACT ATTACK: Gardens full of bacteria!

One teaspoon of garden soil contains 1 billion bacteria. *Yet my brother made me eat it anyway.*

❯ "Fascinating Facts," Microbiology Online. *www.microbiologyonline.org.uk.*

FACT ATTACK: Windshield wipers of death! One study found that unsanitary windshield wiper water could be responsible for as many as 20 percent of cases of Legionnaires' disease in Britain. *Another study found they were caused by wearing puffy shirts.*

❯ Emma Wilkinson, "Windscreen Water Infection Risk," BBC, June 13, 2010. *www.bbc.co.uk.*

FACT ATTACK: Hookworms cure allergies! In 1976, researcher John Turton infected himself with hookworms to replenish his supply of the parasite for study. To his surprise, his lifelong seasonal allergies disappeared. *Leeches could cure cancer, but that doesn't mean I'm going to use them.*

❯ "Parasite Quick Facts," Discovery, *Monster Inside Me.* http://press.discovery.com/ekits/monsters-inside-me.

FACT ATTACK: Dangerous parasite controls mice's brains! Aside from causing birth defects in humans, the protozoan *Toxoplasma gondii* causes mice to behave contrary to their nature. One study found that the parasite, which breeds in felines, caused a group of mice to cease to avoid areas marked with cat urine; some were even attracted to the soiled areas. *All you Jerry fans out there, don't tell Tom.*

> J. Ascensio, "Invasion of the Body Snatchers: 12 Freaky Facts About Toxoplasmosis," Associated Content, February 24, 2010. *www.associatedcontent.com.*

FACT ATTACK: Parasite turns men into idiots, women into divas! Men suffering from toxoplasmosis, a disease caused by a parasitic protozoan, have lower IQs, shorter attention spans, and are more likely to take risks and break rules. Women on the other hand become friendlier, more attractive, and more adventurous sexually. *Pretty sure this holds true regardless of infection status.*

> J. Ascensio, "Invasion of the Body Snatchers: 12 Freaky Facts About Toxoplasmosis," Associated Content, February 24, 2010. *www.associatedcontent.com.*

FACT ATTACK: Cells attack kissing couples! When you kiss your partner, the white blood cells in your mouths attack one another. *Always looking out for me.*

> "Even More Gross Facts You May Have Never Wanted to Know," Associated Content, June 11, 2007, *www.associatedcontent.com.*

FACT ATTACK: Women swallow parasites to lose weight! Because of their tendency to consume many of the calories and nutrients ingested by their host, some nineteeth century women turned to sanitary parasitic tapeworms as a means to lose weight. *Now we use more normal weight loss methods, like eating twenty pounds of bacon in a single sitting and subsisting solely on maple syrup mixed with cayenne pepper.*

> Shana Dines, "The Sanitized Tapeworm Diet! Urban Legend or Fact?" Associated Content, August 30, 2007. *www.associatedcontent.com.*

EXTREME INSECTS

CREEPY CRAWLY CREATURES THAT STING, BITE, KILL, AND MAIM

FACT ATTACK: Bugs outweigh all of humanity!
Springtails, small insects that live in topsoil, are the most abundant insects on earth. There are around 1.5 billion per acre, and their combined biomass would likely outweigh that of humans. *I'm confident the citizens of Wisconsin would tip the scales in our favor.*

> Russell Ash, *Firefly's World of Facts* (Firefly Books, 2007).

FACT ATTACK: Butterflies go the distance! Scientists have tracked butterflies traveling as far as 3,000 miles. *Which means my butterfly chariot idea isn't as crazy as I thought!*

> Russell Ash, *Firefly's World of Facts* (Firefly Books, 2007).

FACT ATTACK: Ants more dangerous than scorpions!
Pound for pound, the world's most venomous insect is the harvester ant. Twelve tiny stings is enough to kill a five-pound mammal. *In a one-on-one battle, I am about 70 percent positive I could win.*

> Sara Wood and Kara Kovalchik, *The Complete Idiot's Guide to Fun FAQs* (Alpha, 2008).

FACT ATTACK: Queen bees ruthless from birth!
A newborn queen bee immediately kills all of the other hatched and unhatched queens in the hive. *But she feels really bad about it afterwards.*

> Liza Lentini, "20 Things You Didn't Know About . . . Bees," *Discover* magazine, March 2007, www.discovermagazine.com.

FACT ATTACK: Killing ants brings bad luck! In Europe, there is a widely held belief that it is unlucky to destroy an ants' nest located in close proximity to one's front door. *You win this round, minister of ant propaganda.*

> L. Patricia Kite, *Insect Facts and Folklore* (Millbrook Press, 2001).

FACT ATTACK: Instead of rice, wedding guests throw butterflies! Butterfly releases are an increasingly popular event at American weddings. Guests at the wedding receive an envelope containing a butterfly that they rip open as the bride and groom exit the church. The butterflies soar overhead in a group and circle for a short time before flying off. *What a waste of perfectly good butterflies.*

> Kamala Nair, "Starting a Butterfly Farm," CNN Money, July 23, 2001, http://money.cnn.com.

> Bill McLain, *Do Fish Drink Water? Puzzling and Improbable Questions and Answers* (William Morrow and Company, 1999), p. 4.

FACT ATTACK: Silkworms eat like pigs! The silkworm consumes 86,000 times its own weight in fifty-six days. *It's easy when you can accomplish that feat by eating an Oreo.*

> Sanjeev Garg, *501 Astonishing Facts* (Pustak Mahal, 2010).

FACT ATTACK: Fireflies make great jewelry! Women in Cuba and other tropical countries pin fireflies to their gowns and hang them around their necks on chains as decorations. *Because jewelry is infinitely cooler when it can die.*

> Sanjeev Garg, *501 Astonishing Facts* (Pustak Mahal, 2010).

FACT ATTACK: Crickets can predict the weather! If you count the number of cricket chirps in a fifteen second time period and add thirty-seven, it will almost exactly equal the current temperature. *If you place a thermometer outside and look at it, it will exactly equal the current temperature.*

❯ Bill McLain, *Do Fish Drink Water? Puzzling and Improbable Questions and Answers* (William Morrow and Company, 1999), p. 275.

FACT ATTACK: **Tiny insects faster than a rocket!** The rate of acceleration for a jumping flea is fifty times greater than a space shuttle at takeoff. *Excuse me, I need to go propose an idea to NASA.*

❯ Joy Masoff, *Oh Yuck! The Encyclopedia of Everything Nasty* (Workman Publishing Company, 2000).

FACT ATTACK: Queen bees biased toward royalty! Unlike worker bees, the queen can sting multiple times without losing her life in the process. However, she will only use her stinger on another queen. *Rather elitist of her, but good to know I'm safe.*

❯ Judith Freeman Clark and Stephen Long, *Weird Facts To Blow Your Mind* (Price Stern Sloan, 1993), p. 10.

FACT ATTACK: Black widows are deadly floozies! The black widow is so named because of the female's habit of eating her suitors shortly after courtship. She can mate with and consume as many as twenty-five male spiders in a single day. *If women did this, I doubt we'd change our habits much.*

❯ Judith Freeman Clark and Stephen Long, *Weird Facts To Blow Your Mind* (Price Stern Sloan, 1993), p. 2.

FACT ATTACK: Tiny bugs live in your lashes! A relative of the spider, the follicle mite spends its entire life roaming around the base of human eyelashes. *When I am done with this book, I think I will have to remove all of my body hair, brush my teeth 172 times, take a bath in boiling water for twenty minutes, lock myself in a hermetically sealed room, and never come out.*

❯ Eric Elfman, *Almanac of the Gross, Disgusting, & Totally Repulsive: A Compendium of Fulsome Facts*, (RGA Publishing Group Inc., 1994), p. 19.

FACT ATTACK: Moth larvae better than steak! Witchetty grubs are a popular survival food in parts of Australia. Found in the roots of the acacia tree, ten large grubs can provide an adult with an entire day's worth of protein. *And an entire lifetime of flashbacks.*

❯ Richard Platt, *They Ate What?! The Weird History of Food* (Two-Can Publishing, 2006), p. 35.

FACT ATTACK: Fleas can jump forever! A flea can jump 30,000 times in succession without stopping. *So far my record is six before I get winded and have to hobble back to the couch to play Mario Kart.*

❯ Joy Masoff, *Oh Yuck! The Encyclopedia of Everything Nasty* (Workman Publishing Company, 2000).

FACT ATTACK: Swarm of grasshoppers frozen in time! A glacier in the Beartooth Mountains of Montana is home to a two-hundred-year-old frozen swarm of grasshoppers. The insects are so well preserved that bears and birds come to feed on them as the ice melts. *Call me when they discover a treasure trove of frozen Hot Pockets.*

❯ Scott Morris, *The Emperor Who Ate the Bible and More Strange Facts and Useless Information* (Main Street Books, 1990).

FACT ATTACK: Cockroaches à la carte! The record for most cockroaches eaten in a minute belongs to Ken Edwards of England. He downed thirty-six on an episode of the British television show *The Big Breakfast* in 2001. *He must get so many women because of that.*

❯ "10 Grossest World Records," Oddee.com, August 31, 2010, *www.oddee.com*.

FACT ATTACK: Russians eat powdered roaches! Individuals in rural Russia still use powdered cockroach to treat dropsy, swelling caused by the accumulation of excess water. *This is probably one of the less strange practices taking place in rural Russia.*

❯ Marion Copeland, *Cockroach* (Reaktion Books LTD, 2003).

❯ "Definition of Dropsy," Medicine.net, *www.medterms.com*.

FACT ATTACK: Europeans discover cockroach cure-all! In some areas of Europe, bruised, boiled, dried, or fried cockroaches treat everything from earaches and poor vision to ulcers. *Nobody said it works though.*

❯ Marion Copeland, *Cockroach*, (Reaktion Books LTD, 2003).

FACT ATTACK: FDA approves maggot therapy! The FDA has approved the medical use of maggots "for cleaning non-healing necrotic skin and soft tissue wounds, including pressure ulcers, venous stasis ulcers, neuropathic foot ulcers, and non-healing traumatic or post surgical wounds." *I'll take my chances with antibiotics, thanks.*

❯ Ben Harder, "Maggot Therapy: How to Find a Doctor Who Will Prescribe Maggots," US News, March 31, 2009, *www.usnews.com.*

FACT ATTACK: Giant millipede invades prehistory! The largest millipede was the *Scolopendra gigantea*, a Paleozoic arthropod that grew up to nine feet long. *Which is why you should never travel back in time.*

❯ Alan Bellows, *Alien Hand Syndrome and Other Too-Weird-To-Be-True Stories* (Workman Publishing, 2009), p. 89.

FACT ATTACK: Worms not invincible! Contrary to popular belief, if you cut an earthworm in half, two will not grow in its place. The wriggling is due to neural impulses during the death throes. *Instead you'll have one dead worm and –2 karma points.*

❯ "Weird Animals," BBC, June 1, 2002, *www.bbc.co.uk.*

❯ "Earthworm," National Geographic, Animals. *http://animals.nationalgeographic.com.*

FACT ATTACK: Earth overrun by beetle infestation! One out of every five species on earth is a beetle. *Which is why I have a beetle costume hanging in my closet in case of an uprising.*

❯ Joy Masoff, *Oh Yuck! The Encyclopedia of Everything Nasty* (Workman Publishing Company, January 2000).

FACT ATTACK: Museums employ beetle assistants!
Dermestid beetles can strip the skin and meat off a carcass in a matter of hours. Museums frequently use them to clean up skeletons they plan to exhibit. *Or to dispose of visitors who ignore the Do Not Touch signs.*

❯ Joy Masoff, *Oh Yuck! The Encyclopedia of Everything Nasty* (Workman Publishing Company, January 2000).

FACT ATTACK: # Termites fight with farts!

Some termites have discovered a way to weaponize flatulence. When confronted by an attacker, the termites pass gas so violently that their abdomens explode, spewing feces and noxious chemicals at the enemy. *We are not so different, you and I.*

❯ Alan Bellows, *Alien Hand Syndrome and Other Too-Weird-To-Be-True Stories* (Workman Publishing, 2009), p. 89.

FACT ATTACK: Termite royalty just won't die!
A single termite queen can live for up to fifteen years. *Which seems a little unfair to the termite princess, who only lives a few weeks.*

❯ Veronica Starovolt, "Facts about Bugs & Insects," Ehow.*com*, May 21, 2010, *www.ehow.com.*

FACT ATTACK: Flies reproduce like rabbits!
One pair of flies can multiply into 191 quintillion in only five months. *Men, grab your swatters. We have work to do.*

❯ Veronica Starovolt, "Facts about Bugs & Insects," Ehow.com, May 21, 2010, www.ehow.com.

FACT ATTACK: Bees are busy, but don't produce much! In their entire lives, twelve bees will produce but a single teaspoon of honey. *Which makes it taste all the sweeter.*

❯ Kendra Meinert, "More People Discover Benefits of Backyard Beekeeping," Greenbay Press Gazette, September 19, 2010, www.greenbaypress gazette.com.

FACT ATTACK: Jar of honey requires millions of trips! To produce a pound of honey a single bee would need to visit 2 million flowers. *So next time you eat honey, please do it in front of a bee and make him watch. Preferably the one that stung me when I was seven.*

❯ Kendra Meinert, "More People Discover Benefits of Backyard Beekeeping," Greenbay Press Gazette, September 19, 2010, www.greenbaypress gazette.com.

FACT ATTACK: Blood-sucking bug attacks you in your sleep! Despite popular belief, bedbugs, a tiny parasitic insect that feeds off the blood of humans, do not usually hide in mattresses. They prefer to lurk in the bed frame and come out at night when we are in deep sleep. *I hear bedbugs hate peanut butter. So if you have bedbugs, slather yourself with peanut butter before you go to bed. And please take pictures. And send them to FactoidAttack@gmail.com.*

❯ Arun Kristian Das, "Bed Bug Facts and Resources," My Fox New York, March 11, 2009, www.myfoxny.com.

❯ "Preventing and Getting Rid of Bed Bugs Safely," New York City Department of Health and Mental Hygiene, www.nyc.gov.

FACT ATTACK: Bedbugs invade Big Apple! Bedbug infestations reached epic proportions in New York City in 2010, with 6.7 percent of adults claiming to have dealt with them in the past year. The city's 311 helpline fielded nearly 40,000 inquiries regarding bedbugs, a 54 percent increase from 2008. *If you ever get bedbugs, keep it to yourself. Otherwise you will lose all of your friends, your sense of self worth, and your dignity.*

> Javier C. Hernandez, "In the War on Bedbugs, a New Attack Strategy," New York Times, July 28, 2010, *www.nytimes.com.*

FACT ATTACK: Bedbugs bite in threes! Bedbug bites generally appear in rows. This is because the host moves in his or her sleep, causing the bedbug to move to another location before it can begin to feed again. *Don't ever get bedbugs. I can't stress this enough.*

> Javier C. Hernandez, "In the War on Bedbugs, a New Attack Strategy," New York Times, July 28, 2010, *www.nytimes.com.*

FACT ATTACK: Spider captures thirty bugs with one web! The Darwin's bark spider spins the world's largest web. It spans twenty-five meters and can capture up to thirty insects at a time. *Or one small child.*

> Claire McCormack, "World's Largest Spider Web Can Catch 30 Insects at a Time," Time, *http://newsfeed.time.com.*

FACT ATTACK: Giant spiderweb catches birds! The golden silk orb-weaver spider spins a web so strong it can capture a bird. *Yet somehow humans remain the dominant species.*

> Bonnie Malkin, "Giant Spider Eating a Bird Caught On Camera," The Telegraph, October 22, 2008, *www.telegraph.co.uk.*

FACT ATTACK: Spiders actually have spidey sense!
Some species of spider can distinguish the vibrations of dangerous insects caught in their web, such as wasps, from that of their usual prey. They can also determine if a vibration indicates a trapped victim or is merely the result of a falling leaf. *That's because leaves tend not to struggle. Mostly.*

> Tom Harris, "How Spiders Work," Howstuffworks.*com*, *http://animals.howstuff works.com.*

FACT ATTACK: **Spiders eat their webs!**

Once a spider's web becomes damaged and unusable, the spider will consume it in order to recycle the protein and create more silk for a new structure. *Tastes like evolution.*

> Tom Harris, "How Spiders Work," Howstuffworks.*com*, *http://animals.howstuffworks.com.*

FACT ATTACK: Jumping spiders weak in the knees!
The muscles in a jumping spider's legs aren't particularly strong; they actually use hydraulic pressure to spring forward. A powerful muscle in the cephalothorax squeezes fluids from the body into the legs to make them expand. *Cue sound effect from the* Six Million Dollar Man.

> Tom Harris, "How Spiders Work," Howstuffworks.*com*, *http://animals.howstuff works.com.*

FACT ATTACK: **Bug dies before it has its first meal!** The male twisted-wing parasite, an insect similar to a fly, has such a short lifespan that it never bothers to feed. Most don't even have functioning mouths. *Eating is overrated anyway.*

❯ Miss Cellania, "The Weirdest Insects in the World," Neat-orama.com, October 8, 2007, *www.neatorama.com.*

FACT ATTACK: **Wasp feeds its young with zombies!** To obtain a fresh source of food for her developing larvae, the emerald jewel wasp subdues a cockroach with venom that leaves it in a catatonic state, but otherwise healthy. She then leads the zombie cockroach to her burrow, lays an egg on its body, and barricades it inside. When the egg hatches, the larvae bores its way into the cockroach and eats it from the inside out. *Jesus tapdancing christ.*

❯ Matthew Hayden, "The 7 Most Horrifying Parasites on the Planet," Cracked.com, March 30, 2009, *www.cracked.com.*

FACT ATTACK: **Flies have eyes in the back of their heads!** In each compound eye, flies have as many as 4,000 lenses. In some fly species, nearly the entire head is made up of compound eyes. *A fly smeared on the side of a newspaper has zero eyes.*

❯ David Lambert, *Super Little Giant Book of Weird Animal Facts* (Sterling Publishing, 2005).

FACT ATTACK: **Spiderwebs span the globe!** A one-pound ball of cobwebs spread out in a straight line would span the diameter of the earth, twice. *Irrelevant, because you'd never get it off your hands to measure.*

❯ Mitchell Symons, *This Book: . . . of More Perfectly Useless Information* (HarperCollins, 2005).

FACT ATTACK: **Nuclear disaster wipes out humanity, insects inherit earth!** Cockroaches are six to fifteen times more resistant to radiation than humans. However, in the insect world they are fairly frail in that regard. Fruit flies, for example, can survive radiation levels nearly double that of even the hardiest cockroach. *Note to self: Invest in fruit fly safety vests for the bomb shelter.*

❯ Dr. Karl, "Cockroaches and Radiation," ABC Science, February 23, 2006. *www.abc.net.au/ science.*

❯ Sue Anne Zollinger, "Cockroaches V. Radiation: Who Wins?" Indiana Public Media, June 14, 2010. *www.indianapublicmedia.org/ amomentofscience.*

FACT ATTACK: **Insects outnumber humans 1.5 billion to 1!** Renowned entomologist Erik J. van Nieukerken estimates the number of insect species in the world to be apprimately 1,017,018. As for the total number of insects worldwide, that number may be as high as 10 quintillion (or about 1.5 billion insects for every one human). *I, for one, welcome our insect masters.*

❯ "Insect," The World Almanac for Kids. *www.worldalmanac forkids.com.*

FACT ATTACK: **Stick bug survives bird attack, regrows severed leg!** Stick insects can shed limbs to avoid predators and regenerate them later. *An important adaptation when your preferred method of self defense is staying completely still and hoping for the best.*

❯ Debbie Hadley, "10 Cool Facts About Stick Insects," About.*com. www.insects .about.com.*

FACT ATTACK: **Unassuming beetle world's first biological cannon!** The bombardier beetle possesses two glands at the end of its abdomen containing hydroquinone and hydrogen peroxide. When threatened, these two chemicals flood into a chamber where they mix with oxygen and other molecules to produce a chemical reaction that propels the substance at predators in a series of around seventy explosions that are audible to the human ear. The secretion is fatal to many insects and can be painful to humans. *If I can get 1,000 of these, I'm totally taking over the office.*

❯ Ross Piper, *Extraordinary Animals: An Encyclopedia of Curious and Unusual Animals* (Greenwood Publishing Group, 2007).

FACT ATTACK: **Don't kill that bee, it could be grandpa!** In Russia it was sacrilegious to kill a bee. Throughout Europe, many believed the souls of men and women returned to earth as bees. *When a bee stings you, it dies. So really it's their own fault.*

❯ L. Patricia Kite, *Insect Facts and Folklore* (Millbrook Press, 2001).

FACT ATTACK: **Honeybee drones used as sex slaves!** In a honeybee hive, drones do not collect nectar or do any work of any kind. Their sole responsibility is to mate with the queen. *Tough life.*

❯ L. Patricia Kite, *Insect Facts and Folklore* (Millbrook Press, 2001).

FACT ATTACK: **Put down that bagel, you could be eating fly vomit!** A house fly regurgitates every time it lands. *And so do I!*

> "House Flies," University of Rhode Island. *www.uri.edu.*

FACT ATTACK: **Ants used as makeshift sutures!** In India, Africa, Honduras, and other countries where large biting ants are prolific, locals use the jaws of the insects as an alternative method for closing wounds. They take several live ants and hold them to the wound where they bite down. They then separate the bodies from the heads, which locks the jaws in place. *Ants: when needle and thread just isn't badass enough.*

> L. Patricia Kite, *Insect Facts and Folklore* (Millbrook Press, 2001).

FACT ATTACK: **Books covered in bugs!** Book lice live primarily in and around paper, but they are also at home in flour or grain. The small insects don't actually feed on the paper, but instead on mold that grows on books. *Good thing nobody reads books anymore. Except you fine people.*

> "Top 10 Gross Things in Your House," Science Channel. *http://science.discovery.com.*

FACT ATTACK: Book bugs reproduce without mating! Book lice are not harmful to humans, but infestations multiply rapidly as the females of the species can reproduce without mating. *Let's hope female humans never develop this ability.*

> "Top 10 Gross Things in Your House," Science Channel. *http://science.discovery.com.*

FACT ATTACK: Termites are egg-laying machines! A single termite queen can lay as many as 30,000 eggs in a single day. *We should stop wasting our time with chickens.*

> "Top 10 Weird Bug Facts," Science Channel. *http://science.discovery.com.*

FACT ATTACK: Cockroaches continue campaign of indestructibility! A cockroach can survive underwater for fifteen minutes. *Unless you step on it first.*

> National Geographic, *Weird But True: 300 Outrageous Facts* (National Geographic Children's Books, 2009).

FACT ATTACK: Midge larvae tough as nails! Midge larvae can survive for up to three days immersed in liquid nitrogen, which is -321°F. *Newspaper > liquid nitrogen.*

> "Top 10 Weird Bug Facts," Science Channel. *http://science.discovery.com.*

FACT ATTACK: Scorpion mostly harmless!

Only thirty to forty species of scorpions are deadly to humans. *The other 1,960 just hurt like hell.*

> Alexandra Hazlett, "The World's Deadliest Animals," *New York Daily News*, February 24, 2010. *www.nydailynews.com.*

FACT ATTACK: Scorpion survives freezing! There are around 2,000 species of scorpion occupying nearly every environment on the planet. The creature is so hardy, scientists have frozen them solid overnight only to watch them thaw and walk away the following day. *They should have tried a blowtorch instead.*

> Alexandra Hazlett, "The World's Deadliest Animals," *New York Daily News*, February 24, 2010 *www.nydailynews.com.*

FACT ATTACK: Makeup contains bug powder! Cochineal extract, or carmine, is a red dye found in candy and cosmetic products. The dye is made from captured cochineal beetles that feed on red cactus berries. The beetles are dried in the sun and ground up into a powder. Only the females suffer this fate, as the males are born with wings and are far more difficult to catch. *The females actually do have wings. They are just too lazy to use them.*

> Karen Schneider, "Bugs in Your Food," American Council on Science and Health, June 12, 2002. *www.acsh.org.*

FACT ATTACK: Bot flies love humans, hate Vaseline! After a human bot fly egg hatches on its host, the maggot borrows into the skin leaving an itchy red bump. To remove the parasite, apply Vaseline or tape over the affected area and cut off the oxygen supply to the developing maggot. Once it dies, you can easily remove it with tweezers. *Removing dead insect larvae from your skin is never "easy."*

> "Parasite Quick Facts," Discovery, *Monster Inside Me.* http://press.discovery.com/ekits/monsters-inside-me-2/template.cfm?page=parasite-quick-facts.

FACT ATTACK: A lot of bugs goes a short way! It takes 70,000 cochineal beetles to make one pound of cochineal. *So much for my business idea.*

> Karen Schneider, "Bugs in Your Food," American Council on Science and Health, June 12, 2002. *www.acsh.org.*

FACT ATTACK: Cockroach gives birth to live babies!

Unlike most insects that lay their eggs and then leave, the female Madagascar hissing cockroach creates a cocoon-like case inside of her body to carry the eggs. She can give birth to as many as sixty live nymph roaches. *See, they're just like us. Only tiny and gross.*

> "Madagascar Hissing Cockroach," National Geographic, Animals. *http://animals .nationalgeographic.com.*

FACT ATTACK: Spider mistaken for bird poop!

The aptly named bird dropping spider, an arachnid native to Australia, evades predators by masquerading as an unappetizing glob of bird poop. When it senses danger, it remains motionless to complete the illusion. *Actually, if I were a bird, I'd be more freaked out if the poop moved.*

> Jonathan Wojcik, "The 9 Most Mind-blowing Disguises in the Animal Kingdom," Cracked.com, September 21, 2010. *www.cracked.com.*

FACT ATTACK: Flightless fly tricks army ants!

The adult female myrmecophilous (ant-loving) phorid fly does not have wings or legs like a normal fly, and instead looks identical to an army ant larvae. Because of the resemblance, the ants pick her up and care for her as one of their own, feeding her and protecting her from predators. *Rich people react the same way if you wear expensive suits.*

> Jonathan Wojcik, "The 9 Most Mind-Blowing Disguises in the Animal Kingdom," Cracked.com, September 21, 2010. *www.cracked.com.*

FACT ATTACK: Spiders fly higher than planes! Young spiderlings can float in the breeze by laying out a line of silk which is picked up by the wind. Some have been sighted at altitudes of 10,000 feet and on ships more than 200 miles from land. *Ladies and gentleman, we have seen the enemy, and there's something on the wing.*

❯ "Spider Facts," How Stuff Works. *http://animals.howstuffworks.com.*

FACT ATTACK: Hippie spider swears off meat! *Bagheera kiplingi* is the only known spider that survives on a predominantly vegetarian diet. Aside from an occasional ant larva, the spider subsists entirely on nutrient-rich nubs called Beltian bodies found on the tips of Acacia trees. *It's probably just a phase.*

❯ Brandon Keim, "Kinder, Gentler Spider Eats Veggies, Cares for Kids," Wired.com, October 12, 2009. *www.wired.com.*

FACT ATTACK: Flying ants discovered in Peru! Peruvian gliding ants possess a unique adaptation that allows them to return to their tree when a gust of wind knocks them off. The ants can perform 180-degree turns in midair. Scientists speculate that the shape of their head acts as a rudder. *The more impressive adaptation would be not to fall off in the first place.*

❯ Robert Sanders, "Discovery of Gliding Ants Shows Wingless Flight Has Arisen Throughout the Animal Kingdom." *UC Berkeley News*, February 9, 2005. *www.berkeley.edu/news.*

FACT ATTACK: Spider's web stronger than Kevlar! Darwin's bark spiders spin webs that span up to thirty square feet and possess a tensile strength ten times greater than Kevlar. *So much evolutionary prowess, yet they are still so easy to squash.*

❯ Brandon Keim, "Gigantic Spider Webs Made of Silk Tougher Than Kevlar," Wired.com, September 20, 2010. *www.wired.com.*

FACT ATTACK: Genital mutilation rampant in butterfly society! Female Parnassian butterflies only mate once in their lives. After a three-hour mating, the male secretes a fluid into her genitals that hardens, forever sealing the opening. *I usually just send flowers.*

> "Top 10 X-Rated Bug Facts," Science Channel. *http://science.discovery.com.*

FACT ATTACK: Katydids prove chivalry not dead! The male katydid produces a nutritious secretion called spermatophyllax along with his sperm that he feeds to his partner while she waits for her eggs to fertilize. *How thoughtful.*

> "Top 10 Weird Bug Facts," Science Channel. *http://science.discovery.com.*

FACT ATTACK: You eat hundreds of bugs every year! The average person consumes 430 insects each year, both intentionally and accidentally. *Only one of mine was ever on purpose, but he was asking for it.*

> "50 Weird Science Tidbits," Science News Review. *www.sciencenewsreview.com.*

FACT ATTACK: Insects evolve decoy naughty bits! To avoid the rather violent mating habits of some members of the species, male and female Africa bat bugs evolved decoy genitals. Some females even have decoy parts for both sexes. *A Do Not Enter sign might be more effective.*

> "50 Weird Science Tidbits," Science News Review. *www.sciencenewsreview.com.*

FREAKY FOOD

EVERYTHING YOU NEVER WANTED TO KNOW ABOUT FOOD

FACT ATTACK: Scottish invent new definition of gross! Haggis is a traditional Scottish dish that consists of a sheep's stomach stuffed with the heart and liver mixed with various spices and onions and boiled for several hours. *Yum.*

> The Sanders Family, *Gross News: Gross (but Clean) Stories from Around the World* (Andrews McMeel Publishing, 2006).

FACT ATTACK: Wendy's serves finger to customer! Anna Ayala received nine years in prison for falsely claiming a Wendy's employee served her chili containing a severed human finger. Scientists analyzed the finger and determined it was not consistent with an object that had been cooked in chili for several hours. *Fresh finger, cooked finger, it's still a finger.*

> The Sanders Family, *Gross News: Gross (but Clean) Stories from Around the World* (Andrews McMeel Publishing, 2006).

FACT ATTACK: The King had massive appetite! Elvis Presley's favorite meal was the Fool's Gold Sandwich. It consists of a French baguette cut lengthwise and filled with one jar of peanut butter, one jar of strawberry jam, and one pound of bacon. *If it's good enough for Elvis, who are you to judge?*

> The Sanders Family, *Gross News: Gross (but Clean) Stories from Around the World* (Andrews McMeel Publishing, 2006).

FACT ATTACK: Moldy strawberries deemed okay! Frozen strawberries may contain an average mold count of 45 percent. *Still better than half.*

> "Food Defect Action Levels," U.S. Food and Drug Administration Center for Food Safety and Applied Nutrition, last updated November 2005, *www.cfsan.fda.gov.*

FACT ATTACK: Oregano full of insect bits! According-ing to the FDA, oregano can contain 1,249 or more insect fragments per ten grams before it is rejected. *Not sure if I'd prefer insect parts, or whole insects.*

❯ "Food Defect Action Levels," U.S. Food and Drug Administration Center for Food Safety and Applied Nutrition, last updated November 2005, www.cfsan.fda.gov.

FACT ATTACK: FDA overlooks maggots in cocktail cherries! A shipment of Maraschino cherries may go out as long as no more than 5 percent of sampled pieces contain maggots. *Good thing nobody over the age of seven actually eats them.*

❯ "Food Defect Action Levels," U.S. Food and Drug Administration Center for Food Safety and Applied Nutrition, last updated November 2005, www.cfsan.fda.gov.

FACT ATTACK: Clevelanders love processed food! There is a street in Cleveland, Ohio, named "Twinkie Lane." *The city knows what its people want.*

❯ http://maps.google.com.

FACT ATTACK: "The feast" puts turducken to shame! The single largest food item known to man is called "the feast." It consists of a roasted camel stuffed with a sheep's carcass, which is stuffed with chickens, which are stuffed with fish, which are stuffed with eggs. *Ladies and gentleman, I have found my Everest.*

❯ "Top 10 Incredible Food Facts," Listverse, December 17, 2007, *www.listverse.com.*

FACT ATTACK: Ancients ate hippo soup! The first documented soup originated in 6000 B.C. and was made from hippopotamus. *No grosser than eating the mechanically separated chicken soup of today.*

❯ "Top 10 Incredible Food Facts," Listverse, December 17, 2007, *www.listverse.com.*

FACT ATTACK: Jell-O is alive! If you hook up Jell-O to an EEG machine it registers movement nearly identical to the human brain. *Who knew our sentient brothers would be so delicious?*

❯ David Hoffman, *Who Knew?: Things You Didn't Know About Things You Know Well* (MJF Books, 2001).

FACT ATTACK: Leave your pots at home when climbing Everest! It is impossible to boil an egg on Mount Everest. *Which is surely the first thing on every climber's mind.*

❯ Bobby Mercer, *How Do You Light a Fart?: And 150 Other Essential Things Every Guy Should Know about Science* (Adams Media, 2009).

FACT ATTACK: Opera singer honored with food! Both the Peach Melba and Melba Toast are named after Australian opera singer Nellie Melba. *That's only because Peach Grzymkowski sounds like a disease.*

❯ Sara Wood and Kara Kovalchik, *The Complete Idiot's Guide to Fun FAQs* (Alpha, 2008).

FACT ATTACK: Charlie Brown sells out! The original airing of *A Charlie Brown Christmas* contained unapologetic promotions for Coca Cola embedded within the cartoon. *The Great Pumpkin would be so disappointed.*

❯ Sara Wood and Kara Kovalchik, *The Complete Idiot's Guide to Fun FAQs* (Alpha, 2008).

FACT ATTACK: Cannibals come in two classes! Exocannibals only eat their enemies, while indocannibals only eat their friends and relatives. *Both are easily offended, so be careful which term you use.*

❯ Noel Botham, *The Mega Book of Useless Information* (John Blake, 2009).

FACT ATTACK: **Pregnancy cravings good for baby!** The stereotype that pregnant women crave odd food combinations—such as pickles and ice cream—may have merit. Pregnant women require more sodium and calcium than other women, and doctors believe odd cravings alert the mother to nutritional deficiencies. *On a related note, toast cream is awesome. Take three spoonfuls of ice cream, spread on toast, enjoy.*

> Sara Wood and Kara Kovalchik, *The Complete Idiot's Guide to Fun FAQs* (Alpha, 2008).

FACT ATTACK: **Super-cold ice cream actually burns calories!** In order to negate the calories in a pint of ice cream, you would need to freeze it to a temperature of -3706°F. The energy your body requires to raise it to a digestible temperature is equivalent to roughly 1,000 calories. *Just find a way around the Third Law of Thermodynamics and you'll be all set.*

> Christoph Niemann, "Unpopular Science," *New York Times*, October 25, 2010, http://niemann.blogs.nytimes.com.

FACT ATTACK: **Americans love their sugar!** The average American consumes sixty-one pounds of refined sugar annually. *The sweet sweet taste of obesity.*

> Rebecca Coffey, "20 Things You Didn't Know About . . . Sugar," *Discover* magazine, October 2009, www.discovermagazine.com.

FACT ATTACK: **Americans continue culture of waste!**

Americans generate 472 billion pounds of trash every year, including 96 billion pounds of food. This only accounts for about 2 percent of the total waste stream. *USA! USA!*

> ❯ Elizabeth Royte, "20 Things You Didn't Know About . . . Garbage," *Discover* magazine, June 2006, www.discovermagazine.com.

FACT ATTACK: **Cranberries have magical healing properties!**

Cranberries contain a host of antibacterial properties and can help prevent bacterial infections, chiefly those affecting the urinary tract. *Why bother going to a doctor when you can get all your medical advice from a bathroom book?*

> ❯ Anahad O'Connor, *Never Shower in a Thunderstorm: Surprising Facts and Misleading Myths About Our Health and the World We Live In* (Times Books, 2007).

FACT ATTACK: **Cheese-chasers unite in sorrow!**

In 2010, organizers of England's annual Cooper's Hill cheese-rolling festival, in which thousands of contestants chase a seven-pound wheel of cheese down a hill, cancelled the event for the first time in hundreds of years. They worried that, due to the increased popularity of the event, the number of injuries could greatly eclipse those incurred during previous years. *At no other point in time during the history of this event did anybody worry that thousands of people running down a hill after wheels of cheese could be dangerous?*

> ❯ "Gloucestershire cheese-rolling off due to safety fears," BBC News, March 12, 2010, http://news.bbc.co.uk.

FACT ATTACK: Never ask a Brit for a cold one! British pub-goers prefer their ale served at room temperature. *Also, the plural of Guinness is Guinness.*

> Bill McLain, *Do Fish Drink Water? Puzzling and Improbable Questions and Answers* (William Morrow and Company, 1999), p. 108.

FACT ATTACK: Science can't beat nature! A 2006 study found that minor burns covered with gauze saturated with honey healed faster than those treated with over-the-counter creams. *Not true. My doctor prescribed me this great medication called Placebo that works better than anything!*

> Anahad O'Connor, *Always Follow the Elephants: More Surprising Facts and Misleading Myths about Our Health and the World We Live In* (Time Books, 2009).

FACT ATTACK: **Gerber sells out to please mommies!** In the 1950s, Gerber added MSG to their baby foods. Not because babies liked it, but because they realized that mothers often tasted baby food before feeding it to their infants. *Why not just put rum in it?*

> Don Vorhees, *Why Do Donuts Have Holes?: Fascinating Facts About What We Eat and Drink* (Citadel Press, 2004).

FACT ATTACK: Farmers feed their chickens flowers! Because it is illegal to use artificial colorings in eggs, farmers often feed their hens marigold petals to produce golden yolks. *I feel scammed.*

> Bill McLain, *Do Fish Drink Water? Puzzling and Improbable Questions and Answers* (William Morrow and Company, 1999), p. 184.

FACT ATTACK: Beer causes disfiguring disease! Ancient Greeks believed drinking beer caused leprosy. *But that didn't stop them.*

> Bill McLain, *Do Fish Drink Water? Puzzling and Improbable Questions and Answers* (William Morrow and Company, 1999), p. 46.

FACT ATTACK: Special effects tool winds up in food! Special effects experts used carrageenan, a seaweed extract, to make the monster in the horror film *The Blob* exceptionally gelatinous. Fast food restaurants use this same substance to make their milkshakes extra thick. *That's actually way less upsetting than what I assumed thickened them.*

> Eric Elfman, *Almanac of the Gross, Disgusting, & Totally Repulsive: a Compendium of Fulsome Facts* (RGA Publishing Group, Inc., 1994), p. 65.

FACT ATTACK: Ground beef more than just meat! Ground meat can contain everything from bones, skin, and gristle to offal, a food industry euphemism for the entrails and internal organs of the butchered animal. *I'd argue that offal is more offensive-sounding than ground-up heart and lung.*

> Richard Platt, *They Ate What?! The Weird History of Food* (Two-Can Publishing, 2006), p. 35.

FACT ATTACK: Fish farmers don't understand math! To produce two pounds of farmed fish requires eat eight pounds of fishmeal . . . a food made from wild fish. *Have to admire a profession that spits in the face of economics.*

❯ Richard Platt, *They Ate What?! The Weird History of Food* (Two-Can Publishing, 2006), p. 27.

FACT ATTACK: Peruvians dine on household pets! Every year, citizens of Peru consume 22 million guinea pigs. *Good for them for treating both cute and ugly animals equally.*

❯ Richard Platt, *They Ate What?! The Weird History of Food* (Two-Can Publishing, 2006), p. 14.

FACT ATTACK: Aztecs pay each other in chocolate! The Aztecs prized chocolate so highly that they would often use it as currency. *If American money were edible, we'd all be doomed.*

❯ Richard Platt, *They Ate What?! The Weird History of Food* (Two-Can Publishing, 2006), p. 10.

FACT ATTACK: Scientists study fossilized poop! Paleoscatologists study fossilized feces called coprolites to determine the diets of ancient animals, including humans. They soak the specimens in paint remover first to dissolve any unwanted material. *Some things just aren't worth knowing.*

❯ Richard Platt, *They Ate What?! The Weird History of Food* (Two-Can Publishing, 2006), p. 5.

FACT ATTACK: Food additives preserving more than our meals! Modern corpses do not decompose as quickly as they used to. Some attribute this to the increased amount of preservatives consumed by modern humans. *Or the bacteria are getting lazier.*

❯ Scott Morris, *The Emperor Who Ate the Bible and More Strange Facts and Useless Information* (Main Street Books, 1990).

FACT ATTACK: **The French love their snails!** The French eat roughly 5 million snails every year. *Unfortunately, the reverse is not also true.*

❯ Della Buckland, "Fun Food Facts," Associated Content, January 28, 2009, *www.associatedcontent.com.*

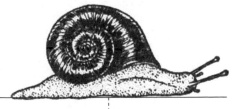

FACT ATTACK: Talk show host receives lunch-meat statue! Chicago artist Dwight Kalb once sent talk show host David Letterman a statue of Madonna constructed out of 180 pounds of ham. *Why feed the hungry when you can be creepy instead?*

❯ Noel Botham, *The Mega Book of Useless Information* (John Blake, 2009).

FACT ATTACK: Pop star's leftovers sold to highest bidder! A half-eaten breakfast of French toast belonging to Justin Timberlake once sold on eBay for $3,000. *I've got a half-eaten chocolate chip pancake belonging to Nick Nolte in my fridge. Ten bucks if anybody is interested.*

> Noel Botham, *The Mega Book of Useless Information* (John Blake, 2009).

FACT ATTACK: Getting high same as eating chocolate! Chocolate and marijuana stimulate the same receptors in the brain. *Which explains why chocolate is so much better under the influence. Or so I've read.*

> Cynthia Kugh, Scott Swartzwedler, Ph.D., Wilkie Wilson, Ph.D., and Leigh Heather Wilson, *Buzzed: The Straight Facts about the Most Used and Abused Drugs from Alcohol to Ecstasy* (The Haddon Craftsmen, Inc., 2003).

FACT ATTACK: **Chocolate can get you high!** To get the same effect as smoking one joint, you would have to consume about twenty-five pounds of chocolate. *Like the munchies, but in reverse.*

> Cynthia Kugh, Scott Swartzwedler, Ph.D., Wilkie Wilson, Ph.D., and Leigh Heather Wilson, *Buzzed: The Straight Facts about the Most Used and Abused Drugs from Alcohol to Ecstasy* (The Haddon Craftsmen, Inc., 2003).

FACT ATTACK: **Hot dogs outlive real dogs!** A hot dog can last twenty years in a landfill. *More upsetting: Who are these people throwing away perfectly good hot dogs?*

> National Geographic, *Weird But True: 300 Outrageous Facts* (National Geographic Children's Books, 2009).

FACT ATTACK: **Ship pelts enemy navy with dairy products!** The Uruguayan army once won a sea battle by firing Edam cheese instead of cannonballs. *Uruguay, you're doing it wrong.*

> Noel Botham, *The Amazing Book of Useless Information: More Things You Didn't Need to Know But Are About to Find Out* (Perigee Trade, 2008).

FACT ATTACK: **Dairy farmers label margarine a drug!** Initially, the dairy industry strongly resisted the advent of margarine. In some states, margarine was not allowed to be yellow, was heavily taxed, and labeled as a harmful drug to dissuade consumers from buying it. *In related news, reading any other book causes cancer. And diabetes.*

> Mike Bellino, *Fun Food Facts* (AuthorHouse, 2008).

FACT ATTACK: **Bloody steaks are a myth!** The red juice that drips from a freshly cooked steak is not actually blood. It is mostly water tainted with red myoglobin from the muscle. *So order your steak myoglobiny instead of bloody.*

> Mike Bellino, *Fun Food Facts* (AuthorHouse, 2008).

FACT ATTACK: **Fake food invades first world stomachs!** If you live in an industrialized country, you eat between thirteen and fifteen pounds of food additives every year. *Mmm, the sweet taste of technological superiority.*

> ❯ Jessica Williams, *50 Facts That Should Change the World* (The Disinformation Company Ltd., 2004), p. 89.

FACT ATTACK: **European cows live better than African humans!** Every cow in the European Union is subsidised by $2.50 a day. Seventy-five percent of Africans live on less. *But to be fair, cows are at least eight times more delicious.*

> ❯ Jessica Williams, *50 Facts That Should Change the World* (The Disinformation Company Ltd., 2004), p. 47.

FACT ATTACK: **Human body full of extra stuff!** It is possible for a human being to survive without a spleen, stomach, one kidney, one lung, 75 percent of the liver, 80 percent of the intestines, and most organs from the pelvic and groin area. *Not sure that's still a human though.*

> ❯ "10 Craziest Facts About the Human Body," Newspick.*com*, *http://news.upickreviews.com.*

FACT ATTACK: **Greeks attracted to useless body part!** Ancient Greeks considered the philtrum, the thin notch between the mouth and the nose, to be one of the most sensitive erogenous zones. *There is nothing sexy about the snot reservoir known as the philtrum.*

> ❯ "10 Craziest Facts About the Human Body," Newspick.com, *http://news.upickreviews.com.*

FACT ATTACK: Chicken nuggets made from pink goo!
Chicken nuggets are often made from a pink gelatinous substance created from mechanically separated chicken parts. Once workers grind up the chicken, they then add artificial flavor and also dye it a natural white color to disguise the pinkish hue. *In no way will this stop me from enjoying chicken nuggets.*

❯ "Chicken Nuggets Are Made from This Pink Goop," Gizmodo, *www.gizmodo.com.*

FACT ATTACK: Burger in a can puts fast food to shame! In 2008, the Swiss-based company Katadyn unveiled Cheeseburger in a Can, a unique food product marketed toward campers. With a shelf life of one year, the meal requires nothing more than boiling water to prepare, but one can even enjoy it cold right out of the can. *"Enjoy" is a bit of a stretch there. Maybe "not die from" instead.*

❯ Mike Hanlon, "The Canned Cheeseburger—Fast Food In the Wilderness," Gizmag.com, January 26, 2008, *www.gizmag.com.*

FACT ATTACK: Beans really are the musical fruit!
The reason beans have a reputation for causing gas is due to their high concentration of oligosaccharides, a sugar molecule that the human stomach cannot digest. The molecules pass through our large intestine intact, where bacteria feast on the sugars and produce gas, which we expel in the form of flatulence. *Science somehow managed to make farts unfunny.*

❯ Alan Bellows, *Alien Hand Syndrome and Other Too-Weird-To-Be-True Stories* (Workman Publishing, 2009), p. 89.

FACT ATTACK: Man's best friend bred for food! The chihuahua is named for the area of Mexico where it was discovered, domesticated, and eaten. *Instead of small dogs, think of them as large rats and you won't feel so bad for them.*

❯ Glen Vecchione, Joel Harris, and Sharon Harris, *The Little Giant Book of Animal Facts* (Sterling Publishing Co., Inc., 2004).

FACT ATTACK: Restaurant serves up breast milk cheese! For a brief time in 2010, the Klee Brasserie restaurant in New York City served cheese made from the owner's wife's breast milk. *Not sure why this is gross. But it just is.*

❯ Lachlan Cartwright and Jeremy Olshan, "Wife's Baby Milk in Chef's Cheese Recipe," *New York Post*, March 9, 2010, www.nypost.com.

FACT ATTACK: Town stages festival around eating mosquitoes! Every year at Cowley's Ridge State Park in Arkansas there is an annual Mosquito Cook-Off in which all of the food contains mosquitoes as the main ingredient. *Now they know how it feels.*

❯ Julie Mooney, *Ripley's Believe It or Not Encyclopedia of the Bizarre* (Black Dog & Leventhal Publishers, Inc., 2002).

FACT ATTACK: New Yorkers pay to eat bugs! In Williamsburg's Brooklyn Kitchen, for the bargain price of $85, patrons can munch on a smorgasbord of insects ranging from live wax moth larvae to yucca frites dotted with mealworms. *As long as I charged more than $50 for it, I'm confident I could shit in a bag and get people to order it in New York.*

❯ Jeff Gordinier, "Waiter, There's Soup in My Bug," *New York Times*, September 21, 2010, www.nytimes.com.

FACT ATTACK: **When mushrooms fight back!** The death cap is responsible for nearly 90 percent of all mushroom-related deaths. Ingesting the fungi causes severe diarrhea and vomiting. *Mushrooms, nature's candy.*

❯ Russell Ash, *Firefly's World of Facts* (Firefly Books, 2007), p. 51.

FACT ATTACK: **Coconut water blood transfusion!** In a pinch, coconut water can be substituted for blood plasma in the event of an emergency. *It won't save your life, but it will certainly make you taste better to the worms.*

❯ "Top 10 Incredible Food Facts," Listverse.com, December 17, 2007, *www.listverse.com.*

FACT ATTACK: **Castor oil carries deadly secret!** Ricin is a substance contained within the seeds of the castor oil plant. It is more poisonous than cyanide and snake venom, and can be fatal even in minute doses. *So grandma wasn't trying to discipline me . . . she was trying . . . oh, dear God, no.*

❯ Russell Ash, *Firefly's World of Facts* (Firefly Books, 2007).

FACT ATTACK: **Coffee made from cat poop!** Some of the world's most expensive coffee makes a pit stop in the digestive system of an animal before it makes its way to your cup. The small, cat-like civet eats only the freshest coffee berries which farmers then harvest from its droppings, clean, roast, and sell for as much as $150 a pound. *Every day, millions of people reach into their wallets and take out money to pay for bottled water. Now ask yourself, "Does cat-poop coffee really surprise me?"*

> Chris Brummit, "Civet Coffee: Good to the Last Dropping," Associated Press, January 20, 2004, *www.usatoday.com*.

FACT ATTACK: **In ironic twist, human eats lions!**
In honor of the 2010 World Cup hosted in South Africa, the owner of a restaurant in Arizona created a hamburger that contained a small amount of lion meat mixed with ground beef. The owner obtained the meat from Czimer's Game & Sea Foods, a company that specializes in exotic meat like camel, llama, and crocodile. *Turnabout is fair play, my feline friends.*

> Annalyn Censky, "Hunting the Lion Burger Butcher," CNN Money, June 23, 2010, *http://money.cnn.com*.

FACT ATTACK: **Lions fair game on menus!**
There are no laws in the United States forbidding the consumption of lion meat. *I doubt the founding fathers anticipated that might be an issue.*

> Annalyn Censky, "Hunting the Lion Burger Butcher," CNN Money, June 23, 2010, *http://money.cnn.com*.

FACT ATTACK: **Hot dogs, silent killers!** Nearly one in five food-related asphyxiations in children younger than age ten are caused by hot dogs. *Natural selection at work.*

❯ Frances Romero, "Top 10 Most Dangerous Foods," *Time*, February 22, 2010, *www.time.com*.

FACT ATTACK: **Researchers try to change shape of hot dogs!** To reduce the risk of hot dog-induced asphyxiation, the American Academy of Pediatrics has proposed manufacturers adjust the shape of the hot dog to make it less dangerous. *The fact that they are 40 percent horse hooves doesn't bother them though.*

❯ Frances Romero, "Top 10 Most Dangerous Foods," *Time*, February 22, 2010, *www.time.com*.

FACT ATTACK: **Jamaica's deadly national fruit!** If not properly eaten, Jamaica's national fruit, the ackee, can cause Jamaican Vomiting Sickness, which can lead to coma and even death. Unripe fruit contains a compound called hypoglycin, which can poison the consumer if he or she doesn't wait until the fruit's protective pods turn red and open naturally. *Stick to bananas and other fruit that won't kill you.*

❯ Frances Romero, "Top 10 Most Dangerous Foods," *Time*, February 22, 2010, *www.time.com*.

FACT ATTACK: **Peanuts stage revolt!** From 1992 to 2002, incidents of peanut allergies in children doubled. *That's because we stepped in and banned PB&J from schools to cater to the allergic kids. Should have let nature run its course. That's right, I said it.*

❯ Frances Romero, "Top 10 Most Dangerous Foods," *Time*, February 22, 2010, *www.time.com*.

FACT ATTACK: **Fast food full of pubes!** Every year, the average person consumes twelve pubic hairs while eating fast food. *Best not to think of how they got there.*

> Ayami Chin, "Gross Facts You May Have Never Wanted to Know," Associated Content, May 24, 2007, *www.associatedcontent.com.*

FACT ATTACK: **Bugs in apple butter!** The FDA permits up to five whole insects per 100 grams of apple butter, excluding mites, aphids, or scale insects. *Hear that, aphids? Party in the apple butter!*

> "Food Defect Action Levels," U.S. Food and Drug Administration Center for Food Safety and Applied Nutrition, last updated November 2005, *www.cfsan.fda.gov.*

FACT ATTACK: **Fecal matter in pepper!** Whole black peppercorns may contain up to one milligram of mammal feces per pound. *It may not seem like much, but when it comes to food, any animal poop is too much animal poop.*

> "Food Defect Action Levels," U.S. Food and Drug Administration Center for Food Safety and Applied Nutrition, last updated November 2005, *www.cfsan.fda.gov.*

FACT ATTACK: **Mysterious meat more popular than ever!** Every four seconds, somebody opens a can of Spam. *And dies a little inside.*

> Noel Botham, *The Book of Useless Information* (Perigee, 2006).

FACT ATTACK: Mona Lisa, in toast form! A Japanese artist once reconstructed the Mona Lisa—completely out of toast. *I'm sure it was just as underwhelming as the original.*

❯ Noel Botham, *The Book of Useless Information* (Perigee, 2006).

FACT ATTACK: Nature hates the color blue! There are no naturally occurring blue foods. Even blueberries are purple. *So Nerds aren't natural?*

❯ Noel Botham, *The Book of Useless Information* (Perigee, 2006).

FACT ATTACK: Foul-smelling fruit banned from hotels! Durian is a popular fruit in Singapore that possesses a tough skin covered in spikes. Beneath the daunting exterior rests a delectable treat that food connoisseurs travel from all over the world to sample—which happens to smell like old gym socks mixed with sewage, according to some. The fruit is so foul-smelling that many hotels and cab companies do not allow patrons to carry it with them. *"I'll take two of the shit fruit please."*

❯ Erica Walsh, "Singapore's Must-Eat Adventures Culinary Experiences You Can't Miss," The Travel Channel. *www.travelchannel.com.*

FACT ATTACK: All-natural moniker meaningless! The FDA has no regulations when it comes to use of the term "all-natural." Products that restaurants tout as "all-natural" often contain everything from high-fructose corn syrup to artificial flavorings. *Next you'll tell me low-fat is a sham. Oh wait . . .*

❯ David Zinczenko, Matt Goulding, and Lauren Murrow, "16 Secrets the Restaurant Industry Doesn't Want You to Know, " *Men's Health.* *www.menshealth.com.*

FACT ATTACK: Deadly delicacy worth the risk! The Japanese delicacy of fugu (raw puffer fish) kills around one hundred people every year. The liver, muscles, ovaries, and skin contain the deadly poison tetrodotin, which is 1,200 times more potent than cyanide. A lethal dose can fit on the head of a pin, and a single fish has enough poison to kill thirty individuals. *If you have to sign a waiver before you eat something, just put down the fork.*

❯ Frances Romero, "Top 10 Most Dangerous Foods," *Time*, February 22, 2010, *www.time.com.*
❯ Dahlia Rideout, "Ten Dangerous & Deadly Foods," Divine Caroline, *www.divinecaroline.com.*

FACT ATTACK: This is why you are fat! Seven percent of Americans eat at McDonald's every day. *Only 2 percent enjoy it.*

❯ Noel Botham, *The Book of Useless Information* (Perigee, 2006).

CIRCUS FREAKS

THE TRUTH ABOUT THE WOLF BOY AND OTHER FREAKS OF NATURE

FACT ATTACK: **Fleas perform for adoring fans!** Original flea circuses employed tiny gold threads to attach the fleas to various props. Because fleas are incredibly strong, the tiny insects were able to move objects across a miniature stage. *But who has time to train them?*

> "How to Build a Flea Circus," Ehow.*com*, *www.ehow.com.*

FACT ATTACK: **Sideshow cashes in on one-offs!** A single-o is a one-exhibit sideshow that often takes place out in the open, as opposed to underneath a tent. One famous example was the "Bonnie and Clyde Death Car," which is still on display today. *Wonder why it's called that.*

> Joe Nickell, *Secrets of the Sideshows* (The University Press of Kentucky, 2005).

FACT ATTACK: **Family of fat ladies births one more!** The Remarkable Baby Ruth, a circus fat lady, came from a long line of circus performers. Her mother was a six-foot tall, 600-pound sideshow act billed as "The Human Blimp." Her grandmother was also rumored to have been a circus fat lady. *Were they expecting the fat woman to give birth to Farrah Fawcett?*

> "The Remarkable Baby Ruth," Sideshow World, *www.sideshowworld.com.*

FACT ATTACK: Baby Ruth refuses to lie! When Baby Ruth discovered that she was being billed as a 700-pound woman—despite her lithe 500-pound frame—she swore to live up to the expectations of her fans. Over the course of several years she ballooned to a staggering 772 pounds at her peak. *A freak maybe, but an honest freak.*

❯ "The Remarkable Baby Ruth," Sideshow World, *www.sideshowworld.com.*

FACT ATTACK: Russia opens first freak museum! In 1719, Peter the Great opened Russia's first museum called the Kunstkamera. The museum housed various curiosities such as mummies and exotic animals, and even included the bodies of several human oddities the czar had encountered in his travels. *Screw art, freaks are way more fun to look at.*

❯ Josh Clark, "What Was in Peter the Great's Cabinet of Curiosities," Howstuffworks.*com,* *www.howstuffworks.com.*

FACT ATTACK: Five-year-old gives birth! The youngest mother in history was Lina Medina, a five-year-old Peruvian girl born in 1933. The circumstances of her impregnation are unknown; however, on May 14, 1939, she gave birth via cesarean section to a healthy 5.92-pound baby boy. *Pedophilia . . . still not funny.*

❯ Reuters, "Six Decades Later, World's Youngest Mother Awaits Aid," *The Telegraph,* August 27, 2002. *www.telegraphindia.com.*

FACT ATTACK: Aztecs keep freaks in cages! Along with the usual menagerie of animals, the zoo of the Aztec king Montezuma contained human oddities such as dwarfs, albinos, and hunchbacks. *Well, he couldn't just let them roam around. That would anger the gods.*

❯ Robert Mullan and Garry Marvin, *Zoo Culture* (University of Illinois Press, 1998), p. 32.

FACT ATTACK: Woman can't stop having babies!
Elizabeth Greenhille of Abbots Langley, Great Britain, allegedly had thirty-nine offspring, thirty-two daughters and seven sons. *Because above all else, God hates birth control and loves overpopulation.*

❯ Richard Torregrossa, *Fun Facts About Babies* (Dell Publishing, 1997).

FACT ATTACK: Feral child returns to society! In the late 1700s, a young boy emerged from the woods near Aveyron, France, having spent his childhood growing up in isolation. Locals displayed the "wild boy" until scientists attempted to educate him. Their efforts were unsuccessful, and the child never progressed beyond a rudimentary understanding of language. *He probably just missed Baloo and Bagheera.*

❯ "9 Children Who Were Raised By Animals," Mother Nature Network, *www.mnn.com*.

FACT ATTACK: Wild boy winds up in zoo! For a short time, the "wild boy" of Aveyron stayed at the Jardin des Plantes in Paris, one of the foremost scientific zoos of the time. *So much for the "Age of Enlightenment."*

❯ Robert Mullan and Garry Marvin, *Zoo Culture* (University of Illinois Press, 1998), p. 32.

FACT ATTACK: Dwarf turns into a giant! At the age of twenty-one, Adam Rainer stood a mere four feet tall. One day he started to grow spontaneously and continued to do so until he reached an astounding eight feet tall. He is the only recorded person to have been both a dwarf and a giant. *Hope all the important bits remained proportional.*

❯ Judith Freeman Clark and Stephen Long, *Weird Facts To Blow Your Mind* (Price Stern Sloan, 1993), p. 5.

FACT ATTACK: Brick-laying machine had no legs!
Willie Boular, a deaf, mute, and legless bricklayer in Atchison, Kansas, once laid 46,000 paving bricks in less than eight hours. *They weren't in any discernible order, but he laid the shit out of them.*

❯ Julie Mooney, *Ripley's Believe It or Not Encyclopedia of the Bizarre* (Black Dog & Leventhal Publishers, Inc., 2002).

FACT ATTACK: **Soap woman on display in Philly!** Visitors to the Mutter Museum in Philadelphia can view, among other medical oddities, the body of a woman that was naturally converted into soap. As she decomposed, chemicals in the soil converted the fat in her body into adipocere, a substance similar to lye soap. *I wash my hands of this nonsense.*

❯ "Woman Turned Into Soap," Canada.*com*, August 2, 2005, *www.canada.com.*

FACT ATTACK: Circus sideshow reborn! In the early '90s, Seattle sideshow enthusiast Jim Rose attempted to resurrect the sideshow with Jim Rose's Circus. The group of performers strayed away from the traditional exploitation of "freaks," and showcased live stunts like the human blockhead. *A freak show without freaks. Sounds grotesquely mediocre.*

❯ "Jim Rose: The Shocking Truth," BBC News, August 17, 1999, *http://news.bbc.co.uk.*

FACT ATTACK: World's tallest man ever! The tallest man in history was Robert Pershing Wadlow, who stood eight feet, eleven inches tall. *We need to stop giving out awards for existing.*

❯ "Tallest Man," Guinness World Records, *www.guinness worldrecords.com.*

FACT ATTACK: Modern flea circus missing key element! Modern flea circuses, dubbed "humbug circuses," use fake fleas and sleight-of-hand tricks to deceive audiences. *May they rot in hell for their unforgivable deception.*

❯ "How to Build a Flea Circus," Ehow.com, *www.ehow.com.*

FACT ATTACK: Human monster decapitates animals! The performance of the sideshow "geek" culminated with his biting the head off of a live chicken or snake. *I'd pay to see that.*

❯ "Geek," Merriam-Webster Online Dictionary, *www.merriam-webster.com.*

FACT ATTACK: Human caterpillar functions without arms or legs! Despite not having any arms or legs, sideshow performer Prince Randian was able to roll his own cigarettes—and light them as well—using only his mouth. *Hands are overrated anyway.*

❭ "Prince Randian," Sideshow World, *www.sideshowworld.com.*

FACT ATTACK: Italian woman births massive freak of nature! The largest baby ever born was a healthy boy weighing in at twenty-two pounds, eight ounces, who came into the world in Aversa, Italy, in September of 1995. *His mother immediately had her tubes tied. Twice.*

❭ Richard Torregrossa, *Fun Facts About Babies* (Dell Publishing, 1997).

FACT ATTACK: **Tiny infant weighs less than a can of Coke!** Born in 2004, Rumaisa Rahman is the world's smallest surviving baby. She weighed just 8.6 ounces and measured less than ten inches long. *Bonus: Mom and Dad could return the car seat and put her in the glove compartment. Gently, of course.*

❭ Barbara Seuling, *You Blink Twelve Times a Minute: and Other Freaky Facts About the Human Body* (Picture Window Books, 2008).

FACT ATTACK: Human mother births alligator children! Esther Parnell and her brother William were both born with ichthyosis, a disease that caused their skin to take on a scaly texture. Dubbed the "Alligator-Skinned Twins" (despite the fact that they weren't actually twins) the two toured the country displaying their unique condition. Esther became "The World's Strangest Mother" in 1948 and later gave birth to six more children, none of whom shared her affliction. *She would later lose the title to Octomom.*

> "The Alligator-Skinned Twins," The Human Marvels, *www.thehumanmarvels.com.*

FACT ATTACK: Not all pinheads are dumb! Many of the circus performers billed as "pinheads" suffered from microcephaly, a congenital disorder that prevented their heads from reaching a normal size. The disorder can cause mental retardation, but some sufferers possess perfectly normal intelligence. *So stop calling your brother a pinhead, as there's a chance it isn't offensive.*

> "Microcephaly—A Disorder of the Nervous System," Bizarre Medical, May 3, 2010, *www.bizarremedical.com.*

FACT ATTACK: Even the unborn find place in freak shows! A "pickled punk" was a popular sideshow attraction that featured a jar containing the body of an unborn fetus preserved in formaldehyde. *As a huge fan of pickles, I find this wildly offensive.*

> "Top 10 Freak Show Acts Of All Time," Toptenz.net, *www.toptenz.net.*

FACT ATTACK: **Freakshow claims tiny conjoined tots!** The Jones sisters, a pair of conjoined infants, toured in sideshows for the majority of their fifteen months of life. *Oh wait, freaks are people.*

❯ "Top 10 Freak Show Acts of All Time," Toptenz.net, *www.toptenz.net.*

FACT ATTACK: **Human Elephant dies in sleep!** When Joseph Merrick was five years old, he developed growths throughout his body that distorted his features. He toured with circuses as "The Elephant Man" until doctors admitted him to Royal London Hospital, where he suffocated in his sleep at the age of 27. *Probably for the best. If you can't stomp around and pick up logs with your trunk, there's no use in being the "Elephant Man."*

❯ "Elephant Man Mystery Unravelled," BBC News, July 21, 2003, *http://news.bbc.co.uk.*

❯ "Top 10 Human Sideshow Freaks," Listverse, *www.listverse.com.*

FACT ATTACK: **Pop star bids on freaky skeleton!** In the 1980s, rumors circulated that eccentric pop star Michael Jackson placed a bid to buy Joseph Merrick's remains. He denied the claims, and Merrick's preserved skeleton remains at the Royal London Hospital. *If only that were the creepiest thing he allegedly did.*

❯ "Music's Misunderstood Superstar," BBC News, June 13, 2005, *http://news.bbc.co.uk.*

❯ "Joseph Merrick—The Elephant Man," The Human Marvels, *www.thehuman marvels.com.*

FACT ATTACK: **Bagelheads turn themselves into freaks!** Young Japanese men have started modifying their bodies using injectable saline to create bagel-shaped bumps beneath the skin. The effect, which the media dubs bagelheads, only lasts twenty-four hours. *Because the best way to be different is to latch onto a trend and do exactly what everybody else is doing.*

❯ Mark Leevan, "Bagelheads and Body Modding Created By Saline Injections Is Hot in Japan," *The Examiner*, June 30, 2009, *www.examiner.com.*

FACT ATTACK: World's first "Siamese Twins" head out west! The term "Siamese Twins" originated with two of the world's most famous conjoined twins, Chang and Eng Bunker. Conjoined at the waist, the two brothers were discovered in Siam and taken to the United States to perform in circus sideshows. *Why be poor in Siam when you can be poor and exploited in the United States?*

> "Chang and Eng Bunker," Answers.*com*, *www.answers.com*.

FACT ATTACK: Two Indian children have twenty-six toes! The record for most fingers and toes on a living person is currently split by two individuals who have fifty digits between them. Both Pranamya Menaria and Devendra Harne of India have twelve fingers and thirteen toes each. *The "Little Piggie" game is especially traumatic.*

> "Most Fingers and Toes— Living Person," Guinness World Records, *www.guinnessworld records.com*.

FACT ATTACK: World's most bearded woman! The record for longest beard on a woman belongs to Vivian Wheeler, whose beard measured eleven inches at its longest point. Born a hermaphrodite, Wheeler gave birth to a son in 1977 despite doctor's insistence that she would not be able to conceive. *Seems kind of like cheating since she was born half a man.*

> Marc Hartzman, "Bearded Lady Reunites with Long-Lost Son," AOL News, September 16, 2010, *www.aolnews.com*.

FACT ATTACK: Amazing X-ray man sees everything! In the early 1900s, a man named Koda Box insisted he had X-ray vision. Audiences would tape quarters to his eyes, but he could still read from pieces of paper held in front of him. Once he navigated a busy New York City street while riding a bicycle and wearing an elaborate blindfold. *The ability to peek undetected does not make you special.*

> "The REAL X-Men," About.com, *http://paranormal .about.com*.

FACT ATTACK: Wolf boy suffers from poor genetics!
Most sideshow performers billed as "wolf boys" suffered from hypertrichosis, a genetic disorder that caused excessive hair to grow all over their bodies. Underneath the hair they were perfectly normal individuals. *Aside from the whole "working as a circus freak" thing.*

❯ Natalie Angier, "Modern 'Wolfmen' May Have Inherited Ancient Gene," *New York Times*, May 31, 1995, *www.nytimes.com.*

FACT ATTACK: World's first freak! The first freak show exhibit took place in 1738 and featured a four-foot-tall woman with a misshapen head. *To think, back then they had to settle for just one freak.*

❯ Kelly Spies, "History of the Freak Show," Associated Content, May 4, 2007, *www.associatedcontent.com.*

FACT ATTACK: Freaks find a home in Hollyweird! In 1932, MGM released the film *Freaks*, a horror film depicting a group of sideshow attractions who band together to stop a trapeze artist from seducing and murdering one of their own for his money. The studio employed actual sideshow performers who had to be secluded between takes to prevent gawkers from swarming the set. *"One of us, one of us! Gooble gobble, gooble gobble!"*

❯ "Freaks," Turner Classic Movies, *www.tcm.com.*

FACT ATTACK: Amazing man eats a plane! Between 1978 and 1980, performer Michel Lotito gradually consumed an entire Cessna 150 airplane. Lotito's stomach lining is twice as thick as a normal human's, which allows him to break down and eat all manner of strange objects ranging from television sets to bicycles. *If he could eat my neighbor's cat, that would be awesome.*

❯ "10 Most Bizarre People On Earth," Oddee.com, December 6, 2006, *www.oddee.com.*

❯ "Frenchman Eats TV, Dinner," CNN, June 12, 1998, *www.cnn.com.*

FACT ATTACK: Barnum cashes in on clever hoax! One of P. T. Barnum's most famous attractions was the body of a creature that appeared to be half monkey and half fish. Billed as the Feejee Mermaid, the oddity was nothing more than a monkey head sewn to the tail of a fish. *But the guy with the top hat said it was real!*

❯ "The Feejee Mermaid," Museum of Hoaxes, *www.museumofhoaxes.com.*

FACT ATTACK: Lizard Man writes book!

To transform himself into a human lizard, Erik Sprague endured more than 700 hours of tattoo work. His body is covered with green scales, and he even has a forked tongue. In 2007 he authored the book *Once More Through the Modified Looking Glass* detailing his experiences with body modification. *Way to break character, dude. A real lizard can't hold a pen.*

❯ Marc Hartzman, "Lizardman Enters Literary World," AOL News, January 17, 2010, *www.aolnews.com.*

FACT ATTACK: Circus freak discovers why men have nipples!
The record for most weight held from one's nipples belongs to the Great Nippulini, a circus performer specializing in lifting heavy objects attached to his two nipple piercings. He successfully suspended forty-eight pounds of weight from his nipple in 2003, and beat his own record with a fifty-five pound anvil the following year. *Well, now you know how much weight a nipple can hold. You can finally sleep at night.*

❯ Marc Hartzman, *American Sideshow* (Penguin Group, 2006).

❯ Marc Hartzman, *American Sideshow* (Penguin Group, 2006).

FACT ATTACK: Freak chooses sideshow over real job! Lionel the Lion-Faced Man originally wanted to be a dentist, but gave it up when he realized he could earn more as a circus freak. *That must have been a depressing realization.*

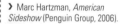

FACT ATTACK: Carnies give free taste of sideshow!
A bally or ballyhoo is a free show that takes place outside of a sideshow to attract a crowd. The term is derived from the Arabic expression *dehalla hoon*, which was used to call Middle Eastern fakirs and dancers to the stage. *The more you know!*

❯ Marc Hartzman, *American Sideshow* (Penguin Group, 2006).

FACT ATTACK: Smallest women pulls in giant paycheck! Lucia Zarate is the world's smallest recorded human. At age seventeen she weighed less than five pounds and stood just two feet and two-and-a-half inches tall. She was so small she could wear a ring as a bracelet. She earned roughly $200,000 during her career. *Which is like $10 billion in today's money.*

❯ Marc Hartzman, *American Sideshow* (Penguin Group, 2006).

FACT ATTACK: Bearded lady births bearded son! Madame Clofullia sprouted facial hair by the age of two and became one of the world's most famous bearded women. In the 1850s she gave birth to a son, who sprouted a beard shortly after his birth. *Some questioned her decision to reproduce and risk passing on her affliction, but to those people I ask an important question: What would you do if there were no more bearded people to condemn?*

❯ Marc Hartzman, *American Sideshow* (Penguin Group, 2006).

FACT ATTACK: Three-legged man survives heart failure! In 1906, circus performer George Lippert's heart gave out. Luckily he had a spare belonging to his parasitic twin, which allowed him to live an additional two weeks. *He probably just let him use the heart so he could be the one to kill him.*

❯ Marc Hartzman, *American Sideshow* (Penguin Group, 2006).

FACT ATTACK: Barnum exploits skin deformity for profit! P. T. Barnum exhibited black sufferers of leucoderma as "leopard boys." The disorder caused irregular depigmentation of the skin, resulting in white patches. To make them sound exotic, he claimed they hailed from the African plains, when in fact many were from America. *Barnum's latest attraction, the full mermaid: a creature with the body of a fish and the head of a fish as well!*

❯ Marc Hartzman, *American Sideshow* (Penguin Group, 2006).

FACT ATTACK: Most Pierced Woman goes overboard!
Elaine Davidson has more than 6,500 piercings,
which has earned her a spot in the *Guinness Book of
World Records* as the most pierced woman. She has
500 piercings in and around her genitalia alone. *I
saw pictures. I wasn't sure what I was looking at.*

❯ "World's Most Pierced
Woman Adds to Her Colleciton,"
The Telegraph, February 23,
2009, *www.telegraph.co.uk.*

❯ "Pierced Lady 'Scared to Go Home,'" *The Sydney Morning Herald*, November 13, 2003,
www.smh.com.au.

**FACT ATTACK: Doctors can't create
freaks!** It is illegal in the United States for doctors
to perform any body modification surgery that alters
the physical appearance of the patient beyond societal
norms. *Correct me if I'm wrong, but I'm pretty
sure there aren't too many women with quadruple
D breasts floating around in nature.*

❯ "Stalking Cat (Dennis Avner)," BBC, *www.bbc.co.uk.*

**FACT ATTACK: Human transforms himself into a
tiger!** Through body modification, Dennis Avner
transformed his figure to resemble that of a tiger.
Stalking Cat's modifications include a cleft lip, whiskers inserted into body piercings, a flattened nose,
tiger stripe tattoos, brow implants, and pointed ears.
*Eccentric people want to be like cats. Crazy people want to be cats.
Batshit crazy people want to have sex with cats. Any questions?*

❯ "Stalking Cat (Dennis Avner),"
BBC, *www.bbc.co.uk.*

FACT ATTACK: Human Owl discovers amazingly mundane gift! Nicknamed the Human Owl, Martin Laurello was born with a twisted spine that allowed him to turn his head 180 degrees. It took him three years to perfect the act, which he displayed both with Barnum & Bailey and Ripley's Odditorium. *Three years to realize, "Holy hell, I can turn my head around!" I'm unimpressed.*

❯ "The Human Owl—Martin Laurello," Bizarre Medical News, August 18, 2010, *www.bizarre medical.com.*

FACT ATTACK: Turtle boy loses shell! Labeled the "Turtle Boy" by his classmates, eight-year-old Maimaiti Hali was born with a thick growth spanning the majority of his back. In the summer of 2010, he underwent surgery to remove a growth that had become as thick as cow hide. Surgeons used skin grafts from his scalp and legs to aid in his recovery. *But not before he learned the ancient art of ninjitsu.*

❯ "Boy Has Surgery to Remove Turtle-Like Shell," Fox News, June 2, 2010. *www.foxnews.com.*

FACT ATTACK: Freaks should steer clear of Michigan! In Michigan, it is illegal to display any human abnormality or freak of nature except for scientific purposes. *Coincidentally, Lady Gaga has never played a show in Michigan.*

❯ Michigan Penal Code (Excerpt), Act 328 of 1931: Section 750.347, Deformed human beings; exhibition, *www.legislature.mi.gov.*

FACT ATTACK: Man removes teeth to win competition! In order to step up his game at the World Gurning Championship in England, where contestants compete to see who can make the most gruesome faces, four-time world champion Peter Jackman removed all of his teeth to make his facial maneuvers easier. *Now that's the difference between an amateur goon and a professional troll.*

❯ Stuart Inamura, "Top 10: Unusual Traditions Around the World," Totally Top 10, July 27, 2010, *www.totallytop10.com*.

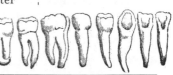

FACT ATTACK: Amazing man missing half his body! Johnny Eck was one of the most famous sideshow performers in the early twentieth century. Born without the vast majority of his lower torso, Eck was otherwise healthy and lived a normal life until he suffered a heart attack in his sleep at seventy-nine. He made for a convincing "saw the man in half" magic trick. *And he never had to iron pants. Bonus!*

❯ Francine Homberge, *Carny Folk* (2005).

FACT ATTACK: Bearded women speaks three languages! Touring as the Victorian Ape Woman, Mexican-born Julia Pastrana suffered from hypertrichosis, a disorder which caused abnormal hair growth all over her body. Despite her outward appearance, Pastrana was quite intelligent and even spoke three languages. After her death during childbirth, her husband and manager mummified her remains as well as the body of her newborn son (who shared her affliction) so he could continue to display them to the world. *Nothing weird about that.*

❯ Christopher Hals Gylseth and Lars O. Toverud, *Julia Pastrana: The Tragic Story of the Victorian Ape Woman* (Sutton, 2003).

FACT ATTACK: Lobster boy gets away with murder! In the late 1970s, Gary Stiles (AKA the Lobster Boy) shot and killed his daughter's fiancé on the night of their wedding. Stiles suffered from ectrodactyly, a disorder that causes the digits of one's hands and feet to fuse together. He openly admitted to the crime; however, because his attorneys argued that no prison could provide for his unique deformity, he was given fifteen years of probation and set free. *Obvious question: How did he hold the gun?*

> "Grady Stiles Jr.—'The Murderous Lobster Man,'" The Human Marvels, *www.humanmarvels.com.*

> "Medical Mystery: Ectrodactyly," ABC News, January 29, 2007, *http://abcnews.go.com.*

FACT ATTACK: Lobster people play odds with mother nature! If an individual suffering from ectrodactyly has a child with an unafflicted individual, there is a 50 percent chance that the child will inherit the disorder. *And a 100 percent chance they will be made fun of if they do.*

> "Medical Mystery: Ectrodactyly," ABC News, January 29, 2007, *http://abcnews.go.com.*

FACT ATTACK: Animals suffer from lobster boy syndrome! Ectrodactyly is not a disorder limited to humans. A range of animals including frogs, dogs, cats, salamanders, and birds can suffer from the disorder. *Lobsters?*

> "Medical Mystery: Ectrodactyly," ABC News, January 29, 2007, *http://abcnews.go.com.*

FACT ATTACK: **Famous artist was a freak!** Some researchers believe Leonardo da Vinci had webbed fingers. *Some researchers waste their time learning useless facts about famous painters.*

❯ "Medical Mystery: Ectrodactyly," ABC News, January 29, 2007, http://abcnews.go.com.

FACT ATTACK: **Human blockhead cons spectators!** While it may appear that the human blockhead hammers a nail directly into his skull, he is actually directing it into the grooves that line the nasal cavity called conchae. *Is nothing sacred?*

❯ Tracy V. Wilson, "How the Human Blockhead Works," Howstuffworks.*com*, www.howstuffworks.com.

FACT ATTACK: **Carny charges for wedding admission!** P. T. Barnum never missed an opportunity to cash in on his sideshow attractions. At the wedding of one of his most famous performers, General Tom Thumb, he reportedly charged guests $75 to attend. *Exploitation is a dish best served lukewarm.*

❯ Stacy Conradt, "The Quick 10: 10 Famous Circus Performers," Mentalfloss.com, November 21, 2008, www.mentalfloss.com.

FACT ATTACK: **Three-legged man gets double the pleasure!** Aside from being born with three legs, four feet, and sixteen toes, sideshow attraction Francesco Lentini also possessed two functioning sets of genitalia, although he rarely revealed this fact during his act. *The half-man must have died a little inside every time he saw him.*

❯ Stacy Conradt, "The Quick 10: 10 Famous Circus Performers," Mentalfloss.com, November 21, 2008, www.mentalfloss.com.

FACT ATTACK: Normal woman labeled a freak!
Prized for her voluptuous body, Saarti Baartman was taken from her home in Africa to Britain in 1810 for sideshow entertainment. Although there was nothing unique about her appearance in her home country, Europeans flocked to gawk at the large buttocks and curves of the "Hottentot Venus." *If a deadly epidemic only afflicts white people, it will be tough to argue we don't deserve it.*

❯ "'Hottentot Venus' Goes Home," BBC News, April 29, 2002, *http://news.bbc.co.uk.*

FACT ATTACK: Skeleton man weds fat lady! In 1924, Pete "Human Skeleton" Robinson married another circus performer named Bunny Smith. Robinson weighed a scant fifty-eight pounds while his bride, the circus fat lady, was more than eight times heavier. *That's more than 464 pounds for those of you scoring at home.*

❯ Marc Hartzman, "One-Legged Acrobat and Fire-Eater Find Love," AOL News. *www.aolnews.com.*

INSANE ASYLUMS AND CRAZY PEOPLE

IT'S NOT A CRIME IF YOUR DOG MADE YOU DO IT

FACT ATTACK: **Ruler carries around corpse!**
When her husband died in the 1500s,
Juana of Castile was so distraught that she
carried his corpse around on a tour of
Spain, lovingly caressing it along the way.
Love: driving people crazy since 100,000 B.C.

> "10 Crazy Royals," Toptenz.
net, *www.toptenz.net.*

FACT ATTACK: **Most serial killers do it for the
nookie!** Sex is the root cause of 69 percent
of all serial murders. *They could not have picked
a funnier number for that statistic.*

> Michael Newton, *Serial
Killers (Criminal Investigations)*
(Chelsea House Publications,
2008).

FACT ATTACK: **First woman executed in United
States!** Mary Surrett, a conspirator in
the assassination of Abraham Lincoln,
was the first woman to be executed in the
United States. She was hanged on July 7,
1865. *Equal rights are no joke.*

> Edward Steers Jr., *Blood on
the Moon: The Assassination of
Abraham Lincoln* (University of
Kentucky Press, 2005).

FACT ATTACK: **Pedophile can't wait to be executed!**
Convicted pedophile and serial killer Albert Fish
looked forward to his execution. He was a masochist
and believed it would be the most thrilling sexual
experience imaginable. *If only he'd thought of the idea
sooner.*

> Tom Philbin, *The Killer Book
of True Crime: Incredible Stories,
Facts and Trivia from the World
of Murder and Mayhem* (Sourcebooks, Inc., 2007).

FACT ATTACK: **Famous criminal only a teenager!** Bonnie Parker, half of the infamous Bonnie and Clyde duo, was only seventeen during her elaborate crime spree which left sixteen people dead, thirteen of them police officers. *Teenagers: more dangerous than Ebola.*

❯ Tom Philbin, *The Killer Book of True Crime: Incredible Stories, Facts and Trivia from the World of Murder and Mayhem* (Sourcebooks, Inc., 2007).

FACT ATTACK: **Child molesters get off too easy!** The average pedophile serves eleven years in prison. *Assuming he or she survives that long.*

❯ Tom Philbin, *The Killer Book of True Crime: Incredible Stories, Facts and Trivia from the World of Murder and Mayhem* (Sourcebooks, Inc., 2007).

FACT ATTACK: **Alleged celebrity killer scams system!** O. J. Simpson was found not guilty for the 1994 murders of Nicole Brown Simpson and Ronald Goldman. However, a subsequent civil court found him liable for their deaths. *Innocent people attempt to flee the country all the time.*

❯ Associated Press, "Judge Orders O. J. Simpson To Stop Spending Book Money," Fox News, February 8, 2007, *www.foxnews.com.*

FACT ATTACK: Quirky scientist was actually crazy!
World renowned scientist Nikola Tesla had an intense fear of dirt and germs. He was also distrusting of anything round, and only stayed in hotel rooms with numbers divisible by three. *In his defense, I'm pretty sure no good has ever come from anything round.*

> ❯ Ian Fortey, "The 10 Craziest Scientific Experiments Ever Conducted," Cracked.com, March 31, 2008, *www.cracked.com.*

FACT ATTACK: **Mysterious disorder makes victims crave paper!** Pica is a rare disorder that causes victims to crave inedible substances like glue, dirt, and paper. The medical community is uncertain as to what causes the disorder, however, some doctors believe the culprit may be a mineral deficiency. *I miss the days when a man could just eat dirt without having to explain himself.*

> ❯ "Top 10 Mysterious Diseases," Live Science, *www.livescience.com.*

FACT ATTACK: Book mocks U.S. judicial system! In 2006, O. J. Simpson authored a "fictional" book titled *If I Did It.* The book described how he would have killed Nicole Brown Simpson and Ronald Goldman had he actually been the murderer. *I hope they catch the real killer someday.*

> ❯ Associated Press, "Judge Orders O. J. Simpson To Stop Spending Book Money," Fox News, February 8, 2007, *www.foxnews.com.*

FACT ATTACK: Prostitute gets back at abusive johns! Aileen Wuornos was a prostitute operating in Florida in 1992. She possessed a deep-seated hatred for men which manifested itself by her leading them into the woods with promises of sex and shooting them to death on seven occasions. Charlize Theron portrayed her in the popular film *Monster*. *If you follow a prostitute into the woods, you deserve to be shot.*

> Tom Philbin, *The Killer Book of True Crime: Incredible Stories, Facts and Trivia from the World of Murder and Mayhem* (Sourcebooks, 2007).

FACT ATTACK: Hitler almost aborted! Hitler's mother seriously considered aborting the unborn dictator, but her doctor talked her out of it. *Way to go, doc.*

> Mitchell Symons, *That Book: . . . of Perfectly Useless Information* (HarperCollins, 2004).

FACT ATTACK: Prince Charming a rapist! In the original Grimm's fairy tale *Sleeping Beauty*, the prince rapes her while she sleeps and leaves before she wakes. *Smart move deviating from the source material, Disney.*

> Shane Mooney, *Useless Sexual Trivia* (Simon & Schuster, 2000).

FACT ATTACK: Ruthless dictators missing manhood! Hitler and Napoleon were both missing a testicle. *It all makes sense now.*

> Noel Botham, *The Book of Useless Information* (Perigee, 2006).

FACT ATTACK: Great leader steals director for monster movie! Dissatisfied with the quality of filmmakers in his own country, North Korean dictator Kim Jong-Il kidnapped world famous director Shin Sang-ok and forced him to produce a propaganda-laced monster film reminiscent of a Godzilla movie. *Spoiler Alert: The Great Leader wins.*

❯ John Gorenfeld, "The Producer From Hell," *The Guardian*, April 4, 2003, *www.guardian.co.uk.*

FACT ATTACK: Dictator builds propaganda city! In the 1950s, Kim Jong-Il's father built the city of Kijong-Dong, on the border of South Korea. It appears to be paradise; however, nobody lives there. It serves as a propaganda piece to convince South Koreans to defect to the North. The city has automatic street lights and street sweepers to maintain the illusion. *To live by myself in a deserted city, I'd defect to North Korea.*

❯ "10 Crazy Facts About Kim Jong II," Listverse.com, *www.listverse.com.*

FACT ATTACK: **Death row makes you hungry!** Before his execution, William Bonin ate a last meal of two sausage and pepperoni pizzas, three servings of coffee ice cream, and fifteen cans of Coke. *His requests for a pretty young virgin with an apple in her mouth were repeatedly ignored.*

❯ Tom Philbin, *The Killer Book of Serial Killers: Incredible Stories, Facts and Trivia from the World of Serial Killers* (Sourcebooks, 2009), p. 11.

FACT ATTACK: **Doctors most likely to kill!** The medical profession has produced the most serial killers. *Which is why I visit a shaman whenever I'm sick.*

> Tom Philbin, *The Killer Book of Serial Killers: Incredible Stories, Facts and Trivia from the World of Serial Killers* (Sourcebooks, 2009), p. 10.

FACT ATTACK: **Psycho with foot fetish keeps souvenirs!** Jerry Brudos had a habit of cutting off the feet of his victims. He had a foot fetish and stored them in his freezer once he removed them from their owners. *Well, where else was he supposed to keep them?*

> Tom Philbin, *The Killer Book of Serial Killers: Incredible Stories, Facts and Trivia from the World of Serial Killers* (Sourcebooks, 2009), p. 95.

FACT ATTACK: **Rock star collects killer mementos!** Jonathan Davis, the lead vocalist of the rock group KoRn, is the proud owner of two of John Wayne Gacy's Pogo the Clown suits as well as Ted Bundy's yellow VW. *Can't say I'm surprised.*

> Tom Philbin, *The Killer Book of Serial Killers: Incredible Stories, Facts and Trivia from the World of Serial Killers* (Sourcebooks, 2009), p. 74.

FACT ATTACK: Killer gets busy with severed head! Serial killer Edmund Kemper took the head of one of his victims and used it as a masturbatory aid in the shower. *There's a visual you will never forget.*

❯ Tom Philbin, *The Killer Book of Serial Killers: Incredible Stories, Facts and Trivia from the World of Serial Killers* (Sourcebooks, 2009), p. 7.

FACT ATTACK: Columbine shooters nearly killed hundreds! On April 20, 1999, Eric Harris and Dylan Klebold stormed into Columbine High School with guns and homemade bombs, and killed twelve students and one teacher. Had several propane explosives they set in the cafeteria gone off, they would have killed hundreds more. *I think everyone can agree that the solution to the school shootings problem is MORE guns.*

❯ Dave Cullen, "The Depressive and the Psychopath," Slate.com, April 20, 2004, *www.slate.com.*

FACT ATTACK: **Kids and teens prone to mental illness!** Ten percent of children and adolescents in the United States suffer from serious emotional and mental disorders. *Which is why you should always approach a teenager with caution.*

❯ "What Is Mental Illness: Mental Illness Facts," National Alliance On Mental Illness, *www.nami.org.*

FACT ATTACK: Jesus Christ reborn, dies again! David Koresh, the leader of a cult group in Waco, Texas, believed he was the reincarnation of Jesus Christ. He lost his life along with seventy-six other cult members after a botched FBI siege of his compound that lasted fifty days. *If he wasn't the son of God, that whole dying thing would have sucked.*

❯ Susan Ellicott, "From the Archive: Bloody Fiasco of Bid to Seize Waco's Sinful Messiah," *The Sunday Times*, May 23, 2010, www.timesonline.co.uk.

❯ "The Brits Waco Survivors," *The Sunday Times*, December 14, 2008, www.timesonline.co.uk.

FACT ATTACK: Cult leader records hit song! In the late '80s David Koresh recorded a rock song called "Madman in Waco" to taunt a sect rival. *Said the pot to the kettle.*

❯ Susan Ellicott, "From the Archive: Bloody Fiasco of Bid to Seize Waco's Sinful Messiah," *The Sunday Times*, May 23, 2010, www.timesonline.co.uk.

FACT ATTACK: Virgin's blood great for the skin! Countess Bathory of Hungary believed she could remain youthful forever by bathing in a steel vat filled with the blood of her prisoners. When the King of Hungary heard of this, he stormed her castle and barricaded the countess in her room behind a wall of bricks, where she spent the rest of her days. *Don't act like you wouldn't be the first in line if that actually worked.*

❯ Noel Botham, *The Mega Book of Useless Information* (John Blake, 2009).

FACT ATTACK: Baldness leads to insanity! Hundreds of years ago, baldness was viewed as a sign of mental illness. The theory stood that a troubled mind could not support a full head of hair. *People don't go bald because they are crazy. People go crazy because they are bald.*

❯ Anahad O'Connor, *Never Shower in a Thunderstorm: Surprising Facts and Misleading Myths About Our Health and the World We Live In* (Times Books, 2007).

FACT ATTACK: The secret ingredient is people! Fritz Haarmann ran a butcher shop in post–World War I Germany where he sold inexpensive, fresh meat to impoverished customers. Some were suspicious of his low prices and discovered that Haarmann had murdered up to fifty boys and men and ground up their bodies into sausage. *Sometimes you have to choose. Do you want cheap meat, or do you want it to not contain humans?*

> Francesca Gould, *Why You Shouldn't Eat Your Boogers and Other Useless or Gross Information About Your Body* (Tarcher, 2008).

FACT ATTACK: Obsessed fan gives up on life! In 1984, a French Michael Jackson fan committed suicide because he could not have surgery to make himself look like the King of Pop. *Michael Jackson couldn't even get surgery to look like Michael Jackson.*

> "Michael Jackson: 100 Facts About the King of Pop," *The Telegraph, www.telegraph.co.uk.*

FACT ATTACK: Murderous narcissist toys with police! In the 1960s, a man known as the Zodiac Killer stalked the San Francisco Bay area, killing at least five people. He taunted police and the public through cryptic letters sent to local newspapers, some of which have never been decoded. *I managed to decode one. It just read "Be sure to drink your Ovaltine."*

> Francisco Bureau, "Zodiac Killer Terrorized, Then Stopped," CNN, October 22, 2002, *www.cnn.com.*

FACT ATTACK: Serial killer still at large! The Zodiac Killer was never caught, but police have gone through as many as 2,500 suspects searching for him. *I think they are getting close.*

> Francisco Bureau, "Zodiac Killer Terrorized, Then Stopped," CNN, October 22, 2002, *www.cnn.com.*

FACT ATTACK: **The real axis of evil!** In 2002, 81 percent of the world's executions took place in either China, Iran, or the United States. *At least we're good at something.*

❯ Jessica Williams, *50 Facts That Should Change the World* (The Disinformation Company, 2004), p. 33.

FACT ATTACK: **Bad boys get all the girls!**

Hybristophilia refers to a disorder whereby one is sexually aroused by those who have committed violent crimes. Prisoners throughout the world receive thousands of love letters and photographs from hybristophiliacs every year. *Except they never write back. Or at least Charles Manson doesn't.*

❯ Denisa Mina, "Why Are Women Drawn to Men Behind Bars?" *The Guardian*, January 13, 2003, *www.guardian.co.uk.*

FACT ATTACK: **Serial killer never lifts a finger!** Charles Manson never killed anybody. He was found responsible for several murders because he instructed his followers to carry them out. *He should have used the "If I told you to walk off a bridge . . . ?" defense.*

❯ Charles Montaldo, "Charles Manson Denied Parole 11 Times," About.com, May 29, 2007, *http://crime.about.com.*

FACT ATTACK: Kidnapped socialite joins her captors! Heiress to a vast publishing fortune, Patty Hearst was kidnapped in 1974 by a group of radicals called the Symbionese Liberation Army. Shortly after her capture, she stunned the world by joining their cause and taking part in a bank robbery. Many believe Hearst suffered from Stockholm syndrome, a disorder where a kidnapping victim begins to sympathize with his or her captors. *Not gonna lie, she was pretty hot holding a machine gun.*

> "Radically Different, Heiress' Life Far Removed from Days of '74 Kidnapping," CNN, *www.cnn.com.*

> Laura Fitzpatrick, "Stockholm Syndrome," *Time*, August 31, 2009, *www.time.com.*

FACT ATTACK: Early asylums more jail than hospital! Medieval insane asylums were more like prisons. Patients were chained up in cells and forced to endure tortures ranging from being swung around in a harness to branding with red-hot pokers in misguided attempts to cure their illness. *If you know a better way to cure ADD, I'd love to hear it.*

> Diane Gray, "The History of Insane Asylums and Mental Illness," Associated Content, April 30, 2007, *www.associatedcontent.com.*

FACT ATTACK: Demon dog advocates murder! Infamous "Son of Sam" serial killer David Berkowitz shot and killed six individuals, allegedly at the behest of his neighbor's dog. *Why don't talking dogs ever tell people to donate to charity or save the rain forest?*

> Dana Chivvis, "'Son of Sam' Denied Parole Again," AOL News, May 11, 2010, *www.aolnews.com.*

FACT ATTACK: Most serial killers not crazy!
Only 2 percent of serial murderers kill because of delusional fantasies similar to those described by the Son of Sam killer. *Well that's because demon dogs don't just talk to every Joe Blow that walks down the street.*

> Michael Newton, *Serial Killers (Criminal Investigations)* (Chelsea House Publications, 2008).

FACT ATTACK: **Mass murder no easy task!** The FBI defines a mass murderer as someone who kills four or more individuals in a single event. Usually the victims are strangers. *Probably tough to get four people who know you are a psycho into a room together.*

> Michael Newton, *Serial Killers (Criminal Investigations)* (Chelsea House Publications, 2008).

FACT ATTACK: Guns are so last season! Sixty-two percent of all killers in the United States use a gun as their weapon of choice. That number shrinks to 22 percent among serial killers, who generally prefer more intimate killing methods like knives or strangulation. *A screwdriver also doesn't alert the government when you purchase it.*

> Michael Newton, *Serial Killers (Criminal Investigations)* (Chelsea House Publications, 2008).

FACT ATTACK: Angel of death only meant well! In the hopes that he could intervene and be seen as a hero, nurse Richard Angelo injected several patients at Long Island's Good Samaritan Hospital with drugs to induce cardiac arrest. Ten of his victims died, and he was sentenced to life in prison. *Seemed like a good idea at the time.*

> "Angels of Death: The Male Nurses," Trutv.*com,* *www.trutv.com.*

FACT ATTACK: Serial murderers popping up in droves! Of the 400 serial killers active in the past century, 80 percent arose after 1950. *I blame video games.*

> Shanna Freeman, "How Serial Killers Work," How Stuff Works, *http://science.howstuff works.com.*

FACT ATTACK: Ruthless killer apologizes to victim! Eight years after he assisted in the 2002 Washington, D.C., sniper attacks that left ten individuals dead and three critically injured, Lee Boyd Malvo sent one of his first victims an apology letter from prison. *"Sorry I got caught. Love, Lee."*

> Elliot C. McLaughlin, "Sniper's Apology Brings Closure, No Justice," CNN, March 4, 2010, *www.cnn.com.*

FACT ATTACK: It takes a lot to be a serial killer! The FBI defines a serial killer as any individual who murders more than three victims with "cooling off" periods between each crime. *My condolences to any of my homicidal readers who didn't make the cut.*

> Shanna Freeman, "How Serial Killers Work," How Stuff Works, *http://science.howstuff works.com.*

FACT ATTACK: **The United States of serial killers!** Eighty-five percent of serial killers come from the United States. *Would have guessed Uzbekistan.*

> "Mook Examines Celebrity and Serial Killers," About.com, *http://crime.about.com.*

FACT ATTACK: **Prison justice swifter than judicial system!** Two years after his conviction for murdering more than a dozen men, Jeffrey Dahmer was beaten to death in prison by another inmate. *Guy should get a medal for saving taxpayer money.*

> Michael Sheridan, "Report: Serial Killer Jeffrey Dahmer May Have Been Behind Kidnapping, Murder of Adam Walsh in 1981," *New York Daily News*, March 30, 2010, *www.nydailynews.com.*

FACT ATTACK: **Beware of the murderous clown!** Serial killer John Wayne Gacy entertained at children's parties as Pogo the Clown. *"Want to see me make the birthday boy disappear?"*

> Charles Montaldo, "John Wayne Gacy the 'Killer Clown,'" About.com, *http://crime.about.com.*

FACT ATTACK: **It sucks to be a woman!** Sixty-five percent of all serial murder victims are female. *So that's why they travel in packs. Safety in numbers.*

> Michael Newton, *Serial Killers (Criminal Investigations)* (Chelsea House Publications, 2008).

FACT ATTACK: The woman who was sixteen people!
One of the most famous cases of multiple personality disorders is that of Shirley Ardell Mason, who psychiatrists believe possessed as many as sixteen unique personas, one of which spoke with a British accent and two of which were young boys. *I have two personalities. The one writing this book, and a funny one.*

❯ Mark Miller and Barbara Kantrowitz, "Unmasking Sybil. (Shirley Ardell Mason, the Real-Life Sybil)," *Newsweek*, January 25, 1999, *www.newsweek.com*.

FACT ATTACK: Deranged killer collects souvenirs! When detectives entered the house of Ed Gein in November of 1957, they hoped to find evidence that would link him to the murder of a local hardware store clerk. Along with her body, they discovered a disturbing collection of human body parts, including a skull fashioned into a bowl, lamps upholstered with human skin, a shoebox containing nine female vaginas, and uncountable other atrocities. *Those were there when he moved in.*

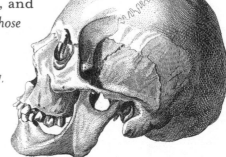

❯ Scott Hassett, "Our Psycho, *The Isthmus*, November 30, 2007, *www.thedailypage.com*.

FACT ATTACK: Multiple personalities spawn multiple movies! Shirley Ardell Mason's life story was the basis for the bestselling book *Sybil* as well as two movies of the same name. *Mason couldn't make the premieres, as she couldn't decide which personality to wear.*

❯ Mark Miller and Barbara Kantrowitz, "Unmasking Sybil. (Shirley Ardell Mason, the Real-Life Sybil)," *Newsweek*, January 25, 1999, *www.newsweek.com*.

FACT ATTACK: **Mass murderer has artistic side!** Charles Manson once recorded an album called *Lie. He shouldn't quit his day job.*

> Noel Botham, *The Book of Useless Information* (Perigee, 2006).

FACT ATTACK: **Rampaging strangler beats record!**
The record for most murders belongs to an Indian man named Behram. Between 1790 and 1840 he strangled 931 individuals with a piece of yellow and white cloth. *If you are going to do something, might as well be the best at it.*

> Noel Botham, *The Book of Useless Information* (Perigee, 2006).

FACT ATTACK: **Ruler keeps head of executed man on mantel!** Peter the Great executed his wife's lover and kept his head in a jar of alcohol in her bedroom. *In his defense, it was a really nice-looking head.*

> Noel Botham, *The Book of Useless Information* (Perigee, 2006).

FACT ATTACK: **Ax murderer kills own parents!** Possibly the original ax murderer, in August of 1892 Lizzie Borden took an ax to her sleeping stepmother's face—forty times. Once she realized what she had done, she proceeded to take the ax to her father as well. *Best not to leave witnesses.*

> Harold Schechter and David Everitt, *The A to Z Encyclopedia of Serial Killers* (Simon and Schuster, 2006), p. 22.

FACT ATTACK: **Mass murderers find peace in art!**

John Wayne Gacy took up oil painting in prison. Louisiana funeral director Rick Staton became Gacy's art dealer and also sells pieces from other murderers like Charles Manson and Richard Ramirez. Some clients include Johnny Depp, Iggy Pop, and John Waters. *In his defense, the works from Manson's green period are exquisite.*

> Harold Schechter and David Everitt, *The A to Z Encyclopedia of Serial Killers* (Simon and Schuster, 2006).

FACT ATTACK: **Vampire kills twenty-eight boys!**

Fritz Haarmann, better known as the "Vampire of Hanover," murdered at least twenty-eight young boys by literally gnawing through their throats. During his trial in 1924, he heckled witnesses while smoking a cigar and joked about the crimes he had committed. *You'd think he'd have figured out he wasn't really a vampire after number twenty-seven.*

> Harold Schechter and David Everitt, *The A to Z Encyclopedia of Serial Killers* (Simon and Schuster, 2006), p. 62.

FACT ATTACK: **Deformed experiments turn on their master!**

According to legend, an Ohio doctor named Dr. Crowe was commissioned by the government to treat a group of children suffering from hydrocephalus, a disorder which caused their heads to swell with fluids, leaving them with the unfortunate nickname "melonheads." Instead of curing their ailment, he enhanced the feature by injecting them with more fluid, until the group turned on him, tore his body to pieces, and burned down his laboratory. *Freak justice is swift, but fair.*

> Mark Moran and Mark Scuerman, *Weird U.S.* (Sterling Publishing, 2005), p. 61.

FACT ATTACK: **Real-life Hannibal Lecter consumes victim's lung!**

Nicolas Cocaign was sentenced to thirty years in prison for strangling his cellmate, ripping out one of his lungs—which he mistook for his heart—and frying it up with some onions. Prior to the murder, Cocaign plead with prison officials to put him in isolation due to his violent nature. *Can't say he didn't warn them.*

> ❯ Meena Hartenstein, "Nicolas Cocaign, Real-Life Hannibal Lecter, Sentenced to 30 Years for Brutal Murder, Cannibalism," *New York Daily News*, June 24, 2010. *www.nydailynews.com.*

FACT ATTACK: **Time-traveling car turns driver invisible!**

Mark Paul Warren was awarded an insanity plea after he killed two motorists while driving erratically on a New Zealand highway. He later told police he was traveling in a time machine and believed he would become invisible if he reached 100 km/h (62 mph). *What a lunatic. Everyone knows you have to go 88 mph to initiate the Flux Capacitor.*

> ❯ Rachel Tiffen, "Insane Driver Who Killed Two Committed for Treatment," *NZ Herald*, July 31, 2009, *www.nzherald.co.nz.*

FACT ATTACK: **Boy kills parents to save them from disappointment!**

After school officials discovered a gun in Kipland Kinkel's locker on May 21, 1998, the fifteen-year-old was so distraught by the embarrassment his imminent expulsion would cause his parents that he opted to shoot and kill them both. *New rule: If they find a gun in your locker, you don't get to go home and "pick up a few things" before they cart you away.*

> ❯ Nicole Fancher, "8 Years Later: Thurston and Kinkel Revisited," *The Daily Emerald*, October 2, 2006, *www.dailyemerald.com.*
>
> ❯ "Chronology: Kip Kinkel's Life and the Events Leading Up to the Horror of May 20–21, 1998," PBS, *www.pbs.org.*

FACT ATTACK: **Ruthless killer a sucker for romance!**

After he killed his parents, Kipland Kinkel spent the evening alone at home listening to the soundtrack of the film *Romeo & Juliet* on repeat. *Marilyn Manson, you are off the hook. We have a new scapegoat.*

> ❯ "Chronology: Kip Kinkel's Life and the Events Leading Up to the Horror of May 20–21, 1998," PBS, *www.pbs.org.*

FACT ATTACK: Poetry drives artists crazy! Colin Martindale of the University of Maine studied fifty-two contemporary poets, discovering that nearly 50 percent had some psychological problem and 15 percent could be defined as psychopaths. For example, Percy Shelley had frequent hallucinations of a man attacking him with a revolver, and John Keats was susceptible to inexplicable fits of weeping and hysterical laughter. *Good thing I just write snarky humor books.*

> Bruce Felton and Mark Fowler, *The Best, Worst, & Most Unusual: Noteworthy Achievements, Events, Feats & Blunders of Every Conceivable Kind* (Galahad, 1994).

FACT ATTACK: Author marks pages with human skin! Charles Dickens had a piece of skin belonging to deceased serial killer William Burke that he used as a bookmark. *Well, what else was he supposed to use it for?*

> Greta Garbage, *That's Disgusting!: An Adult Guide to What's Gross, Tasteless, Rude, Crude, and Lewd* (Ten Speed Press, 1999), p. 24.

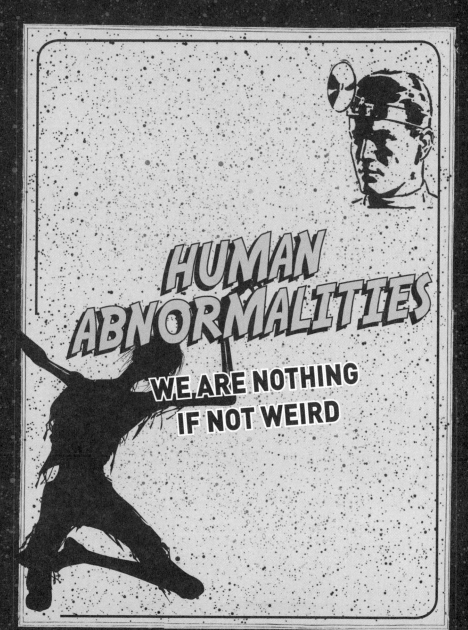

HUMAN ABNORMALITIES

WE ARE NOTHING IF NOT WEIRD

FACT ATTACK: Ancient doctors bore holes in your head! Trepanation, a practice that dates back to 3,000 B.C., was a medical procedure whereby a doctor removed pieces of the skull using a sharpened stone. The practice still exists today, and proponents claim it cures everything from headaches to depression. *I hope their tool of choice has improved.*

❯ Francesca Gould, *Why You Shouldn't Eat Your Boogers and Other Useless or Gross Information About Your Body* (Tarcher, 2008).

FACT ATTACK: Babies poop human hair! Meconium is the name given to an infant's first defecation. It is a greenish-black substance composed of materials ingested while in the uterus, including bile, water, mucus, amniotic fluid, and hair. *Grossest fact so far. And that's saying something.*

❯ Francesca Gould, *Why You Shouldn't Eat Your Boogers and Other Useless or Gross Information About Your Body* (Tarcher, 2008).

FACT ATTACK: Certain people smell like rotting fish! Fish odor syndrome is an unfortunate genetic condition that causes the sufferer to ooze the smell of rotting fish from their sweat, saliva, and urine. The patient's liver is unable to break down a substance called trimethylamine, resulting in the unpleasant odor. There is no cure. *Suddenly, being the Tree Man doesn't seem so bad, does it?*

❯ Francesca Gould, *Why You Shouldn't Eat Your Boogers and Other Useless or Gross Information About Your Body* (Tarcher, 2008).

FACT ATTACK: Human flesh tastes like beef! Survivors of the Uruguayan plane crash of 1972 were forced to cannibalize their fellow passengers to survive. They later confessed that human flesh tasted like beef when cooked. *Call me crazy, but I think I may have solved our overpopulation problem.*

❯ Francesca Gould, *Why You Shouldn't Eat Your Boogers and Other Useless or Gross Information About Your Body* (Tarcher, 2008).

FACT ATTACK: Autistic employees ten times more precise! In 2004, Thorkil Sonne started Speciali-sterne to create jobs for those diagnosed with autism and other disorders that make it difficult for them to function in work environments. Customers include companies like Microsoft, who have found the individuals five to ten times more precise than the average person. *Note to self: Hide this fact from boss.*

❯ Thorkil Sonne, "First Person: Founder of Specialisterne," ABC News, April 1, 2010, *http://abcnews.go.com.*

❯ Robert Evans and Philip Moon, "5 Horrible Diseases That Changed The World (For the Better)," Cracked.com, June 14, 2010, *www.cracked.com.*

FACT ATTACK: Our ears set us apart! The outer ears of no two humans are exactly alike. Some believe this distinction could serve as a better means of identification than fingerprints. *Except criminals don't typically drag the sides of their heads all over crime scenes.*

❯ Amit Garg, *501 Astonishing Facts* (Pustak Mahal, 2010).

FACT ATTACK: **Women's favorite subject: men!** Women talk about men three times more often than men talk about women. *It's just that sports and video games are so much more interesting.*

❯ Amit Garg, *501 Astonishing Facts* (Pustak Mahal, 2010).

FACT ATTACK: Allergy sufferers can't escape the sun! Sufferers of actinic prurigo develop painful blisters if they venture out into the sun for even a short while. *I'm no doctor, but it sounds like they are vampires.*

> Simon De Bruxelles, "The Boy Who's Allergic to Summer Sun," *The Sunday Times*, June 29, 2006, *www.timesonline.co.uk.*

FACT ATTACK: **"I have a headache" defense proven invalid!** The endorphins released during sex can actually relieve a headache. *No more excuses.*

> "Ten Weird Human Sex Facts," Divine Caroline, *www.divinecaroline.com.*

FACT ATTACK: Women more sexually ambiguous than men! Research shows that women may be inherently bisexual. When exposed to pornographic material containing only women, a large percentage of heterosexual female subjects were aroused even when there were no men present in the films. The same was not true for the male test subjects. *See, porn can teach us things.*

> Wing Sze, "10 Things You Didn't Know About Sex," *Fashion*, *www.fashionmagazine.com.*

FACT ATTACK: Sleepwalkers shouldn't get special treatment! Contrary to popular belief, there is no danger to waking up a sleepwalker. They will merely be confused and disoriented. *But it's way more fun to watch and see what they do.*

❯ "Sleep Disorders and Parasomnias," WebMD.com, *www.webmd.com.*

FACT ATTACK: Night terrors no joke! A person experiencing a night terror may appear to wake suddenly in a terrifed state, but does not respond to voices and is difficult to fully awaken. This state generally lasts about fifteen minutes, after which the sufferer usually lies down and appears to fall back asleep. *Nine times out of ten, they're faking.*

❯ "Sleep Disorders and Parasomnias," WebMD.*com,* *www.webmd.com.*

FACT ATTACK: Human brain hogs oxygen! The brain accounts for only 2 percent of our body mass, but consumes 20 percent of the oxygen we inhale. If deprived of oxygen, the brain will begin to die within four minutes. *Which is why autoerotic asphyxiation is so dangerous. If only I'd known sooner. . . .*

❯ Rich Maloof, "7 Weird-But-True Facts About the Human Brain," MSN, *health.msn.com.*

FACT ATTACK: **Organic computer barely needs power!** The human brain functions on the equivalent of just ten watts of power. *Unless your brain is a Mac.*

> Kate Wong, "You're a Dim Bulb (And I Mean That in the Best Possible Way)," *Discover* magazine blog, March 23, *http://blogs.discovermagazine.com.*

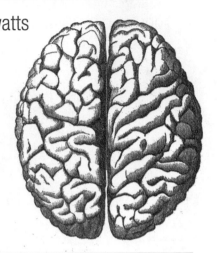

FACT ATTACK: **Some people can taste music!** Sufferers of synesthesia find that they do not experience the world using their five senses in the same way that others do. Because of crossovers in their neural wiring, they describe being able to taste sounds and hear certain colors. *In case you are wondering, Marilyn Manson tastes like strawberries. And so does his music.*

> "Top Ten Little-Known Mental Disorders," Science Channel, *http://science.discovery.com.*

FACT ATTACK: **Man celebrates record-sized tumor!** After doctors removed one of Eugene Tyner's kidneys that had developed a malignant tumor, he celebrated the successful surgery by submitting the massive 332-gram tumor to the *Guinness Book of World Records. I certainly hope he just sent a picture.*

> Associated Press, "Man Pursues World Record for Kidney Tumor," MSNBC, November 1, 2010, *www.msnbc.msn.com.*

FACT ATTACK: Stress-free humans sleep longer!
If removed from the stress of the modern world, the average human will sleep for about ten hours a day. *More reason to quit your job.*

❯ Bill McLain, *Do Fish Drink Water? Puzzling and Improbable Questions and Answers* (William Morrow and Company, 1999), p. 143.

FACT ATTACK: We swallow a lot of snot! The human nose produces about one liter of mucus every day. The vast majority of it drips down the throat into the stomach. *Might as well eat your boogers then. Cut out the middleman.*

❯ C. S. Larsen, *Crust & Spray: Gross Stuff in Your Eyes, Ears, Nose, and Throat (Gross Body Science)* (Millbrook Press, September 2009).

FACT ATTACK: The blind still dream! People who are blind from birth do dream, but not in the same way as sighted individuals. Instead of seeing shapes and colors in their dreams, they often report hearing sounds and experiencing feelings of being touched. Those who lose their sight later in life still dream in pictures, but they often fade as time goes on. *Not sure if hearing yourself in front of a classroom in your underwear is quite as powerful as seeing it.*

❯ Bill McLain, *Do Fish Drink Water? Puzzling and Improbable Questions and Answers* (William Morrow and Company, 1999), p. 142.

FACT ATTACK: **Even royal urine is special!**

The urine of King George III was a deep shade of purple. *What a gifted man.*

> Bill McLain, *Do Fish Drink Water? Puzzling and Improbable Questions and Answers* (William Morrow and Company, 1999), p. 79.

FACT ATTACK: **Dead babies turn into mummies!**

Because human infants contain very little bacteria in their bodies, they will often mummify naturally instead of decomposing like adults. *I'm skeptical. Only one way to find out.*

> Eric Elfman, *Almanac of the Gross, Disgusting, & Totally Repulsive, a Compendium of Fulsome Facts* (RGA Publishing Group, Inc., 1994), p. 29.

FACT ATTACK: **Corpses give off flammable gas!**

Before morticians began refrigerating bodies, they would poke holes in corpses bloated with excess gases and set a candle to them. The gases would ignite and produce a blue flame that could last for days. *I really want to test that, but hate myself because I do.*

> Eric Elfman, *Almanac of the Gross, Disgusting, & Totally Repulsive, a Compendium of Fulsome Facts* (RGA Publishing Group, Inc., 1994), p. 28.

FACT ATTACK: **Cysts grow their own hair!**

If you suffer from a dermatoid cyst in your bladder, it is possible to urinate hair. A range of organic matter can form in the cyst such as teeth, fat, and even bone that can leak out if ruptured. *To my bald readers: If you could then attach said hair to your head, would it be worth it?*

> Eric Elfman, *Almanac of the Gross, Disgusting, & Totally Repulsive, a Compendium of Fulsome Facts* (RGA Publishing Group, Inc., 1994), p. 15.

FACT ATTACK: Doctors inject patients with skin of the dead! The filler alloderm is derived from the skin of cadavers. Doctors use it cosmetically to create fuller lips for their patients. *At least it's natural.*

❯ Francesca Gould, *Why You Shouldn't Eat Your Boogers and Other Useless or Gross Information About Your Body* (Tarcher, 2008).

FACT ATTACK: Boxers' brains turn to mush! When Dr. Milton Halpern opened the skulls of boxers who died in the ring, their brains oozed out of their heads. The repeated blows to the head had liquefied their gray matter. *Not like they were using them anyway.*

❯ Eric Elfman, *Almanac of the Gross, Disgusting, & Totally Repulsive, a Compendium of Fulsome Facts* (RGA Publishing Group, Inc., 1994), p. 7.

FACT ATTACK: Doctors remove tree from man's lungs! When surgeons operated on Artyom Sidorkin's lung, they were shocked to discover a five-inch fir tree embedded within his soft tissue. Because the tree was too large to have been inhaled, doctors inferred that he must have inhaled a spore that took root and germinated in his lungs. *So a watermelon can grow in your stomach if you swallow a seed!*

❯ Will Stewart, "Shocked Russian Surgeons Open Up Man Who Thought He Had a Tumour . . . To Find A Fir Tree Inside His Lung," *Daily Mail,* April 15, 2009, *www.daily-mail.co.uk.*

FACT ATTACK: Baby poop doesn't smell like burnt hair! Babies who feed solely on a mother's milk do not have poop that smells offensive. *It may not smell, but baby poop is still the ultimate birth control.*

> Joy Masoff, *Oh Yuck! The Encyclopedia of Everything Nasty* (Workman Publishing Company, 2000).

FACT ATTACK: If it's yellow, don't let it mellow! Generally, urine does not contain any bacteria unless it sits around for a while. When urine first leaves the body it is completely sanitary and is actually potable. In fact, Mahatma Gandhi started each morning with a sip of his own urine. *Bottoms up.*

> Joy Masoff, *Oh Yuck! The Encyclopedia of Everything Nasty* (Workman Publishing Company, 2000).

FACT ATTACK: **Humans produce a load of shit!** The average human defecates 2.6 tons of feces in a lifetime. *Thankfully, the average human does not save it.*

> Karl Shaw, *The Giant Bathroom Reader* (Magpie Books, 2006).

FACT ATTACK: Farts add up to atomic proportions! If you farted nonstop for six years and nine months, you would expel enough gas to produce the energy of a nuclear bomb. *By that logic, if I can get 299,635,200 people to fart simultaneously, I can control the world!*

> Noel Botham, *The Mega Book of Useless Information* (John Blake, 2009).

FACT ATTACK: Candy man buried in edible coffin! Roland Ohisson, a Swedish purveyor of sweets, was buried in a coffin made entirely of chocolate. *What a waste.*

> Noel Botham, *The Mega Book of Useless Information* (John Blake, 2009).

FACT ATTACK: Overzealous masturbation hazardous to your manhood! More than half of men who experience penile fracture will do so as a result of overly rigorous masturbation. *All of them wish they'd just gone blind or caused the birth of a two-headed kitten.*

> Shane Mooney, *Useless Sexual Trivia* (Simon & Schuster, 2000).

FACT ATTACK: Sexual deviants are cuddly critters! The term "furry" refers to those who derive sexual pleasure from dressing up as animals and imitating their behavior. The sexual encounters, called "yiffing," often focus on rubbing and petting one another's costumed bodies. *Before you pass judgment, think of the strangest thing you've done sexually and compare it to wearing a rabbit costume and grinding on a guy in a bear suit.*

> George Gurley, "Pleasures of the Fur," *Vanity Fair*, March 2001, *www.vanityfair.com*.

FACT ATTACK: **Developing babies plagued by tiny boners!** A male fetus is capable of sustaining an erection in the third trimester. *And he doesn't even have a book to cover it up. Poor little fella.*

> Shane Mooney, *Useless Sexual Trivia* (Simon & Schuster, 2000).

FACT ATTACK: **Humans win animal kingdom sweat-off!** Aside from chimpanzees, humans have more sweat glands proportional to our body size than any other animal. *Damn you, chimps!*

> Kathy Boake, *You Are Weird: Your Body's Peculiar Parts and Funny Functions* (Kids Can Press Ltd, 2009).

FACT ATTACK: **Penises flee from paranoid owners!** Although it is not a physical affliction, those suffering from genital retraction syndrome have a very real belief that their genitalia are retracting into their body, a fact which they assume will result in their death. The disorder primarily affects men, some of whom attempt to alleviate the phantom symptom by stretching their penises or clamping them down to prevent them from receding. *Back whence it came.*

> Christine Taylor, "Genital Retraction Syndrome," Associated Content, February 9, 2010, *www.associatedcontent.com.*

> "Koro—The Genital Retraction Syndrome," BBC, September 7, 2001, *www.bbc.co.uk.*

FACT ATTACK: Vomit champion emerges! The longest recorded projectile vomit was twenty-seven feet. *The shortest was me a few seconds ago. Just a little in my mouth.*

❯ "Gross Facts You May Have Never Wanted to Know," Associated Content, May 24, 2007, *www.associatedcontent.com.*

FACT ATTACK: Living zombies troubled by skepticism! Suffers of the Cotard delusion, also known as Walking Corpse Syndrome, believe that they have died. They insist their organs have ceased to function, and many refuse to eat due to the futility of such actions. *That would be an interesting intellectual argument. Patient: "I'm dead." Doctor: "Then how are you talking to me?" Patient: "Next question."*

❯ Alan Bellows, *Alien Hand Syndrome and Other Too-Weird-To-Be-True Stories* (Workman Publishing, 2009), p. 282.

FACT ATTACK: Case of the Mondays causes heart attacks! A ten-year study conducted in Scotland found that 20 percent of heart attacks occur on Mondays. *When you run out of sick days, sometimes you have to resort to drastic measures.*

❯ "Mondays Bring Heart Attacks," BBC News, January 20, 2000, *http://news.bbc.co.uk.*

FACT ATTACK: Longest sleepless session lasts for weeks! The longest recorded sleepless session is 264 hours. *By the time you read this, I will have beaten that record.*

❯ "10 Craziest Facts About the Human Body," Newspick.com, *http://news.upickreviews.com.*

FACT ATTACK: Guinness eliminates record category! Due to fears of the negative health effects caused by sleep deprivation, *The Guinness Book of World Records* no longer recognizes the record for longest stretch without sleep. *Yet the most chainsaws juggled simultaneously doesn't scare them?*

❯ "Man Claims New Sleepless Record," BBC News, May 25, 2007, *http://news.bbc.co.uk.*

FACT ATTACK: Scientists discover memory eraser molecule! By suppressing an enzyme in the brain called alpha calcium/calmodulin-dependent protein kinase II (CaMKII) at different stages of the memory process, scientists can prevent the transfer of new memories from short-term to long-term storage and even selectively erase specific individual memories. *I can finally unsee Two Girls, One Cup!*

❯ Moheb Costandi, "The Power of the Memory Molecule," *Scientific American*, November 11, 2008, *www.scientific american.com.*

❯ "Twenty-five Things You Probably Didn't Know About Your Body and Health," MSN Health, *www.health.msn.com.*

FACT ATTACK: Love conquers all, except paraplegia! One out of every three people would not go through with a marriage if their fiancé was involved in an accident that left them paraplegic. *The other two thirds are saps.*

❯ Bernice Kanner, *Are You Normal about Sex, Love, and Relationships?* (Macmillan, 2004).

FACT ATTACK: ADHD keeps nomads on their toes!
Attention deficit hyperactivity disorder is more prevalent among nomadic people, which has led scientist to believe that the disease evolved as a means to keep individuals from becoming too complacent and encourage them to seek out new food sources. *The mellow hunter/gatherers were quickly eaten by smilodons.*

> Ewen Callaway, "Did Hyperactivity Evolve as a Survivial Aid for Nomad?," New Scientist, June 10, 2008, *www.newscientists.com.*

FACT ATTACK: OCD good for babies! Some scientists believe obsessive compulsive disorder (OCD) evolved as a way of encouraging new mothers to better care for their offspring. The incessant attention to hygiene would have given the children of OCD sufferers a better chance of survival. *And a better chance to creep out their friends and family later in life.*

> Robert Evans and Philip Moon, "5 Horrible Diseases That Changed The World (For the Better)," Cracked.com, June 14, 2010, *www.cracked.com.*

FACT ATTACK: Stomach has its limits! The human stomach can hold about thirty-two ounces of food at any given time. *Or about fifty-five hot dogs.*

> Angela Royston, *Puke and Poo (Read Me!)* (Heinemann-Raintree, 2009).

FACT ATTACK: Can't do much without a tongue!
The only letter sounds one can make
without using the tongue are m, p, h, f,
and v. *You are trying now, aren't you?*

❯ Barbara Seuling, *You Blink Twelve Times a Minute: and Other Freaky Facts About the Human Body* (Picture Window Books, 2008).

FACT ATTACK: Jungles crawling with tiny humans! The average height of a pygmy is four feet six. *It's not the size of the pygmy that matters, but how you use it.*

❯ Bill McLain, *Do Fish Drink Water? Puzzling and Improbable Questions and Answers* (William Morrow and Company, 1999), p. 256.

FACT ATTACK: Miniature women have giant babies!
Pygmy women are the smallest full-grown females
on earth, but they produce the largest babies. New-
borns average more than eight pounds at birth. *Like
pushing a watermelon out of a hole the size of a thimble.*

❯ Barbara Seuling, *You Blink Twelve Times a Minute: and Other Freaky Facts About the Human Body* (Picture Window Books, 2008).

FACT ATTACK: Researchers uncover world's most annoying sound! A study conducted by England's Salford University determined that the most irritating sound known to man is that of another person vomiting. Microphone feedback came in second with multiple babies crying coming in at number three. *Gotta go with the sound of somebody asking me to clean something.*

> Roger Kaplinsky-Dwarika, "'Most Annoying Sound' Is Stomach Turning," ABC News, January 25, 2007, *http://abcnews.go.com.*

FACT ATTACK: Human beings shed! Humans shed about 600,000 skin particles every hour. At that rate, the average person loses around fifty pounds of skin by age thirty-five. *That's half an Olsen twin!*

> "Sixteen Unusual Facts About the Human Body," HowStuff-Works.*com, www.health.howstuffworks.com.*

FACT ATTACK: Crippling phone phobia strikes Britain! Nomophobia is a fear of being without mobile phone service. Sufferers panic if they can't get a signal, misplace their phone, or if the battery is low. According to one study, the phobia could affect up to 53 percent of British mobile phone users. *Gotta love first-world problems.*

> Alexandra Gekas, "10 Fascinating Phobias," *Woman's Day*, September 14, 2010. *www.womansday.com.*

FACT ATTACK: Nicole Kidman reveals irrational fear! Nicole Kidman is terrified of butterflies. *I'm sure they feel the same way.*

> "100 Things We Didn't Know This Time Last Year," BBC News, December 30, 2005. *http://news.bbc.co.uk.*

FACT ATTACK: **Real life blue man discovered!**

Fifty-seven-year-old Californian Paul Karason suffers from argyria, a rare condition that turns his skin a deep blue. Karason drinks a homemade dermatitis remedy called colloidal silver which he produces by running an electrical current through distilled water with a sliver of silver in it. It is the silver in the concoction that causes the blue tint. *I'm no doctor, but I'd say step one is to stop drinking silver.*

❯ Mike Celizic, "Real-life 'Blue Guy' Shrugs Off His Skin Color," *Today*, January 7, 2008. *http://today.msnbc .msn.com.*

FACT ATTACK: **Underwear model missing navel!**

Underwear model Karolina Kurkova does not have a belly button. Magazines often insert one digitally in post-production. While she has not acknowledged the anatomical abnormality publicly, her agent merely insists, "She is not an alien." *Yes, she is.*

❯ "Who Doesn't Have a Belly Button?" BBC News, November 20, 2010. *http://news.bbc.co.uk.*

FACT ATTACK: **Finger length linked to aggression!**

The ratio of a man's index finger compared to his ring finger can determine how aggressive he might be. If he has a short index finger and long ring finger, he is more likely to be especially boisterous. The phenomenon does not extend to verbal hostility. *Next time you pick a fight, ask to hold hands first.*

❯ "Finger Length 'Key to Aggression'", BBC News, March 4, 2005. *http://news.bbc.co.uk.*

FACT ATTACK: **Man survives nail gun to the head!**
Construction worker Travis Bogumill survived having a three-and-a-half-inch-long nail driven into his skull in July of 1998. The gun drove the nail so deeply into Bogumill's brain that no piece of the nail was visible. Despite the horrific nature of his injury, the only adverse effect was a decreased ability to perform simple mathematics. *3 + 7 = hamster.*

❯ "Wisconsin Worker Survives Removal of Nail," *Chicago Tribune*, July 17, 1998. *www.chicagotribune.com.*

FACT ATTACK: **Susceptibility to mosquito bites genetic!** Genetics account for 85 percent of our attractiveness to mosquitoes. Other contributing factors include cholesterol levels, acid buildup on the skin, and the amount of carbon dioxide we exhale. *Thanks, Mom and Dad.*

❯ Elizabeth Heubeck, "Are You a Mosquito Magnet?" WebMD. *www.webmd.com.*

FACT ATTACK: **Screaming children damage ears!** Human children can scream at up to 90 decibels. Levels above 85 decibels can damage the hearing of anyone close by. *I find it's best to ignore them.*

❯ Noel Botham, *The Best Book of Useless Information Ever: A Few Thousand Other Things You Probably Don't Need to Know (But Might as Well Find Out)* (Perigee, 2007).

FACT ATTACK: **Setting farts on fire, still funny!** A fart is about 4 percent oxygen, 7 percent methane, 9 percent carbon dioxide, 21 percent hydrogen, and 59 percent nitrogen. The combination of hydrogen and methane is what makes them flammable. *There is no single greater accomplishment for a young man than lighting his very first fart on fire.*

> Mark Leyner and Billy Goldberg M.D., *Why Do Men Have Nipples?* (Three Rivers Press 2005), pp. 139–140.

FACT ATTACK: **Babies dumber than chimps!** Scientists believe that human babies are less intelligent than chimpanzee babies. *But more intelligent than human adults.*

> Bart King and Chris Sabatino, *The Big Book of Boy Stuff* (July 2004).

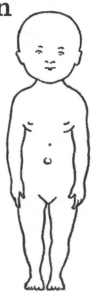

FACT ATTACK: **Fish medicine good for humans!** The tetracycline sold for use in fish tanks to treat bacterial infections is often supplied in the same dosage humans receive by prescription. Despite the similarity, doctors don't recommend patients self-medicate with the over-the-counter fish product. *I'll be damned if I'm going to let some "doctor" tell me what I can and cannot shove down my pie hole.*

> Mark Leyner and Billy Goldberg M.D., *Why Do Men Have Nipples?* (Three Rivers Press 2005), p. 103.

FACT ATTACK: Not all humans smell asparagus pee! Scientists used to believe that certain individuals digested asparagus differently than others, which resulted in the sulfuric smelling urine many expel after consuming the vegetable. But almost all humans produce the odoriferous phenomenon, however, not everyone has the sensory cells necessary to smell it. *How weird is it if you secretly like the smell?*

❯ Karen Marriott, "Peter Barham on Asparagus Pee: Why Does My Wee Smell When I've Eaten Asparagus?" *The Guardian*, September 23, 2005, *www.guardian.co.uk*.

FACT ATTACK: Elderly humans lose sense of taste! Starting at around age forty-five, human beings begin to lose their sense of taste. We start life with apprimately 9,000 taste buds and end up with nearly half that. Some elderly people lose their ability to taste bitter or salty flavors altogether. *Good, I won't be able to taste the terrible food in whatever second-rate home my kids stick me in.*

❯ Mark Leyner and Billy Goldberg M.D., *Why Do Men Have Nipples?* (Three Rivers Press 2005), p. 203.

FACT ATTACK: Corpses demonstrate optical illusion! Despite the popular myth, human hair and nails do not continue to grow after death. In reality, the skin dries out and contracts, giving the impression that these body functions continue post-mortem. *Which explains why the world isn't overrun with fingernails.*

❯ Mark Leyner and Billy Goldberg M.D., *Why Do Men Have Nipples?* (Three Rivers Press 2005), p. 206.

FACT ATTACK: Oral sex can be nutritious! The average ejaculate contains between 200 and 300 million sperm, five calories, vitamin C, zinc, phosphate, and other nutrients. *Hungry? Why wait?*

❯ Mark Leyner and Billy Goldberg M.D., *Why Do Men Have Nipples?* (Three Rivers Press 2005), p. 82.

FACT ATTACK: **Medical community shits on under-endowed men!** If a flaccid penis is more than two and a half times the standard deviation below the average length when stretched, it is medically dubbed a micropenis. *Proof that doctors really are assholes.*

❯ Mark Leyner and Billy Goldberg M.D., *Why Do Men Have Nipples?* (Three Rivers Press 2005), p. 91.

FACT ATTACK: **Tibetans are world's fastest evolving humans!** The award for fastest case of human evolution goes to inhabitants of Tibet, who in just 3,000 years evolved the ability to live in high altitudes without experiencing mountain sickness. *Next time let's evolve something useful, like bottle openers instead of pinky toes.*

❯ Nicholas Wade, "Scientists Cite Fastest Case of Human Evolution," *New York Times*, July 1, 2010, *www.nytimes.com.*

FACT ATTACK: **If your pee smells like waffles, find a hospital!** Maple syrup urine disease is a disorder that causes the urine of the afflicted to smell like maple syrup. Unfortunately, it also causes lethargy, food avoidance, coma, and mental retardation if left untreated. The disorder affects one out of every 120,000 births. *Wait a second, not everyone's pee smells like pancakes?*

❯ Natalie Josef, "Six Diseases and Infections You Don't Want," Divine Caroline, *www.divinecaroline.com.*

FACT ATTACK: **Neanderthal DNA discovered in modern humans!** A genetic analysis of 2,000 people conducted by researchers at the University of New Mexico revealed that, before Neanderthal man went extinct nearly 30,000 years ago, several members of the species interbred with Homo sapiens, leaving their genetic imprint on modern-day humans. *I always thought I had an abnormally large brow ridge.*

❯ Rex Dalton, "Neanderthals May Have Interbred with Humans," *Nature*, April 20, 2010, *www.nature.com.*

WHAT'S THIS THING DO?

DUMB DISCOVERIES AND TERRIFYING CONTRAPTIONS WE WISH WE COULD UNINVENT

FACT ATTACK: Google cars drive themselves! In 2010 Google revealed that it had been developing artificially intelligent computer software that could operate an automobile without the need for a human driver. Initial tests were flawless, with the only accident occurring when a Google car was rear-ended while sitting at a traffic light. *I wonder if you can program it to brake angrily and tailgate other drivers.*

> John Markoff, "Google Cars Drive Themselves, In Traffic," *New York Times*, October 9, 2010, *www.nytimes.com.*

FACT ATTACK: New body armor painted on skin! Israeli scientists have developed a method for assembling nanospheres into fixed patterns stronger than steel and even Kevlar. The technology could be used to create super-thin body armor that conforms to the wearer's body. *Better solution: Don't hang out near people with guns.*

> Clay Dillow, "New Nanospheres Are the Stiffest Biological Materials Ever Created, Surpassing Kevlar," Popsci.com, October 22, 2010, *www.popsci.com.*

FACT ATTACK: **Government plans ultimate weapon!** The U.S. government has plans to develop a flying Humvee. The program, dubbed Transformer, has more than $9 million in government funding. *So, like a Hummer, but several times more unnecessary.*

> "A Flying Humvee? Don't Scoff, Pentagon Wants One," *LA Times*, October 19, 2010, *www.latimes.com.*

FACT ATTACK: Tiny inventor sets record! In 1989, four-year-old John J. Stone-Parker and his sister invented a star-shaped gadget that prevented ice from slipping from a drinking glass. He is the world's youngest patent holder. *His sister is the world's most bitter sibling.*

❯ Russell Ash, *Firefly's World of Facts* (Firefly Books, 2007).

FACT ATTACK: Anatomically correct robots invade sex industry! In January of 2010, Truecompanion unveiled the world's first artificially intelligent sex robot at the AVN Adult Entertainment Expo in Las Vegas. The robot responds to human touch and can even engage in conversation with its owner. Unfortunately, Roxxxy can't move her limbs independently, as movement is reserved for "the three inputs" and a mechanical heart that powers a liquid cooling system. *You had me at sex robot. You lost me at conversation.*

❯ "Roxxxy, the World's First Life-Size Robot Girlfriend," Fox News, January 11, 2010, *www.foxnews.com.*

FACT ATTACK: Bug zapper does more than just zap! The electrical current from a bug zapper doesn't just electrocute the insects, it actually causes their bodies to explode. The internal juices can spray as far as eight feet. *I'm waiting for the inhumane version that pins them down and hits them with mild micropulses to stun them before tiny tweezers appear to rip off their wings. That's a product I can get behind.*

❯ The Sanders Family, *Gross News: Gross (but Clean) Stories from Around the World* (Andrews McMeel Publishing, 2006).

FACT ATTACK: Bathroom tissue conglomerate goes green! Researchers at Kimberley-Clark developed a toilet paper roll that does not require a cardboard insert. The company polled its customers and discovered that 50 percent toss the cardboard tubes in the trash instead of recycling them. *Hear that? It's the sound of 10 million kindergarten teachers sighing in despair.*

❯ Jonathan Bardelline, "Scott Dumps Toilet Paper Waste with Tubeless Rolls," Greenbiz.com, October 27, 2010, *www.greenbiz.com.*

FACT ATTACK: The bed that kicks you out! In the early twentieth century, inventor Ludwig Ederer invented an alarm mechanism that was built into the bed. At a predetermined time the bed rotated to a forty-five degree angle and ejected the sleeper onto the floor. *I just pay somebody to rip the covers off and throw them into the hallway every morning.*

❯ Sarah Houghton and Elaine Lally, *Inventions: Great Ideas and Where They Came From* (Red Bricklearning, 2002).

FACT ATTACK: First roller skates missing key component! When Joseph Merlin invented the first roller skates in the 1760s, he neglected to install a braking mechanism. He realized his error while showing off his new invention at a party after crashing into a full-length mirror. *It's the little things that get you.*

❯ Sarah Houghton and Elaine Lally, *Inventions: Great Ideas and Where They Came From* (Red Bricklearning, 2002).

FACT ATTACK: Special diaper takes guesswork out of changing time! Using mild electrical conduction, the diaper alarm activates blinking lights and a siren if it senses moisture on a baby's skin. *If you can't hear the alarm over the sound of your child's screams, you know it's working.*

❯ Ted VanCleave, *Totally Absurd Inventions: America's Goofiest Patents* (Andrews McMeel Publishing, 2001).

FACT ATTACK: A cure-all pill for whiny kids!

Obecalp is a pill manufactured to FDA standards marketed as a treatment for children's mild complaints. *Read the name backwards and watch your dreams wither and die.*

> Rebecca Coffey, "20 Things You Didn't Know About . . . Sugar," *Discover* magazine, October 2009, *www.discovermagazine.com.*

FACT ATTACK: Gunpowder made from elixir of life!

In the ninth century, a team of Chinese alchemists searching for the "elixir of immortality" combined saltpeter, sulfur, realgar, and dried honey, and instead invented gunpowder. *Close enough.*

> Sean Markey, "20 Things You Didn't Know About . . . Lab Accidents," *Discover* magazine, November 2006, *www.discovermagazine.com.*

FACT ATTACK: Lightning strikes twice for Fleming!

Alexander Fleming, famous for the accidental discovery of penicillin, inadvertently uncovered an antibiotic enzyme in nasal mucus several years later. When he sneezed onto a bacterial sample, he discovered that his discharge kept the microbes in check. *Wonder what he could have accomplished had he ever tried to do anything on purpose.*

> Sean Markey, "20 Things You Didn't Know About . . . Lab Accidents," *Discover* magazine, November 2006, *www.discovermagazine.com.*

FACT ATTACK: **Ancients ignored soap's true potential!** Ancient peoples used soap to disinfect wounds as early as 2,000 B.C.; however, they did not use it for bathing. *These are the same people who used shovels every day, but never made the leap to invent spoons.*

> Bill McLain, *Do Fish Drink Water? Puzzling and Improbable Questions and Answers* (William Morrow and Company, 1999), p. 188.

FACT ATTACK: **Pubic wig disguises STDs!** A merkin, or pubic wig, was a popular device employed by prostitutes in the 1600s. Women afflicted with sexually transmitted diseases like gonorrhea and syphilis would use the merkin to disguise the outward signs of the disease, such as open sores or yellow discharge. *And they also made great hand warmers.*

> Francesca Gould, *Why You Shouldn't Eat Your Boogers and Other Useless or Gross Information About Your Body* (Tarcher, 2008).

FACT ATTACK: **L.A. has more cars than people!** The city of Los Angeles contains three times more cars than it does people. *Hedonism at its best.*

> Bill McLain, *Do Fish Drink Water? Puzzling and Improbable Questions and Answers* (William Morrow and Company, 1999), p. 244.

FACT ATTACK: First vacuum too big to carry!
The first vacuum cleaner was so large it had to be pulled to the owner's house by a team of horses. *Unfortunately, the vacuum could not clean up after its escorts.*

❯ Bill McLain, *Do Fish Drink Water? Puzzling and Improbable Questions and Answers* (William Morrow and Company, 1999), p. 182.

FACT ATTACK: Vacuums don't actually suck!
Vacuums don't actually "suck" anything. Instead, they merely create spaces into which the surrounding atmosphere pushes matter. *I'm not sure of anything anymore.*

❯ LeeAundra Temescu, "20 Things You Didn't Know About . . . Nothing," *Discover* magazine, June 2007, *www.discovermagazine.com.*

FACT ATTACK: Without stimuli, the mind wanders into risqué territory! To determine what would happen if a person's body were cut off from external stimuli, John Lilly built the first sensory deprivation tank in 1954. Floating in lukewarm water for hours on end produced hallucinations in Lilly that were "too personal to relate publicly." *The average person does not require a special chamber to achieve this effect.*

❯ "Top 10 Mad Scientists in History," Oddee.com, October 13, 2008, *www.oddee.com.*

FACT ATTACK: Inventor wrongly steals credit!
Galileo did not invent the telescope; he was merely the first to use it to formally observe the sky. *Everybody else had just been using it to make their balls look massive.*

❯ Liza Lentini, "20 Things You Didn't Know About . . . Galileo," *Discover* magazine, July 2007, *www.discovermagazine.com.*

FACT ATTACK: Pencils dangerous to astronauts!
Astronauts on early American and Russian space missions used pencils because of their ability to function in zero gravity. However, NASA engineers worried about the flammability of pencils in a pure-oxygen atmosphere and switched to Paul Fisher's pressured Fisher Space Pen after the *Apollo* 1 fire. *See, pencils are dangerous.*

❯ Dean Christopher, "20 Things You Didn't Know About . . . Pencils," *Discover* magazine, May 2007, *www.discover magazine.com*.

FACT ATTACK: Technology improves ancient weapon!
Modern archery bows produced from advanced materials, like Kevlar and magnesium fiberglass, shoot arrows at speeds greater than 150 miles per hour. *Have they invented a way to compete in archery without getting made fun of?*

❯ Dean Christopher, "20 Things You Didn't Know About . . . Sports Technology," *Discover* magazine, August 2008, *www.discovermagazine.com*.

FACT ATTACK: Cannon accuracy more important than weather! To avoid debtors' prison, Galileo made a living designing a military device to aim cannonballs. His earlier invention—the first thermometer to measure temperature variations—was a financial failure. *Knowing the temperature is wildly overrated anyway.*

❯ Liza Lentini, "20 Things You Didn't Know About . . . Galileo," *Discover* magazine, July 2007, *www.discovermagazine.com*.

FACT ATTACK: New invention simulates floating in thin air! In the summer of 2010, pilot Christian Brown developed a hot air balloon with a glass bottom so passengers could look down at the world below them while they flew. Brown described riding in his invention as a "terrifying experience" that "isn't for the faint-hearted." *Well, I'm sold.*

Jesus Diaz, "Glass-Bottomed Hot Air Balloon Is a Terrifying Experience," Gizmodo, August 13, 2010, *www.gizmodo.com.*

FACT ATTACK: Napalm killed thousands long before Vietnam! In 1942, Harvard chemist Louis Fieser combined naphthenic acid and palmitic acid to create a substance that clung to any surface and burned violently. The military first used the substance, called napalm, on March 9, 1945 when Air Force bombers dropped nearly 2,000 tons of it on Tokyo, killing at least 83,000 people and leaving up to 1 million homeless. *Dear Japan, thanks for giving us sushi and ramen. Sorry about the 1940s. xoxo, your friends across the Pacific.*

Joey Green, *Contrary to Popular Belief: More Than 250 False Facts Revealed* (Broadway Books, 2005).

FACT ATTACK: Sandwich history shrouded in misinformation! Contrary to popular belief, the Earl of Sandwich did not invent the popular lunch item. The first recorded sandwich was invented by Rabbi Hillel between 70 B.C. and 10 C.E. and consisted of fruits, nuts, honey, and bitter herbs between two pieces of matzah. *The Twinkie was still invented by the Duke of Twinkieton, though.*

Joey Green, *Contrary to Popular Belief: More Than 250 False Facts Revealed* (Broadway Books, 2005).

FACT ATTACK: **Cheeky gag bad for the copy machine!** People sitting on photocopiers and scanning their buttocks are responsible for more than 23 percent of photocopier malfunctions. *This knowledge will not stop me, and only strengthens my resolve.*

> Noel Botham, *The Mega Book of Useless Information* (John Blake, 2009).

FACT ATTACK: **Iron maiden invention way worse than band of same name!** The iron maiden was a torture device shaped like a vertical sarcophagus with spikes lining the interior. The torturer would close the doors, forcing the spikes into the victim's body. The spikes were arranged in such a way so that they would miss vital organs and the victim would bleed to death. *And people get uppity about waterboarding.*

> "12 of the Most Horrifying Torture Devices in History," Listaholic.com, *www.listaholic.com.*

FACT ATTACK: **Benign-sounding device anything but!** Simply dubbed "the pear," this medieval torture device consisted of a bulbous end with a crank at the top of the machine. One would insert the contraption into the victim's mouth, anus, or vagina. As one cranked the top portion, the bulbous end would open up gradually and tear the victim apart from the inside. *This is why I always carry a cyanide pill in my cheek. Never know when it might come in handy.*

> "12 of the Most Horrifying Torture Devices in History," Listaholic.com, *www.listaholic.com.*

FACT ATTACK: Torture victims split in twain! The
Spanish Donkey was a simple torture device consisting of a large wedge affixed to four legs. Victims
straddled the device with weights attached to their
feet, which eventually split their bodies in half on
the wedge. *Because humans are sick, twisted individuals.*

> "12 of the Most Horrifying
Torture Devices in History,"
Listaholic.com,
www.listaholic.com.

FACT ATTACK: Company replicates a mother's touch!
The Zaky Infant pillow is a device filled with plastic
pellets shaped to mimic a set of human hands. The
shape of the pillow helps soothe the baby when a
loving touch isn't available. *If your child is into disembodied
limbs, that is.*

> "A Great Gift For Baby . . .
If He Likes Friday the 13th
Films," *San Francisco Chronicle,*
www.sfgate.com.

**FACT ATTACK: Miracle pesticide kills everything
it touches!** Dichloro-diphenyl-trichloroethane
(DDT) was a popular pesticide used to stop the
spread of mosquito-borne illnesses like malaria.
The substance was found to cause fertility and neu-
rological problems in humans, and also had a dev-
astating effect on bird populations in areas where it
was sprayed. *Birds are overrated, anyway.*

> Dan Fletcher, "The 50 Worst
Inventions," *Time,* May 27, 2010,
www.time.com.

FACT ATTACK: Roman army thwarted by science! In
212 B.C., the Roman army sailed to the city of Syra-
cuse to take it from the Greeks. According to legend,
the mathematician Archimedes used copper mirrors
to reflect the sun and set their ships aflame, dubbed
the "Archimedes Death Ray." Scientists have determined that the device is theoretically possible. *When I
hear "death ray," I don't imagine an overrated magnifying glass.*

> Alan Bellows, *Alien Hand
Syndrome and Other Too-Weird-
To-Be-True Stories* (Workman
Publishing, 2009), p. 89.

FACT ATTACK: **Media giant outdone by magic marker!** In 2002, Sony began encrypting its compact discs with software that made it impossible to transfer the music to a computer. Unfortunately for the company, customers could bypass the deterrent if they drew a ring around the edge of the CD with a magic marker. *Epic fail.*

> Dan Fletcher, "The 50 Worst Inventions," *Time*, May 27, 2010, *www.time.com*.

FACT ATTACK: **Nerdy gadget transforms into death ray!** Most laser pointers are harmless devices used to highlight items during presentations. However, companies have started marketing versions strong enough to burn holes through paper and ignite matches. If pointed directly at one's eyes, these powerful lasers can cause permanent damage. *For my own sake, I am glad my brother never got ahold of one of these.*

> Serena Gordon, "Kids Playing with Laser Pointers May Be Aiming for Eye Trouble," Businessweek, September 8, 2010, *www.businessweek.com*.

FACT ATTACK: **Robot suit creates super soldiers!** Engineers at Raytheon Company have developed an exoskeleton robotic suit that enables soldiers to lift 200 pounds several times without tiring and punch through three inches of wood. The suit is agile enough to allow the wearer to kick a soccer ball or climb stairs. *If our enemies challenge us to a no-holds-barred game of soccer, we want our soldiers to be prepared.*

> Samantha Murphy, "New Exoskeleton Robot Suit Is Faster, Stronger," Live Science, September 27, 2010, *www.livescience.com*.

FACT ATTACK: **President coins coffee slogan!** The tagline "Good to the last drop" for Maxwell House coffee was coined by President Theodore Roosevelt while sampling their coffee before the brand went national. *Whatever you do, though, for the love of God, don't drink the last drop.*

> Charles Reichblum, *Dr. Knowledge Presents: Strange & Fascinating Facts about Famous Brands* (Black Dog & Leventhal Publishers, Inc., 2004), p. 164.

FACT ATTACK: Lame company name becomes slightly less lame! The original name for the Yahoo! search engine was "Jerry's Guide," after one of its creators, Jerry Yang. He and his partner later settled on "Yet Another Hierarchical Officious Oracle!" or Yahoo! for short. *Something tells me they didn't get invited to very many parties growing up.*

❯ Charles Reichblum, *Dr. Knowledge Presents: Strange & Fascinating Facts about Famous Brands* (Black Dog & Leventhal Publishers, Inc., 2004), p. 164.

FACT ATTACK: Crapper never invented the Crapper! Despite popular belief, Thomas Crapper did not invent the toilet, although he did manufacture them. The true inventor was John Harrington, who developed the flush toilet for Queen Elizabeth I in 1596. *My whole life is based on a lie.*

❯ John Townsend, *Outrageous Inventions (Weird History of Science)* (Raintree, 2007).

FACT ATTACK: Pop star's mom revolutionizes office supplies! Liquid Paper was invented by the mother of Michael Nesmith, the lead guitarist for the pop band the Monkees. He left the band shortly after she sold her company to Gillette for $47 million. *There is not enough White Out in the world to erase the awfulness that is the Monkees.*

❯ Paul Niemann, *Invention Mysteries (Invention Mysteries Series)* (Horsefeathers Publishing, 2004), p. 38.

FACT ATTACK: **Tiny toilet lights save marriages!** Men who consistently miss the toilet when urinating in the dark can find solace in Johnny Lights, a string of lights that rests underneath the rim of the toilet and illuminates when the lid is up. The tiny beacons also protect women from falling in should someone neglect to put the seat down. *I generally prefer the "sonar" method to pissing in the dark. Just keep shifting until you hear water.*

❯ Buck Wolf, "Toilet Landing Lights . . . and Other Strange Valentine's Day Gifts," ABC News, *http:// abcnews.go.com.*

❯ Ted Vancleave, *Totally Absurd Inventions: America's Goofiest Patents* (Andrews McMeel, 2001).

FACT ATTACK: **Bed keeps you safe from terrorists!** The Quanum Sleeper is a coffin-like bed that hermetically seals its occupants inside in the event of a biological terrorist attack. The bed is also lined with polycarbonate bulletproof panels, in case of armed robbery. *Congratulations terrorists, you've won.*

❯ Cory Doctorow, "Bulletproof 'Anti-terrorist' bed with air-supply, toilet," Boing Boing, March 28, 2008, *www.boingboing.net.*

FACT ATTACK: **Intelligent fork curbs obesity!** To prevent eaters from gorging themselves too fast, the alarm fork comes equipped with red and green lights that alert the diner to slow down their rate of consumption and then indicate when it's safe to start eating again. *If you ignore the red light, it calls you a fatass and reminds you that this is why you are eating alone.*

❯ Ted Vancleave, *Totally Absurd Inventions: America's Goofiest Patents* (Andrews McMeel, 2001).

FACT ATTACK: Face piercings hold glasses! Tired of dealing with the annoying bands that hold glasses on one's ears, inventors James Sooy and Oliver Gibson invented a pair that attach to piercings embedded into the bridge of the wearer's nose. *I'll stick with contacts, thanks.*

❯ Bill Christensen, "New Glasses Require Piercing Bridge of Nose," Live Science, May 22, 2006, *www.livescience.com.*

FACT ATTACK: Eighteenth century medical kit included scythe! In the eighteenth century, doctors used curved knives on the battlefield when removing limbs. This made it easier to make a circular cut around the appendage and saw through the bone with a hacksaw. *Or a set of keys, whichever was more painful.*

❯ "20 Scary Old Surgical Tools," Vital Signs, *www.surgicaltechnologists.net.*

FACT ATTACK: Super substance 200 times stronger than steel! In 2004, scientists discovered graphene, a substance that is 200 times stronger than steel and conducts energy more efficiently than any other known substance. *Why are we still using steel as a barometer for strength?*

❯ Kichio Kaku, "Graphene Will Change the Way We Live," Bigthink.com, October 6, 2010, *www.bigthink.com.*

FACT ATTACK: Graphene succumbs to elephants! It would take an elephant standing on a pencil to break through a sheet of graphene as thin as plastic wrap. *Where am I supposed to get a pencil?*

❯ Kichio Kaku, "Graphene Will Change the Way We Live," Bigthink.com, October 6, 2010, *www.bigthink.com.*

FACT ATTACK: Scientists weaponize mother nature!
In 1994, scientists at the Wright Laboratory proposed a weapon that would coat enemy troops with bee pheromones. Soldiers would then disperse hives around the battlefield in the hopes that the bees would sting the enemy and leave them unharmed. *Good idea, unless, of course, the enemy tries to hug you.*

> Alan Bellows, *Alien Hand Syndrome and Other Too-Weird-To-Be-True Stories* (Workman Publishing, 2009), p. 16.

FACT ATTACK: Blowing smoke up your ass does not cure drowning! In the 1700s, smoke enemas were a popular medical procedure for resuscitating victims of drowning. The doctor inserted a rectal tube connected to a fumigator into the anus and forced smoke towards the rectum. Doctors believed the warmth of the smoke promoted respiration, but skepticism about the procedure gave rise to the phrase, "blowing smoke up one's ass." *From the people who brought you bloodletting.*

> Mickey Z., "22 Weird & Somewhat Useful Bicycle Facts for Staying Green on 2 Wheels," Planetgreen.com, December 2, 2009, *http://planetgreen.discovery.com.*

FACT ATTACK: Gun shoots around corners! Guns with barrels that curve ninety degrees, such as the German Kummlauf, have been around since the 1800s. The concept returned in 2003 when the Israeli army started using the Corner Shot, a modern machine gun version. *Any cartoon–inspired firearm is okay in my book.*

> Russ Kick, *Disinformation Book of Lists: Subversive Facts and Hidden Information in Rapid-fire Format* (The Disinformation Company, 2004).

FACT ATTACK: **Hands-free helmet gun!**
The Brow Beater is a specially designed gun fitted directly into a soldier's helmet. The soldier fires the gun by opening his mouth, activating a trigger located on the chin strap. *Whatever you do, don't yawn.*

❯ Russ Kick, *Disinformation Book of Lists: Subversive Facts and Hidden Information in Rapid-fire Format* (The Disinformation Company, 2004).

FACT ATTACK: **Inherent sadistic streak in dentists confirmed!** The electric chair was invented by a dentist, Dr. Alfred Southwick. *Not surprising; dentists have been perfecting torture devices for centuries.*

❯ Craig Brandon, *The Electric Chair: An Unnatural American History* (McFarland & Company, 1999).

FACT ATTACK: **Man buried alive, saved by bell!** To avoid the terrifying prospect of being buried alive without a means of escape, coffins in the 1800s were sometimes designed with safety devices ranging from air tubes and food chutes to pieces of string attached to bells on the surface to alert cemetery goers of the error. *Coffin technology is one flat screen TV away from me faking my own death.*

❯ Jan Bondeson, *Buried Alive: The Terrifying History of Our Most Primal Fear* (W. W. Norton & Company, 2002).

FACT ATTACK: Ancients discover electricity 2,000 years before Edison! Artifacts known as the Baghdad Batteries consisted of clay jars containing a copper cylinder encased in an iron rod. Scientists theorize that the addition of an electrolyte such as lemon juice or vinegar would have produced an electrical current. *If they also invented the first Game Boy to go with the batteries, then I'd be impressed.*

> "Extraterrestrials on Earth," *Is It Real?: Ancient Astronauts*, National Geographic, *http://channel.nationalgeographic.com/series/is-it-real.*

FACT ATTACK: Toilet paper replaces stones and snow! Before the invention of toilet paper, people improvised with everything from wool and lace to wood shavings, grass, stones, seashells, and snow. *Using sandpaper is a mistake you only make once. Trust me.*

> Russell Ash, *Firefly's World of Facts* (Firefly Books, 2007).

FACT ATTACK: Torture device stretches victims! The rack was an ancient torture device frequently used as a means of interrogation. Victims were strapped to the machine which gradually pulled their arms and legs out of their sockets. *You know it's working when the victim confesses to things they couldn't possibly have done.*

> Russell Ash, *Firefly's World of Facts* (Firefly Books, 2007).

FACT ATTACK: Worldwide nuclear arsenal dwindling! In 1985, there were apprimately 65,000 nuclear warheads stockpiled throughout the world. That number has since dwindled to less than 30,000. *Good work, guys. Now we can only destroy the earth 1,000 times instead of 3,000.*

> Russell Ash, *Firefly's World of Facts* (Firefly Books, 2007).

FACT ATTACK: Bacteria hiding in neckties! To combat the prevalence of germs, bacteria, and other contaminants that hide out in the neckties of hospital workers, April Strider of Safesmart Inc. invented "safety ties," which are coated with an anti-microbial substance that repels contaminants. *Or they could, ya know, stop wearing ties.*

❯ Elizabeth Armstrong Moore, "Germ Alert: Attack of the Killer Necktie!", CNET, November 19, 2009, http://news.cnet.com.

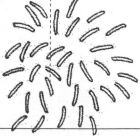

FACT ATTACK: U.S. and Russia holding onto nukes! The United States and Russia account for more than 90 percent of all remaining nuclear weapons. *Best we keep a few. Just in case Australia gets uppity.*

❯ Russell Ash, *Firefly's World of Facts* (Firefly Books, 2007).

FACT ATTACK: New lamp runs on blood! The Blood Lamp is a single-use device that requires the owner sacrifice a drop of blood in order to turn it on. The secret ingredient that fuels the lamp, aside from blood, is luminol, a chemical used by forensics experts that glows blue when it reacts with the iron in blood. *Would be much more exciting if it ran on semen instead of blood. But certainly not both.*

❯ Jaymi Heimbuch, "A Lamp with an Alternative Energy Source—Your Blood," Treehugger.com. *www.treehugger.com.*

FACT ATTACK: Prankster-proof fire alarm a death trap! The February 1938 issue of *Modern Mechanix* had an idea for a new type of fire alarm to deter pranksters. To activate the alarm, an individual passed their hand through a metal handcuff to reach the signal dial. The handcuff would then close, and only a police officer or fireman with a special key could open it. *Great idea, unless, of course, there's a real fire.*

❯ "Fire B Traps Pranksters," *Modern Mechanix*, February 1938, *http://blog.modern mechanix.com*.

FACT ATTACK: Baby Cage provides piece of mind! In the 1920s, parents in the United States whose infants were taking up too much space in their apartments found a solution in the form of the Baby Cage. The wire contraption hung from a window and "securely" housed baby, leaving Mom and Dad free to tend the house. *Not responsible for inevitable emotional scarring.*

❯ Dan Fletcher, "The 50 Worst Inventions," *Time*, May 27, 2010, *www.time.com*.

FACT ATTACK: Agent Orange kills thousands! A potent herbicide used from 1961 to 1971 in the Vietnam War, Agent Orange was employed to cut through the thick jungle canopy to reveal the location of enemy troops. The chemical worked, but exposure caused cancers, birth defects, and numerous other disorders in humans. The United States dumped about 21 million gallons of it on Vietnam during the war, resulting in hundreds of thousands of injuries and birth defects to Vietnamese citizens. *Sometimes saying "Our bad" just isn't enough.*

❯ Dan Fletcher, "The 50 Worst Inventions," *Time*, May 27, 2010, *www.time.com*.

FACT ATTACK: Device repels loitering teenagers! To protect store owners from gangs of unruly teenagers, Howard Stapleton invented the Mosquito. The device emits an irritating high-pitched sound that is unbearable to young people, but can't be heard by anyone older than 25. *I've found a paintball gun works too. And it's more fun.*

> "Mosquito Targets Teens With Audio Repellent," NPR, September 1, 2010, *www.npr.org.*

FACT ATTACK: Fake fur terrible for environment! It takes a gallon of oil to produce three faux fur coats. *And only 300 chinchillas to produce three real ones!*

> "100 Things We Didn't Know This Time Last Year," BBC News, December 30, 2005, *http://news.bbc.co.uk.*

FACT ATTACK: Play-doh for your poop! The Turd Twister is a plastic device with various shapes cut into the center that one can use to make designs with one's feces. Shapes include lightning bolts, shamrocks, and spaghetti. *Finally, a useful one.*

> Neha Grey, "What Were They Thinking? Eleven Weird Inventions," Divine Caroline, *www.divinecaroline.com.*

FACT ATTACK: Motorists drive over little girl repeatedly! To encourage motorists to slow down near schools, a Vancouver district is testing out speed bumps that produce optical illusions. As a driver approaches the bump, he or she encounters a three-dimensional image of a little girl chasing after a ball to remind them why they need to slow down. *Or speed up, if they hate kids.*

> Clay Dillow, "Optical Speed-bumps Create Illusion of Little Girl Darting Out in Front of You," Popsci.com, September 8, 2010, *www.popsci.com.*

FACT ATTACK: **Scientist eats mysterious chemical, discovers Splenda!** An Indian scientist named Shashikant Phadnis accidentally discovered the sweetening properties of sucralose, more commonly known as Splenda, in 1976. Phadnis's partner asked him to *test* a particular chemical, but Phadnis misheard and thought he wanted him to *taste* the substance. Before anyone could stop him, Phadnis popped the chemical into his mouth and discovered it to be astonishingly sweet and not noticeably harmful to humans. *In reality he didn't mishear, his partner was just a dick.*

> "Splenda History, Uses of Splenda," Splenda Info, *www.splendainfo.com.*

FACT ATTACK: **Scientists invent tractor beam!** Researchers have developed a small-scale tractor beam that can move objects 100 times larger than a bacterium in water. The machine works by passing a hollow laser around tiny glass particles. As the air around the particles heats up, the cool dark center of the laser keeps them in place. A second laser can then manipulate the location of the particles. *Doesn't sound so hard.*

> Mike Lucibella, "Tractor Beams Com to Life," Physorg.com, September 8, 2010, *www.physorg.com.*

FACT ATTACK: **Ubiquitous kitchen appliance discovered by chance!** The concept for the microwave oven was realized when a researcher walked past a high-powered radar tube and a chocolate bar melted in his pocket. *Good thing he didn't have a mouse in there.*

> "50 Weird Science Tidbits," Science News Review. *www.sciencenewsreview.com.*

Myths, Urban Legends, and Hearsay

If Enough People Saw It, It Must Be True

FACT ATTACK: Project Deepscan proves futile! In 1987, a fleet of twenty-four ships probed the waters of Loch Ness hoping to find evidence to prove the existence of the Loch Ness Monster. Dubbed Project Deepscan, the week-long investigation did produce three peculiar sonar blips, however, nothing concrete was ever discovered. *Not true. They concretely determined that their lives have no meaning.*

> "1987: Search Ends For Loch Ness Monster," BBC News, *http://news.bbc.co.uk.*

FACT ATTACK: Multiple Loch Ness Monsters! Given the length of time that individuals have reported Nessie sightings, scientists speculate that—assuming she is real—there must be a significant number of the creatures to serve as a breeding population. *She's as real as you and me. Assuming we aren't real.*

> "The Loch Ness Monster: Facts and Theories," Wyrdology.com, *www.wyrdology.com.*

FACT ATTACK: **Science embraces Loch Ness Monster!** Although no hard evidence has been uncovered to support the existence of the Loch Ness Monster, it received the scientific name *Nessiteras rhombopteryx* in 1975. *It's Latin for "It's probably just a fish."*

> "The Loch Ness Monster: Facts and Theories," Wyrdology.com, *www.wyrdology.com.*

FACT ATTACK: 50% zebra, 50% giraffe, 100% real!

Until its discovery in the early 1900s, scientists refused to believe in the existence of a strange creature in the Congo that possessed zebra stripes on its hind quarters and a head and neck similar to a giraffe's, albeit shorter. The elusive creature, known as the okapi, can now be found in zoos around the world. *Score one for the lunatic monster hunters!*

❯ Loren Coleman, "Replica Cryptia: Okapis," Cryptomundo, September 15, 2009, *www.cryptomundo.com.*

FACT ATTACK: **The okapi, a symbol of hope!**

Before the group disbanded due to financial reasons, the International Society of Cryptozoology used the okapi as its logo. *Funny, I always assumed monster hunters were swimming in cash.*

❯ Loren Coleman, "Replica Cryptia: Okapis," Cryptomundo, September 15, 2009, *www.cryptomundo.com.*

FACT ATTACK: **Lake Travis monster actually an Indian!**

In 2007, after a college professor developed a photo he'd snapped near Lake Travis, Texas, he noticed an odd figure in the corner. Once he adjusted the image, he uncovered a massive bipedal animal. Experts speculate its identity could be anything from an alien, to Bigfoot, to a Native American wearing a headdress. *Well, obviously it's manbearpig.*

❯ Eddie Middleton, "Humanoid Night Creature Pic Declared Authentic By Brad Steiger's Photo Expert," *The Examiner,* June 8, 2009. *www.examiner.com.*

FACT ATTACK: **Giant snake evades capture!**

The anaconda generally doesn't grow larger than twenty feet, but myths abound of giant snakes in the Amazon rain forest more than 100 feet long. The New York Zoological Society offers a $50,000 reward for anyone who can produce a snake of any species that is longer than thirty feet, but so far no one has claimed the reward. *I'll go call Ice Cube and John Voight.*

❯ "Snakes on Demand," National Geographic, *www.natgeotv.com.*

FACT ATTACK: Bigfoot on Mars! In 2008, NASA's *Spirit Rover* snapped a picture of what appeared to be a large humanoid creature on the surface of Mars. Upon further investigation, it was merely a rock. *That's just what Bigfoot wants you to think.*

> "NASA Photo Shows Humanoid Figure on Mars," Fox News, January 23, 2008, *www.foxnews.com.*

FACT ATTACK: Genie masquerades as tiny lizard! Natives of Madagascar believe that the stump-tailed chameleon is a forest genie that brings bad luck. *They give the wish-giving variety a bad name.*

> Peter Tyson, "Legends of Madagascar," PBS, *www.pbs.org.*

FACT ATTACK: Malaysian ghosts attack with their boobs! The Malaysian hantu hetek (breast ghost) is a voluptuous creature who smothers unsuspecting victims with her massive mammary glands. In a strange twist, her breasts are located on her back. *Because it wasn't weird enough without the last bit.*

> Jonathan Wojcik, "The 7 Most Ridiculous Ghost Stories From Around the World," Cracked.com, October 31, 2010, *www.cracked.com.*

FACT ATTACK: Dishonest mariners sell fake unicorn horns! For centuries, enterprising sea merchants sold the tusks of narwhals as unicorn horns. *Wonder what they did with all the unicorn horns, then.*

> Peter Tyson, "Fantastic Creatures," PBS, *www.pbs.org.*

FACT ATTACK: Buddha hung around with mythical creatures! The Tibetan flag contains a depiction of two snow lions, mythical white beasts said to prowl the mountains of Tibet. Larger than normal lions and possessing big shaggy manes and bushy tails, legend has it that the massive cats were protectors of the Buddha. *Why, pray tell, does an enlightened being need protection?*

❯ "Mythical Creatures," BBC, www.bbc.co.uk.

FACT ATTACK: British monsters used to be pets!

Many mythical creatures found in the British Isles can be traced back to the Dangerous Wild Animals Act of 1976, which made owning large cats such as pumas illegal. Rather than euthanize the animals, many wealthy individuals simply released them into the wild.

Smooth move, England.

❯ "Mythical Creatures," BBC, www.bbc.co.uk.

FACT ATTACK: The Great Sphinx is smarter than you! The Great Sphinx of Giza is a monument situated on the west bank of the Nile River that depicts a mythical animal Egyptians believed acted as a guardian of ancient tombs. It was fond of riddles, and if a person could not answer correctly the sphinx devoured them immediately. *Whatever he asks, the answer is forty-two.*

❯ "Top 10 Mythical Animals," Animal Planet, http://animal.discovery.com.

FACT ATTACK: **Sea cows victims of mistaken identity!** Sailors once mistook manatees for mermaids. *Fat, blubbery sea-faring mammal = enchanting vixen of the sea.*

❯ "Sea Cow, Origin of Mythical Mermaid, Threatened with Extinction, UN Warns," United Nations News Center, *www.un.org*.

FACT ATTACK: **Mermaids tempted ancient mariners!** The first mermaid stories date back as far as 3,000 year ago. Some stories described the creatures as helpful, saving mariners who fell overboard. Others, however, insisted mermaids were sirens of the deep, coaxing sailors into the water to their deaths. *Million-dollar question: You have to marry someone who is half fish. Which half do you choose?*

❯ "Top 10 Mythical Animals," Animal Planet, *http://animal .discovery.com*.

FACT ATTACK: **All CPR dummies have the same name!** A myth states that CPR training dummies are named Annie at the behest of an unnamed billionaire whose daughter died because nobody could perform CPR on her. While most CPR training dummies are manufactured with a tag displaying the moniker "Anne," it is in honor of a popular doll manufactured in Europe. *I just call her Sweet Cheeks.*

❯ Jan Harold Brunvand, *Encyclopedia of Urban Legends* (W. W. Norton & Company, 2002).

FACT ATTACK: **Explorer discovers Yeti-sized foot-prints!** The first Westerner to find evidence of the Yeti was Charles Howard-Bury, who discovered large footprints in the snow while exploring Mount Everest in 1921. *It turned out to just be two chupacabras walking close together.*

❯ Brenda Rosen, *The Mythical Creatures Bible: The Definitive Guide to Legendary Beings* (Sterling, 2009).

FACT ATTACK: **Chinese dragons fly without wings!** Mythical Chinese dragons rarely have wings, and instead ride on clouds or spouts of water into the heavens. *Which is why one should never fly in a Chinese plane.*

❯ Brenda Rosen, *The Mythical Creatures Bible: The Definitive Guide to Legendary Beings* (Sterling, 2009).

FACT ATTACK: **KFC does (not?) contain real chicken!** Despite popular belief, the fast food chain Kentucky Fried Chicken did not shorten its name to KFC because its food could not legally be classified as "chicken." The company never gave a public reason for the switch, but the company has since reverted back to its original name. *A wing by any other name would still taste as artery-clogging.*

❯ Jamie Frater, *The Ultimate Book of Top Ten Lists: A Mind-Boggling Collection of Fun, Fascinating and Bizarre Facts on Movies, Music, Sports, Crime, Celebrities, History, Trivia and More* (Ulysses Press, 2009).

FACT ATTACK: **Call 1-800-They-Stole-My-Kidneys!** The myth of falling asleep at night and waking up in a hotel bathtub full of ice—minus one kidney—has been around for some time, and the United States government takes the threat very seriously. They set up a hotline for victims of organ harvesting; however, they have yet to receive a single call. *That's because they don't sew too many people back up when they are done.*

❯ Dennis O'Connell, "Top 10 Urban Legends," Askmen.com, *www.askmen.com*.

FACT ATTACK: **Scuba divers can rest easy!** Throughout the years, several urban legends surfaced claiming rescue workers discovered the body of a scuba diver hanging from a tree hundreds of miles from the nearest ocean. The conclusion is generally that an airtanker scooped up the diver along with ocean water to fight a forest fire, but in reality the planes used for this purpose do not have the capacity to suck a human through their suction vent. *But the one about Pop Rocks and soda is totally true.*

❯ Dennis O'Connell, "Top 10 Urban Legends," Askmen.com, *www.askmen.com.*

FACT ATTACK: **Monster killed by holy bullet!** In 1765 a fanged monster with a taste for human blood roamed the French region of Gévaudan. The king's personal gun carrier, Antoine De Beauterne, set out to kill the beast and returned with the body of a rare species of wolf. The killings continued until Beauterne shot another wolf with a bullet blessed by a priest. *Which he just happened to have laying around.*

❯ H. G. Carlson, *Mysteries of the Unexplained* (Contemporary Books, 1994), p. 58.

FACT ATTACK: **There is no Frankenstein monster!** "Frankenstein" is not the name of a monster, but instead the name of the scientist who gave him life. In the novel, Dr. Frankenstein named the monster Adam, and in the films he had no name. *Correct your friends if they get it wrong. They'll love that.*

❯ Joey Green, *Contrary to Popular Belief, More Than 250 False Facts Revealed* (Broadway Books, 2005).

FACT ATTACK: First star to the right, and straight on 'til Sydney! Neverland, the fictional realm inhabited by Peter Pan, is a real place. Australians use the term "Never Never Land" to refer to the outback, because visitors will "never never" want to return. Although the term "Never Never Land" did not appear in James Barrie's original play, people often use the two interchangeably. *Not exactly good tourism PR.*

❯ Joey Green, *Contrary to Popular Belief, More Than 250 False Facts Revealed* (Broadway Books, 2005).

FACT ATTACK: **Hunt for legendary creatures actually a science!** The study of legendary creatures is known as cryptozoology. *Proof that adding "oology" to the end of words makes them sound important.*

❯ "Cryptozoology," Merriam-Webster Online Dictionary, *www.merriam-webster.com.*

FACT ATTACK: Gorilla once believed to be a hoax! While many criticize the field, defenders of cryptozoology are quick to point out that many common animal species, like the gorilla and giant squid, were once believed to be superstitious hoaxes. *Not sure I'd put the Jersey Devil on par with gorillas.*

❯ Ker Than, "Rumor or Reality," Live Science, *www.livescience.com.*

FACT ATTACK: Deformed monster ruins summer for rich socialites! In the summer of 2008, the body of a strange creature washed up on the shore of Long Island, New York. Dubbed the Montauk Monster, the animal was hairless, had a beak like a bird, a tail like a dog, and an elongated front paw. Although nobody is certain what the animal actually was, theories range from a sea turtle without its shell to a genetically altered dog escaped from a animal-disease research facility. *Not the ugliest thing to ever wind up on a beach in Long Island.*

> Paul WagenSeil, "'Montauk Monster' Has Hamptons in a Tizzy," Fox News, July 31, 2008, *www.foxnews.com.*

FACT ATTACK: Jersey devil has a bounty on its head!
There is a $10,000 reward for the capture of the New Jersey Devil, a creature with bat-like wings, a horse's head, hooves, and glowing eyes that stalks the pine barrens of New Jersey. Although many have tried, no one has yet to claim the prize.
I once drugged Snookie and tried to pass her off as the Jersey Devil to claim the reward, but nobody believed the real creature could be that hideous.

> "Top 10 Cryptids," Toptenz.net, *www.toptenz.net.*

FACT ATTACK: Armpit state embraces monster!
The Jersey Devil is the state's unofficial mascot, and the official mascot of the New Jersey Devils hockey team. *Somehow I'm not surprised.*

> Loren Coleman and Jerome Clark, *Cryptozoology A To Z: The Encyclopedia of Loch Monsters, Sasquatch, Chupacabras, and Other Authentic Mysteries of Nature* (Fireside, 1999).

FACT ATTACK: **Flying humanoid creature predicts catastrophes!** Every year citizens of Point Pleasant, West Virginia, gather to honor the Mothman, a mythical being with the body of a man, wings like a moth, and red glowing eyes. Sightings of the creature began in the 1960s just before the collapse of a suspension bridge that killed forty-six people, and then ceased. This led some to speculate that the Mothman only appears before catastrophic events. *Then why was there no sign of him before* Star Wars: The Phantom Menace *came out?*

> "Top 10 Cryptids," Toptenz.net, *www.toptenz.net.*

FACT ATTACK: **Developers scam town with monster hoax!** A series of Jersey Devil sightings in 1909, complete with hoofprints in the snow and more than a hundred eyewitness reports, is now believed to be an elaborate real estate hoax. Developers hoped to convince terrified residents to sell their homes for considerably less than they were worth. *But don't worry, chupacabras are still real.*

> Loren Coleman and Jerome Clark, *Cryptozoology A To Z: The Encyclopedia of Loch Monsters, Sasquatch, Chupacabras, and Other Authentic Mysteries of Nature* (Fireside, 1999).

FACT ATTACK: **Dinosaur meat poisons villagers!** Locals in the Congo tell stories of a dinosaur-like creature with the body of an elephant and a serpentine neck called Mokele-Mbembe. Hunters claim to have killed the beast with spears and cooked it, but all who ate from it allegedly died soon after. *Based on what I learned from the documentary* The Land Before Time, *I'm pretty sure Mokele-Mbembe's scientific name is Littlefoot.*

> "Top 10 Cryptids," Toptenz. net, *www.toptenz.net.*

FACT ATTACK: Dog-faced monster terrorizes Canada! Not all lake cryptids resemble large aquatic dinosaurs. The Igopogo of Canada is said to have the face of a dog and move around in the water like a seal. *I'm no cryptozoologist, but I'd say that's a seal.*

> Loren Coleman and Jerome Clark, *Cryptozoology A To Z: The Encyclopedia of Loch Monsters, Sasquatch, Chupacabras, and Other Authentic Mysteries of Nature* (Fireside, 1999).

FACT ATTACK: Neanderthals still out there! Some cryptozoologists believe Neanderthal man may still be roaming around parts of Europe. They attribute many sightings of Bigfoot-like creatures to small populations of the ancient hominid species. *I'm still a fan of the "guy in monkey suit" theory.*

> Loren Coleman and Jerome Clark, *Cryptozoology A To Z: The Encyclopedia of Loch Monsters, Sasquatch, Chupacabras, and Other Authentic Mysteries of Nature* (Fireside, 1999).

FACT ATTACK: Madagascar man-eater is a plant! Natives of the island of Madagascar speak of a giant tree with tendril-like branches capable of ensnaring a human being and crushing it to death. Czech explorer Ivan Mackerle encountered the man-eating tree in 1998, but nobody has been able to confirm his discovery. *Thankfully, trees are fairly easy to evade.*

> Karl P. N. Shuker, *The Beasts That Hide from Man: Seeking the World's Last Undiscovered Animals* (Paraview Press, 2003).

FACT ATTACK: Deadly worm kills victims with a thought! In the early '90s, scientists embarked on a mission to track down the elusive Mongolian Death Worm, a creature that allegedly patrols deserts and emerges from the sand to spew acid at its victims. Locals believe the cryptid has psychic powers and can kill a man merely by looking at him. No specimens were ever found. *Clearly they didn't try looking on Tatooine.*

> "Top 10 Cryptids," Toptenz. net, *www.toptenz.net.*

FACT ATTACK: Pastafarian numbers swell! Ten million people worldwide classify themselves as Pastafarian. Followers believe the Flying Spaghetti Monster has an affinity for pirates and caused global warming in reaction to the general lack of pirates these days. *Death to the nonbelievers! Science damn them!*

❯ Dan Vergano, "'Spaghetti Monster' Is Noodling Around with Faith," *USA Today*, March 26, 2006, *www.usatoday.com*.

FACT ATTACK: Earth possibly created by Flying Spaghetti Monster! In an open letter to the Kansas Board of Education addressing their decision to teach intelligent design in schools, twenty-five-year-old Bobby Henderson insisted the school also teach the equally plausible notion that a Flying Spaghetti Monster (FSM) created the universe. The letter spawned a religion dubbed Pastafarian. *R'amen.*

❯ Dan Vergano, "'Spaghetti Monster' is Noodling Around with Faith," *USA Today*, March 26, 2006, *www.usatoday.com*.

FACT ATTACK: Navy discovers giant sea monster! Maybe! In the summer of 1997, U.S. naval microphones detected an ultra low-frequency sound emitted by a large aquatic animal too big to be a whale. Scientists are still at a loss to explain what it could have been. *My money is on the chupacabras, strapped to Bigfoot, riding the Loch Ness monster.*

❯ Varla Ventura, *Beyond Bizarre: Frightening Facts and Blood-Curdling True Tales* (Weiser Books, 2010).

FACT ATTACK: Searching for monsters becomes all the rage! Middle class members of society in Victorian England thought it was fashionable to go "monster spotting," or trolling for sea creatures. *They also felt the same way about corsets, so let's not give them too much credit.*

❯ Varla Ventura, *Beyond Bizarre: Frightening Facts and Blood-Curdling True Tales* (Weiser Books, 2010).

FACT ATTACK: **Christian missionaries discover Nessie!** The first recorded sighting of the Loch Ness Monster occurred in 565 c.e. during the travels of Saint Columba. After the missionaries sailed into the Loch, a giant sea creature appeared to one of Columba's assistants as he swam in the water. The man ordered the monster back in the name of the Lord and it retreated into the depths. *Apparently sea monsters are God-fearing creatures.*

❯ Nathan Robert Brown, *The Complete Idiot's Guide to the Paranormal* (Alpha, 2010), p. 130.

FACT ATTACK: Scientists search for human-like living fossils! In 1973, Russian researcher Dmitri Bayanov coined the term "huminology" to refer to the study of humanoid cryptids like the Yeti, Bigfoot, and the Chinese Wild Man. *I'm a uselessfactologist. It's very scientific work.*

❯ Loren Coleman and Jerome Clark, *Cryptozoology A To Z: The Encyclopedia of Loch Monsters, Sasquatch, Chupacabras, and Other Authentic Mysteries of Nature* (Fireside, 1999).

FACT ATTACK: **Hunt is on for the Chinese Wild Man!** In 2010, the Hubei Wild Man Research Association (HWMRA) announced it was recruiting researchers to track down a Bigfoot-like creature dubbed the "Wild Man" that allegedly inhabits the forests of China. There have been more than 400 reported sightings of the creature since the 1970s, but so far no one has found conclusive evidence of its existence. *If anybody needs me, I'll be in China wearing a bear costume giving the HWMRA false hope.*

> David John Walker, "Chinese Group Will Relaunch 'Bigfoot' Search," Seer Press, October 10, 2010, *www.seerpress.com.*

FACT ATTACK: **Balls of fire baffle scientists!** Each October, spectators gather to watch glowing spheres rise from the Mekong River in Thailand. Locals insist the phenomenon is the breath of the Naga, a mythical serpent that lives in the river, but scientists think it may be caused by natural gases expelled from decaying plant life. *I believe there's a giant version of my friend Mike resting at the bottom of the river, farting towards the heavens.*

> Alan Bellows, *Alien Hand Syndrome and Other Too-Weird-to-Be-True Stories* (Workman Publishing, 2009), p. 157.

> "5 Natural Events That Science Can't Explain," Mother Nature Network, *www.mnn.com.*

FACT ATTACK: **Woman with bad teeth drowns British children!** Jenny Greenteeth is a character of British folklore who hides in lakes and rivers and pulls unsuspecting victims into the water to drown them. Some believe the character is actually a euphemism for duckweed, a type of vegetation known to entangle careless children playing at the water's edge. *I'd rather my friends think I was killed by a demon than by swampgrass.*

> "Jenny Greenteeth, Folklore Character," BBC, September 10, 2004, *www.bbc.co.uk.*

> Carole G. Silver, *Strange and Secret Peoples: Fairies and Victorian Consciousness* (Oxford University Press, 1999).

FACT ATTACK: Kangaroo-man pesters London populace! Between 1808 and 1904, a creature dubbed Spring Heeled Jack terrorized the streets of London. Resembling a man with pointy ears and horns, he molested young women and evaded capture by leaping over high fences and tall buildings. To this day, nobody knows who or what he was. *A supervillain with a limited scope for evilness?*

❯ Alan Bellows, *Alien Hand Syndrome and Other Too-Weird-To-Be-True Stories* (Workman Publishing, 2009), p. 118.

FACT ATTACK: Alien pet acquires taste for goat blood! El Chupacabra ("goat sucker") is a mythical creature that feeds on the blood of livestock. The creature leaves the animal drained with several puncture marks. Most commonly sighted in Puerto Rico, the speculated origins of the animal range from genetically altered vampire bats to the cast-away pets of aliens. *Leave it to aliens to have a pet blood-sucking monster.*

❯ Katherine Neer, "How Chupacabras Work," HowStuffWorks.com, *www.health.howstuffworks.com.*

FACT ATTACK: Angels save more than half of Americans! In a study of 1,700 Americans, 55 percent believed they had been aided at some point in their lives by a guardian angel. *The other 45 percent attributed their good fortune to the Flying Spaghetti Monster.*

❯ David Van Biema, "Guardian Angels Are Here, Say Most Americans," *Time*, September 18, 2008, *www.time.com.*

FACT ATTACK: Lizard man terrorizes South Carolina swamp! The Lizard Man of Scape Ore Swamp was first reported by a South Carolina teenager in the '80s and has been terrorizing the area ever since. The seven-foot-tall creature is said to have glowing red eyes, pads on its hands and feet that allow it to cling to surfaces, and is incredibly strong, capable of ripping open cars. *The Geiko gecko has gone rogue.*

❯ "Lizard Man," Animal Planet, *http://animal.discovery.com.*

FACT ATTACK: Lake Champlain home to a monster! There are 300 eyewitness accounts of Champ, an aquatic animal similar to the Loch Ness Monster, inhabiting Lake Champlain. In 2003, scientists recorded echolocation from the lake and discovered sounds similar to many whale species, but not identical to any known animal on earth. *If they ever find this thing, whatever will the "scientists" do with themselves?*

❯ Lohr McKinstry, "Lake Champlain Expedition Searches for Champy," *The Press Republican,* September 28, 2008. *www.pressrepublican.com.*

❯ "Champ, the Famed Monster of Lake Champlain," Lake Champlain Land Trust. *www.lclt.org.*

❯ "Lake Champlain Research," Fauna Communications. *www.animalvoice.com/lakechamplain.*

FACT ATTACK: Comets mistaken for dragons! The myth of winged dragons with long tails transcends many different cultures. Some speculate that their prevalence stems from ancient sightings of comets. A streak flying through the night sky with an icy tail might have resembled a living creature to ancient civilizations. *That's because the guy who said, "I think it's a burning ball of ice hurtling through space" was always thrown into the volcano.*

❯ "Top 10 Beasts and Dragons: How Reality Made Myth," Live Science, *www.livescience.com.*

FACT ATTACK: Extinct ape resurfaces in legend! Some scientists believe that the creature known as Bigfoot may actually be a living Gigantopithecus, a giant ape that died off around 100,000 years ago. *Knowing what he is doesn't make him any easier to find.*

❯ "Top 10 Creatures of Cryptozoology," Live Science, *www.livescience.com.*

FACT ATTACK: **Elusive cryptid leaves massive footprints!** Bigfoot hunters claim to have discovered enormous footprints as large as twenty-four inches long that could not possibly belong to any known animals. By contrast, the average human foot is only about ten inches long. *It's not the size that counts. . . .*

> "Sasquatch," *Encyclopaedia Britannica*, 2008.
> Hawes and Sovak, "Quantitative Morphology of the Human Foot in a North American Population," *Ergonomics*, July 1994.

FACT ATTACK: **Human/dog/rat hybrid revealed!** In 2003, disturbing pictures surfaced on the Internet of a human/dog/rat hybrid nursing a litter of interspecies babies. Some speculated the creature was a product of a genetics experiment gone horribly wrong. The images were actually a sculpture created by artist Patricia Piccinini, titled "The Young Family." *John Candy is still the original Mog.*

> "Animal-Human Hybrid / Human Dog,'" About.com. http://urbanlegends.about.com.

FACT ATTACK: **Giant fish returns from extinction!** In 1938, a South African museum curator spotted an odd fish when sorting through the daily catch of a local fisherman. The creature was a coelacanth, an ancient fish scientists believed had been extinct for millions of years. The fish was well known to local inhabitants, who called it "gombassa" or "mame." *Natives: 1, Science: 0.*

> "Top 10 Creatures of Cryptozoology," Live Science, www.livescience.com.

FACT ATTACK: **Tabloid hoax scams major newspapers!** In 2001, the *Birmingham Sunday Mercury* reported that proofreader George Turklebaum passed away at his desk at a New York publishing house, a fact that went unnoticed by his coworkers for five days while the body remained at his work station. The story turned out to be a hoax perpetrated by the supermarket tabloid *Weekly World News*, but not before it was picked up by various other publications including *The Guardian* and the BBC. *I don't want to live in a world where we can't trust supermarket tabloids.*

> David Emery, "George Turklebaum, R.I.P." About.com, January 31, 2001. *http://urbanlegends.about.com.*

FACT ATTACK: **Rival humanoid species discovered!** Folktales from the island of Flores in Indonesia tell of a peculiar race of tiny human-like creatures called the Ebu Gogo who abduct children and speak in murmurs. Scientists dismissed the claims until 2003, when archaeologists discovered the remains of a new hominid species called *Homo floresiensis* in caves on the island. The species lived alongside modern humans as recently as 12,000 years ago, but some believe they may still exist on the island today. *Just what the earth needs, more humans.*

> "Top 10 Creatures of Cryptozoology," Live Science, *www.livescience.com.*

FACT ATTACK: Headless chicken survives for 18 months! After a botched decapitation in 1945, a headless chicken nicknamed "Miracle Mike" roamed around a Colorado farm for a year and a half until he choked to death in an Arizona motel room. *Not sure what's weirder, a chicken living without a head or a chicken without a head renting a motel room.*

> Guinness World Records, *www.guinnessworldrecords.com.*

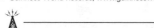

FACT ATTACK: Sea serpent myth debunked! Scientists speculate that the oarfish, a thin, fifty-foot-long deep-sea creature, could be responsible for many alleged sightings of sea serpents. The creature normally does not leave the deep ocean, but does occasionally come to the surface when near death. *So like a sea serpent, but significantly less magical.*

> "Top 10 Cryptids That Turned Out To Be Real," Listverse.com, *www.listverse.com.*

FACT ATTACK: Giant lizard morphs into giant ape! The 1926 expedition to confirm the myth of giant lizards inhabiting the island of Komodo served as the inspiration for the film *King Kong*. *It was also the inspiration for the less popular film* Bride Wars.

> "Top 10 Cryptids That Turned Out To Be Real," Listverse.com, *www.listverse.com.*

FACT ATTACK: Elusive devil bird revealed! Natives of Sri Lanka tell legends of a creature that gives off blood-curdling screams that they call the Devil Bird. The creature was rarely seen by locals, and western scientists wrote it off as fallacy. That is, until 2001, when scientists encountered the spot-bellied eagle owl and heard it give off the same characteristic screech. *Children of the Mothman, perhaps?*

> "Top 10 Cryptids That Turned Out To Be Real," Listverse.com, *www.listverse.com.*

ANIMAL ODDITIES

IN NATURE, FACT IS ALWAYS STRANGER THAN FICTION

FACT ATTACK: In Egypt, kill a cat and get killed!
Ancient Egyptians considered cats to be sacred animals. The animals shared the mummification ritual, and the penalty for killing one was death. *I refuse to venerate any creature that thinks it's better than me.*

> Judith Freeman Clark and Stephen Long, *Weird Facts To Blow Your Mind* (Price Stern Sloan, 1993), p. 39.

FACT ATTACK: Piss on a jellyfish sting does nothing! Despite popular opinion, urinating on a jellyfish sting will not alleviate the pain. *Vinegar works better, but urine will always be funnier.*

> Anahad O'Connor, *Always Follow the Elephants: More Surprising Facts and Misleading Myths about Our Health and the World We Live In* (Time Books, 2009).

FACT ATTACK: Snakes attracted to alcohol!
One in three snakebite victims is drunk. *In other news, fire is hot, water is wet, and knives are sharp.*

> Noel Botham, *The Mega Book of Useless Information* (John Blake, 2009).

FACT ATTACK: Snails can slide anywhere! A snail can traverse the length of a razor blade without cutting itself. *Unless it is listening to Dashboard Confessional at the time.*

> Sanjeev Garg, *501 Astonishing Facts* (Pustak Mahal, 2010).

FACT ATTACK: **Fish has see-through head!** The head of the barreleye fish is completely transparent. *Not that there's much to see.*

❯ "Researchers Solve Mystery of Deep-Sea Fish with Tubular Eyes and Transparent Head," Monterey Bay Aquarium Research Institute, *www.mbari.org.*

FACT ATTACK: **Pandas should be eating meat!** Despite the fact that 99 percent of their diet consists of bamboo, giant pandas possess the digestive system of a carnivore which is ill-suited to breaking down vegetation. To compensate, a single panda must consume as much as forty pounds of bamboo a day to survive. *Why do we even bother trying to save these momos?*

❯ Jane McGrath, "Why Don't Pandas Hibernate?" Howstuffworks.com, *http://animals.howstuffworks.com.*

FACT ATTACK: **Even monkeys fake orgasm!** If the female macaque does not scream during intercourse, her partner will almost never ejaculate. *Ladies, learn from the monkey.*

❯ Charles Q. Choi, "Study Reveals Why Monkeys Shout During Sex," MSNBC, December 19, 2007, *www.msnbc.com.*

FACT ATTACK: Anteaters are true kings of the jungle! Aardvarks are very aggressive and have been known to attack and kill lions when provoked. *Did not see that one coming.*

> Judith Freeman Clark and Stephen Long, *Weird Facts To Blow Your Mind* (Price Stern Sloan, 1993), p. 10.

FACT ATTACK: Invisible sharks roaming the ocean! Some shark species can emit light from their bodies that essentially renders them invisible to predators and prey below. They produce the shimmering effect from light-emitting organs called photophores located underneath their bodies. *As if visible sharks weren't terrifying enough.*

> Jennifer Viegas, "Sharks Can Become Invisible," Discovery News, May 25, 2010, *http://news.discovery.com.*

FACT ATTACK: Running of the Bulls not really dangerous! Despite the inherent risk associated with fleeing from stampeding bulls in a confined space, between 1924 and 2004 only thirteen individuals died during the annual Running of the Bulls in Pamplona, Spain. *That's unfortunate.*

> Joey Green, *Contrary to Popular Belief: More Than 250 False Facts Revealed* (Broadway Books, 2005).

FACT ATTACK: The dog that ate deer balls! Weimaraner dogs were originally bred to hunt stags. They pursued the intended victim low and from behind and were trained to leap at the animal's genitals and remove them in a single bite. Some members of the breed still perform this maneuver instinctively if given the opportunity. *It wasn't an effective method for killing the stag, but it sure was funny to watch.*

> David Louis, *2201 Fascinating Facts* (Wing Books, 1988).

FACT ATTACK: Fragile African mammal defies nature! Mostly found in eastern Africa, the naked mole rat is the only known mammal that is completely hairless. When a young naked mole rat enters the world, its wrinkled skin is so thin that one can see its internal organs. *If you have a grandma fetish, you will love these guys.*

❯ Joy Masoff, *Oh Yuck! The Encyclopedia of Everything Nasty* (Workman Publishing Company, 2000).

FACT ATTACK: Dinner option turns deadly for sea turtles! When sea turtles consume some species of jellyfish, they give off a scent that attracts sharks, who in turn devour the turtle. *The circle of life is an awe-inspiring thing.*

❯ Joy Masoff, *Oh Yuck! The Encyclopedia of Everything Nasty* (Workman Publishing Company, 2000).

FACT ATTACK: Jesus lizard walks on water! When startled, the basilisk lizard can run across a body of water for the distance of a quarter mile. Its large feet, lightweight body, and rapid pace allow it to skim across the surface without sinking. *When I read something like this, I feel so inadequate.*

❯ Sheila De La Rosa, *The Encyclopedia of Weird* (Tom Doherty Associates, 1998).

FACT ATTACK: Elephants can perform acrobatics! Aside from humans, the Asian elephant is the only animal that can stand on its head. *File this under: How the hell did we discover this?*

❯ Erin Barret and Jack Mingo, *Random Acts of Factness: 1001 (or so) Absolutely True Tidbits About Everything* (Conari Press, 2005).

FACT ATTACK: Marsupial genitalia come in pairs!
Most male marsupials have bifurcated penises. This
configuration evolved to match the dual vaginas
most female marsupials possess. *We have a hard enough
time preventing one penis from getting us into too much trouble.
Two would require more control than the average man possesses.*

❯ Erin Barret and Jack Mingo,
*Random Acts of Factness: 1001
(or so) Absolutely True Tidbits
About Everything* (Conari Press,
2005).

**FACT ATTACK: President turns White House into
zoo!** President John Quincy Adams kept
an alligator in the White House. *More accu-
rately: An alligator let John Quincy Adams live in the
White House.*

❯ Erin Barret and Jack Mingo,
*Random Acts of Factness: 1001
(or so) Absolutely True Tidbits
About Everything* (Conari Press,
2005).

FACT ATTACK: **Octopuses can't handle
pressure!** If an octopus becomes
stressed, it will often eat one of its
own tentacles. *Way worse than eating a
whole package of Ding Dongs.*

❯ Varla Ventura, *Beyond Bizarre: Frightening Facts and Blood-Curdling True Tales* (Weiser Books, 2010).

FACT ATTACK: Ancient ostrich myth busted! Despite popular belief, ostriches do not bury their heads in the sand when threatened. Instead, they flop to the ground and remain motionless. Because their head is a light color, it blends in with the sand, giving the illusion that they have buried it. *Playing dead is only marginally less pathetic.*

> "Birds: Ostrich," San Diego Zoo, *www.sandiegozoo.com.*

FACT ATTACK: **Bottom-feeding mollusk sees everything!** A sea scallop can have as many as 100 eyes. *So, more eyes = more delicious.*

> David Denning, "How Many Eyes Can One Animal Have?" Biomedia Associates, *www.ebiomedia.com.*

FACT ATTACK: Bats: man's true best friend! A colony of 500 bats can eat 250,000 insects in the span of one hour. *Better than a bug zapper, but with the machine you know the mosquito suffered.*

> Joy Masoff, *Oh Yuck! The Encyclopedia of Everything Nasty* (Workman Publishing, January 2000).

FACT ATTACK: Mysterious animal smells like snack food! The Binturong, an animal native to the rain forests of southeast Asia, has the face of a cat, the body of a bear, stiff white whiskers, a prehensile tail like a monkey, and gives off an odor reminiscent of freshly popped popcorn. It uses its strange musk to mark its territory. *And to give hikers false hope.*

> "Binturong," San Diego Zoo, *www.sandiegozoo.org.*

FACT ATTACK: Polish army enlists bear! During World War II, a 500-pound brown bear named Wojtek served in the Polish army. He was the unofficial mascot for the 22nd Army Corps, and provided much-needed entertainment for the troops. *Proof that even bears hate Nazis.*

> Dave Thier, "Scotland Honors Nazi-Fighting Polish Army Bear," AOL News, October 13, 2010, *www.aolnews.com.*

FACT ATTACK: Howler monkeys dying to be heard! The call of a howler monkey carries for up to three miles. *If you discovered they were screaming, "Every time you masturbate, a howler monkey dies," would you stop?*

> "Howler Monkey," National Geographic Animals, *http://animals.nationalgeographic.com.*

FACT ATTACK: Dog has its day in court! The bloodhound is the only animal whose evidence is admissible in court. *Because everyone knows beagles are liars.*

> Glen Vecchione, Joel Harris, and Sharon Harris, *The Little Giant Book of Animal Facts* (Sterling Publishing, 2004).

FACT ATTACK: Koalas don't need water! Koalas obtain all of their water from eating eucalyptus leaves. In fact, the word "koala" is an aboriginal word that means "no drink." *The Aboriginals are not very creative.*

> Glen Vecchione, Joel Harris, and Sharon Harris, *The Little Giant Book of Animal Facts* (Sterling Publishing, 2004).

FACT ATTACK: Impalas practically asking to be eaten! When impalas find a fresh water source, they immediately mark their new territory with potent urine. Unfortunately, this makes it especially easy for predators to find them. *Luckily, they can run fast.*

> Glen Vecchione, Joel Harris, and Sharon Harris, *The Little Giant Book of Animal Facts* (Sterling Publishing, 2004).

FACT ATTACK: Dinosaur fools scientists for decades! Paleontologists now believe that one of the most popular dinosaurs might never have existed. The dinosaur we all know as triceratops may actually have been a juvenile version of torosaurus, another dinosaur similar in appearance to the triceratops, but slightly larger. *And so my childhood died.*

> Charles Cooper, "Scientists: Triceratops May Not Have Existed," CBS News, August 3, 2010, *www.cbsnews.com.*

FACT ATTACK: **Dog owners reach out and touch their pets!** Thirty-three percent of dog owners talk to their pets on the phone and leave them messages on answering machines. *Thirty-three percent of dogs are smarter than their owners.*

> Glen Vecchione, Joel Harris, and Sharon Harris, *The Little Giant Book of Animal Facts* (Sterling Publishing, 2004).

FACT ATTACK: Sniper fish attacks targets on land!
The archer fish hunts prey that generally don't hang out in the water, like small lizards and insects. To get them within reach, the fish shoots a jet of water that knocks them off of low-hanging trees into the water, adjusting the force of the spray based on the size of the target.

❯ Charles Q. Choi, "Fish Shoot Prey with Precise Water Guns," Live Science, October 9, 2006, www.livescience.com.

FACT ATTACK: Rest easy, squirrels still not dangerous!
Squirrels are immune to rabies. *For some reason, I still don't trust them. They always look like they're up to something.*

❯ Dane Sherwood, Sandy Wood, and Kara Kovalchik, *The Pocket Idiot's Guide to Not So Useless Facts* (Penguin Group, 2006).

FACT ATTACK: Animal named through miscommunication! When British explorer Captain James Cook traveled to Australia in 1770, he and his men noticed a strange animal bounding across the outback. When they asked a native Aborgine what they called the creature the man replied "Kannaguru," which means "I do not understand you." *Interesting enough, "buffalo" actually means "Get off my land, white devil."*

❯ Bart King and Chris Sabatino, *The Big Book of Boy Stuff* (Gibbs Smith, 2004).

FACT ATTACK: Cats pee ultraviolet urine! Cat urine is sensitive to black light. *This is why it is always good to have a cat around, in case somebody shows up in your room with a black light and starts asking questions.*

❯ Dane Sherwood, Sandy Wood, and Kara Kovalchik, *The Pocket Idiot's Guide to Not So Useless Facts* (Penguin Group, 2006).

FACT ATTACK: **The amazing bird that thinks it's a bear!** The North American Whippoorwill is the only bird that hibernates. While it rests, its internal temperature drops from 105°F to 55.4°F. *I slept for an entire year once. Nobody made a fuss.*

❯ Russell Ash, *Firefly's World of Facts* (Firefly Books, 2007), p. 58.

FACT ATTACK: **Dog's saliva better than antibacterial soap!** Dog saliva contains lysozyme, an enzyme that destroys harmful bacteria. *Screw going to the hospital. Come here, Bandit.*

❯ Nicole Adams, "Why Would a Dog Lick the Pads of Their Feet?" Ehow, June 28, 2010, *www.ehow.co.uk.*

FACT ATTACK: **Fish replaces tongue with parasite!** The tongue-eating louse is a small crustacean that attaches itself to a passing fish, bores its way into its host through the gills, and slowly ingests the fish's tongue. Once the organ is gone, the parasite is able to fuse with the fish and take the place of the missing appendage. *If you find a nice warm home, you don't just up and leave. Gotta lock that down.*

❯ Matthew Hayden, "The 7 Most Horrifying Parasites on the Planet," Cracked.com, March 30, 2009, *www.cracked.com.*

FACT ATTACK: **Sloths stay close to home!**

On average, the sloth travels only fifteen feet per day. *But that's like 100 miles in cat years.*

❯ "Unusual Animal Facts," Buzzle.com, *www.buzzle.com.*

FACT ATTACK: **Scorpions hate booze!** If you put a drop of liquor on a scorpion, it will sting itself to death. *Almost went out and bought a scorpion just to test this.*

❯ "Unusual Animal Facts," Buzzle.com, *www.buzzle.com.*

FACT ATTACK: **Lesbian lizards reproduce without men!** The New Mexico whiptail lizard is an all-female species that reproduces despite the lack of male sexual partners. Some of the lizards do simulate sex acts with one another, and those that do reproduce more successfully than their abstemious sisters. *I invoke Internet rule 34.*

❯ "20 of the World's Weirdest Endangered Species," Webecoist.com, *www.webecoist.com.*

❯ "Unisexual Whiptail Lizards," American Museum of Natural History, *www.amnh.org.*

FACT ATTACK: **Creepy subterranean salamander lives to 100!** The olm is an amphibian that lives in the subterranean waters of Italy, Croatia, and Herzegovenia. It is blind, lives to 100 years old, and can go ten years without food. *In short, it's your grandma.*

❯ "20 of the World's Weirdest Endangered Species," Webecoist.com, *www.webecoist.com.*

FACT ATTACK: **Bat small enough to fit on your finger!** The bumblebee bat is one of the world's smallest, measuring just one inch. The tiny mammals can hover like hummingbirds and easily perch on the tip of a human thumb. They are one of the most endangered species in the world, with only 200 estimated in the wild. *Start breeding, you lazy shits. I don't want my kids growing up in a world without tiny bats.*

❯ "20 of the World's Weirdest Endangered Species," Webecoist.com, *www.webecoist.com.*

FACT ATTACK: **Lions mate like rabbits!**

A lion can mate up to fifty times in a day. *But only if they don't cuddle afterwards.*

> "Unusual Animal Facts," Buzzle.com, *www.buzzle.com.*

> "Top 10 Animal Oddities," Animal Planet, *http://animal .discovery.com.*

FACT ATTACK: **Giant pet rabbits escape and breed with locals!** When bred in captivity, rabbits can weigh more than thirty pounds and grow to more than three feet long. Giant rabbits do not occur in the wild, but they have been known to escape captivity and breed with local wild rabbit populations. *Coincidentally, their feet are twice as lucky.*

FACT ATTACK: **Scientists create super salmon!** The ocean pout, a species of fish, produces a protein that acts as antifreeze and keeps its blood from forming ice crystals. In the hopes of producing a superior Atlantic salmon, scientists took genetic material from the pout and spliced it into salmon, along with growth hormones from another, larger species of salmon. *Not because they needed to, but they were really bored that day.*

> Scott Hensley, "Weird Facts About Genetically Engineered Salmon," NPR, September 20, 2010, *www.npr.org.*

FACT ATTACK: Sea creature eats own brain! The sea squirt has a very simple brain which it only uses to select a suitable spot to root itself for the duration of its life. Once it settles down, it consumes the now useless organ. *I should consider that course of action next time I'm hungry. I'm certainly not using it.*

❯ "Weird Animals," BBC, June 7, 2002, *www.bbc.co.uk.*

FACT ATTACK: **Hippo sweat a natural mood ring!** When a hippopotamus is irritated, its sweat turns red. *A moment of silence for all the noble biologists who died bringing you this useful bit of trivia.*

❯ Mitchell Symons, *That Book: . . . of Perfectly Useless Information* (HarperCollins, 2004).

FACT ATTACK: Cat survives 360-foot drop! It takes a cat about two-and-a-half feet of free fall to orient itself to land feet first. The record for longest fall belongs to a cat named Voodoo who survived a drop of thirty-six stories. *In 2006, my courageous cat Sophie and I nearly beat that record (RIP Sophie: 2001–2006).*

❯ Alan Bellows, *Alien Hand Syndrome and Other Too-Weird-To-Be-True Stories* (Workman Publishing, 2009), p. 118.

FACT ATTACK: **Giant frog bests miniature antelope!** The world's largest frog is bigger than the world's smallest antelope. *As long as they're both bigger than the world's largest cockroach, I can rest easy.*

❯ Mitchell Symons, *That Book: . . . of Perfectly Useless Information* (Harper-Collins, 2004).

FACT ATTACK: **Alcoholic cattle produce superior beef!** To reproduce the coveted Kobe beef popular in Japan, Cornish farmers feed their cattle up to 40 pints of beer a day. They also provide the cows with water, but the farmers insist they prefer the beer. *They also prefer not being made into hamburgers, but if we give them everything they want then the terrorists win.*

❯ "Cattle on 40 Pints a Day of Beer," BBC News, February 9, 2007. *http://news.bbc.co.uk.*

FACT ATTACK: **Animal kingdom harnesses power of electricity!** Electric eels can deliver a 600-volt shock to stun their prey. This is equivalent to five times the power of a standard U.S. wall socket. Human deaths are rare, but victims of multiple shocks can experience respiratory failure or drown as a result of the shocks. *Step 1: Capture hundreds of electric eels. Step 2: ??? Step 3: Profit!*

❯ "Electric Eel," National Geographic Animals, *http://animals .nationalgeographic.com.*

FACT ATTACK: **Poisonous frogs: adorable or alarming?** With enough venom to kill ten grown humans, the golden poison dart frog is pound for pound one of the most dangerous animals on earth. Scientists are unsure what makes the frogs poisonous, as specimens raised in captivity never develop venom. *Hate to be the intern who had to verify that last bit.*

❯ "Golden Poison Dart Frog," National Geographic Animals. *http://animals.national geographic.com.*

FACT ATTACK: **Barnyard animals pilot hot air balloon!** A sheep, a duck, and a rooster were the first passengers on a hot air balloon. *Poor sheep. Why not stick with animals that can fly?*

> National Geographic, *Weird But True: 300 Outrageous Facts* (National Geographic Children's Books, 2009).

FACT ATTACK: **Bulls indifferent to color, hate all matadors equally!** The color of a matador's cape, or muleta, is traditionally red, which is widely believed to irritate the bull. In reality, bulls are colorblind, so it is irrelevant what color cape a matador uses to antagonize them. *Shot in the dark, but maybe it's the being stabbed with swords bit that pisses them off.*

> Larry Smith II, "How Texas Longhorns See the World and Reducing the Stress of Handling," International Texas Longhorn Association. *www.itla.net.*

> Alexander Fiske-Harrison, "A Noble Death," *Prospect* magazine, September 28, 2008. *www.prospectmagazine.co.uk.*

FACT ATTACK: **Catfish: tongues with fins!** Unlike most animals that taste with their tongues, catfish have taste buds covering their entire bodies. A six-inch-long catfish can have as many as 250,000 taste buds from head to tail fin. *Still don't feel bad eating them.*

> "Understanding Catfish Senses," Indiana Game and Fish. *www.indianagameandfish.com.*

FACT ATTACK: Frogs can hear with their lungs!
Frogs don't have an external eardrum and instead rely on two membranes called the tympanum which reside just behind each eye. They can also hear through their lungs, which are directly connected to the tympanum and respond to vibrations caused by sound waves. *Explains why my frog is such a good listener. No one understands me like he does. . . .*

> Regina Bailey, "Fascinating Animal Facts," About.com. *http://biology.about.com.*

> "Frog Ears," Animal Planet. *http://animal.discovery.com.*

FACT ATTACK: Snakes' eyes always open!
Snakes never close their eyes, even when they are asleep. They lack movable eyelids like many other animals. *When snakes develop opposable thumbs, we're fucked.*

> Regina Bailey "Fascinating Animal Facts," About.com. *http://biology.about.com.*

FACT ATTACK: Elephant poop measured in gallons! An elephant can defecate in a 7-gallon pile. *Given enough time, I think I could top that.*

> "Even More Gross Facts You May Have Never Wanted to Know," Associated Content, June 11, 2007, *www.associatedcontent.com.*

FACT ATTACK: Bat sticks to glass ceilings! A bat species found only in Madagascar secretes a modified sweat from its ankles that allows it to stick to smooth surfaces like palm leaves or even glass ceilings. Scientists mistakenly believed its feet acted like suction cups, and gave it the Latin name *Myzopoda* or "sucker foot." *FlyMouseGekko: It's half fly, half mouse, half gekko. Or maybe half flymouse, half gekko. Or half fly, half mousegekko.*

> Kert Than, "Sucker-Footed Bat Hangs Upright Via Sweat, Not Suction," National Geographic News, December 17, 2009, *http://news.national geographic.com.*

FACT ATTACK: Mammals that lay eggs! The echidna and platypus, both animals native to Australia, are the only two mammals that lay external eggs. Once the eggs hatch, the young crawl into a small pouch located on the mother's abdomen where they nurse from milk secreted through pores in the lining. *Watch some videos of the babies crawling around the pouch. It's creepier than* Alien.

❯ "Monotremes," Animal Planet. *http://animal.discovery.com.*

FACT ATTACK: Fish fuses with its mate! To mate with a female, the male angler fish latches onto the side of his partner with his teeth and releases an enzyme that causes his body to fuse with hers. Eventually, her body completely absorbs his until nothing but his gonads remain dangling on her side. *It's not a tumor.*

❯ "Weird Wonders: 15 of the World's Strangest Animals," Webecoist.com, October 5, 2009, *www.webecoist.com.*

FACT ATTACK: Animals master war strategies! Ants, crows, and humans share one common characteristic—they are the only animals that fight in formation. *We should really team up with them. We'd be unstoppable!*

❯ "Top 10 Weird Bug Facts," Science Channel. *http://science.discovery.com.*

FACT ATTACK: Sea turtles unfazed by jellyfish! Sea turtles are immune to jellyfish venom and eat them as a regular part of their diet. *Helps when you have a shell.*

❯ Alexandra Hazlett, "The World's Deadliest Animals," *New York Daily News*, February 24, 2010, *www.nydailynews.com.*

FACT ATTACK: **Baboons terrible at baseball!** Baboons cannot throw overhand. *But they have a mean sidearm.*

> Noel Botham, *The Best Book of Useless Information Ever: A Few Thousand Other Things You Probably Don't Need to Know (but Might as Well Find Out)* (Perigee, 2007).

FACT ATTACK: **Freshwater stingrays pierce bone!** Scientists have only been aware of the freshwater stingray since the early 1990s. The massive invertebrates are so strong they have been known to ram boats and bend fishhooks straight. Their barbs can pierce skin and even bone. *Somebody should have warned Steve Irwin.*

> Alexandra Hazlett, "The World's Deadliest Animals," *New York Daily News*, February 24, 2010, www.nydailynews.com.

FACT ATTACK: **Humans far more dangerous than sharks!** In 2008, there were fifty-nine unprovoked shark attacks recorded throughout the world. That same year, there were 40 million sharks killed by humans. *Retribution was swift, my comrades.*

> Alexandra Hazlett, "The World's Deadliest Animals," *New York Daily News*, February 24, 2010, www.nydailynews.com.

FACT ATTACK: **Master of disguise fools ocean predators!** Many animals can imitate the physical attributes of other creatures to evade predators, but the mimic octopus is the first ever discovered that can adopt the characteristics of multiple animals. Among its preferred subjects are venomous sea snakes, seahorses, stingrays, anemones, crabs, and starfish. *The seahorse one seems like he's just showing off.*

> Jonathan Wojcik, "The 9 Most Mind-blowing Disguises in the Animal Kingdom," Cracked.com, September 21, 2010, www.cracked.com.

FACT ATTACK: **Blind mole rats not so blind!** Blind mole rats can actually see, albeit not very well. One study determined they had some sensitivity to light and were even able to detect certain colors. *"Legally blind mole rats" just sounds stupid though.*

❯ Wynne Parry, "'Blind' Mole Rats Can See, Study Confirms," Live Science, August 10, 2010, www.livescience.com.

FACT ATTACK: **Attack of the flying squid!** Certain squid species can jettison themselves out of the water and take flight. Utilizing the same propulsion method they employ to evade predators, the squid shoot out of the water and glide for up to ten meters. *Way to steal the flying fish's thunder.*

❯ Ferris Jabr, "Fact or Fiction: Can a Squid Fly Out of the Water?" *Scientific American*, August 2, 2010, www.scientificamerican.com.

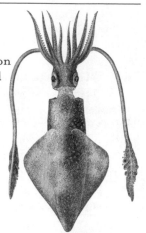

FACT ATTACK: **Giant cat hybrid stalks zoos!** Assumedly nonexistent in the wild, the crossbreeding of lions and tigers does occasionally occur in captivity. The resulting offspring are called ligers if the mother is a lion, and tigons if the mother is a tiger. *Bred for their skills in magic.*

❯ Maryann Mott, "Ligers Make a 'Dynamite' Leap Into the Limelight," National Geographic News, August 5, 2005. http://news.nationalgeographic.com.

FACT ATTACK: **Jellyfish species lives forever!** The *Turritopsis nutricula* is more commonly known as the immortal jellyfish, because as far as scientists can tell, the creature lives forever. Once the jellyfish matures and reproduces sexually, it reverts back to its juvenile state and begins the maturation process anew. There does not appear to be a limit to the number of times it can repeat this process. *Kill it with fire!*

❯ "'Immortal' Jellyfish Swarming Across the World," Telegraph, www.telegraph.co.uk.

PARANORMAL PHENOMENA

THE UNEXPLAINABLE WORLD OF THE WEIRD

FACT ATTACK: **First frozen chicken appears as ghost!**
To prove that meat would keep longer if frozen, the scientist Sir Francis Bacon killed a chicken, plucked out its feathers, and stuffed it with snow. He later caught pneumonia and died. There have been many ghost sightings at the site of his death, but not the ghost of Bacon. Instead, many report seeing a headless chicken pecking at the ground with its neck. *Miracle Mike would be so proud.*

❯ Jonathan Wojcik, "The 7 Most Ridiculous Ghost Stories From Around the World," Cracked.com, October 31, 2010, *www.cracked.com.*

FACT ATTACK: **Ghosts appear in photographs!** Believers in the paranormal often cite odd objects of light found in photographs as evidence that ghosts walk among us. However, the phenomenon, known as "orbs," is most likely caused by refractions of light from the flash of the camera. *Besides, everyone knows ghosts are shaped like triangles, not balls.*

❯ Richelle Hawks, "5 Things That Are Not Paranormal," Associated Content, November 16, 2009, *www.associated content.com.*

FACT ATTACK: **Humans not welcome in nature!** After hikers enter certain sections of wooded areas, they often hear a faint buzzing sound, sense a malevolent presence, and experience the feeling that they are not welcome. Some insist the experience—known as *panic,* named for the Greek god Pan, protector of wild places—is evidence that nature is self-aware. However, others dismiss it as tricks of the mind. *Mother Nature is real, and she's pissed.*

❯ "Top 10 Bizarre Modern Phenomena," Listverse.com, *www.listverse.com.*

FACT ATTACK: Filmmakers discover tiny flying fish!
In the mid-1990s, several filmmakers slowed down their footage and noticed small undulating objects floating past the camera. Dubbed "rods" or "sky-fish," no one is quite sure if these strange objects are living creatures, or if they are merely tricks of the camera. *Two words: tiny aliens.*

❯ Stephen Wagner, "Top 10 Earth Mysteries," About.com. *http://paranormal.about.com.*

FACT ATTACK: Death not the end! Fifteen percent of all Americans who find themselves in near-death situations report having a "near-death experience." This includes feeling like one is floating above one's body, the sensation of entering another realm or dimension, or the presence of spiritual beings. *The other 85 percent are godless heathens.*

❯ Ed Grabianowski, "How Near-Death Experiences Work," Howstuffworks.com, *http://science.howstuffworks.com.*

FACT ATTACK: Near-death experience caused by CO2!
While studying a group of fifty-two heart attack victims, researchers discovered that all eleven that reported near-death experiences had increased levels of carbon dioxide in their blood. This was the only factor that affected whether or not an individual reported a near-death experience. *Clearly Satan messed with the tests to cloud our judgment.*

❯ James Owen, "Near-Death Experiences Explained?" National Geographic News, April 8, 2010, *http://news.nationalgeographic.com.*

FACT ATTACK: Teens try to end World War II with voodoo! In 1941, a group of Maryland youth gathered together in a remote cabin with the intent to kill Hitler with a voodoo hex. Despite their best efforts, their plan did not work. *Oh really? Do you see any Hitlers running around?*

❯ "Putting a Hex On Hitler," Life, *www.life.com.*

FACT ATTACK: Fish fall from sky over Australia! In March of 2010, residents of the small town of Lajamanu in Australia were bombarded with hundreds of small fish literally raining down from the sky. The fish were still alive when they hit the ground. *Doubt they were alive for long after.*

❯ Richard Shears, "Residents Stunned as Hundreds of Fish Fall Out of the Sky Over Remote Australian Desert Town," *The Daily Mail*, March 2, 2010, www.dailymail.co.uk.

FACT ATTACK: Animals rain down from heaven all the time! The occurrence of creatures like fish and frogs falling from the sky is actually not all that uncommon. Scientists speculate that tornadoes suck the creatures into the atmosphere where they freeze before falling back to earth. *Not sure where the scientists come from, but in Boston it generally only rains water. And sometimes vomit.*

❯ Richard Shears, "Residents Stunned as Hundreds of Fish Fall Out of the Sky Over Remote Australian Desert Town," *The Daily Mail*, March 2, 2010, www.dailymail.co.uk.

FACT ATTACK: Spooky lights disappear before your eyes! When citizens of Marfa, Texas, stand near Route 90 and peer off into the distance, they see eerie lights floating in the distance. When they approach them, however, they disappear. Referred to as spooklights, this phenomenon has been documented in numerous other locations throughout the world. *Ghosts really need to find less creepy hobbies.*

❯ Stephen Wagner, "Top 10 Earth Mysteries," About.com, http://paranormal.about.com.

FACT ATTACK: Cow mutilations baffle ranchers! Since the 1970s, ranchers have complained of mutilations performed on their cattle with surgical precision. Often only the eyes, tongue, or genitals are removed, and there is a lack of blood on the scene. Theories range from satanic cults and alien experimentation to bizarre diseases. *The question isn't who would ever want a cow's penis, the question is who wouldn't?*

❯ Stephen Wagner, "Top 10 Earth Mysteries," About.com, http://paranormal.about.com.

FACT ATTACK: Entombed lizards spring back to life!
Since the 1700s, geologists have been shocked to discover perfectly preserved lizards and amphibians encased in solid rock. More shocking, however, are the few documented cases where the entombed creature sprang back to life several minutes after exposing it to air. *I think I saw that in a cartoon once.*

❯ Stephen Wagner, "Top 10 Earth Mysteries," About.com, *http://paranormal.about.com.*

FACT ATTACK: People relive Christ's crucifixion!

There were no instances of stigmata, the spontaneous appearance of wounds that mimic those endured by Jesus Christ during his crucifixion, before the thirteenth century. *Spoiler Alert: There weren't any after either.*

❯ "Mystical Sigmata," *Catholic Encyclopedia, www.newadvent.org.*

FACT ATTACK: Psychic octopus predicts future! During the 2010 World Cup, a German octopus named Paul successfully predicted the outcome of all seven of Germany's matches by opening the lid of one of two jars containing a mussel and a team flag. Paul died in his tank several months after the completion of the games. *Well, you can't just let something that powerful live.*

❯ Nesha Starcevic, "World Cup Soccer's Psychic Octopus Dies," MSNBC, October 26, 2010, *http://nbcsports.msnbc.com.*

FACT ATTACK: **Time-travelling woman appears in silent film!** During a scene in the 1928 Charlie Chaplin film *The Circus*, a woman walks through the background holding a device to her ear much in the same way one might hold a cellular telephone today. *Droid does.*

> Suzanne Choney, "Cell Phone Time Traveler From 1928?" MSNBC, October 26, 2010, *http://technolog.msnbc.msn.com.*

FACT ATTACK: **Low-frequency sounds masquerade as ghosts!** Experiments have shown that low-frequency sound waves may be responsible for phenomena associated with ghosts. The sounds can cause feelings of nervousness as well as a sense of a presence in the room. They may also vibrate the human eye, causing people to see things that are not there. *Which doesn't do us much good if it's the ghosts making the sounds.*

> Tracy V. Wilson, "How Ghosts Work," Howstuffworks.com, *http://science.howstuff works.com.*

FACT ATTACK: **Large minority believe in ghosts!** According to a 2005 Gallup poll, more than one third of Americans believe it is possible for a house to be haunted, with around 32 percent believing specifically in ghosts. *The disparity there tells me that about 1 percent think a house can be haunted by Gary Busey.*

> Tracy V. Wilson, "How Ghosts Work," Howstuffworks.com, *http://science.howstuff works.com.*

FACT ATTACK: History's greatest thinkers all same person! The Count of St. Germain appeared in the eighteenth century as a skilled musician, artist, and alchemist, and many believed he discovered the coveted elixir of life. Unfortunately, he disappeared without a trace before anyone could verify his discovery. Some believe he has appeared throughout history as important historical figures ranging from Plato and St. Joseph to philosopher Roger Bacon. *You can live forever, but you have to begin each sentence with "Don't cross the streams." Would you do it?*

> Jamie Frater, *The Ultimate Book of Top Ten Lists: A Mind-Boggling Collection of Fun, Fascinating and Bizarre Facts on Movies, Music, Sports, Crime, Celebrities, History, Trivia and More* (Ulysses Press, 2009).

FACT ATTACK: Vast majority believe in telepathy! More than 70 percent of people believe it is possible to send messages telepathically. *Right now you are thinking, "I wonder if I have enough toilet paper."*

> H.G. Carlson, *Mysteries of the Unexplained,* (Contemporary Books, 1994), p. 132.

FACT ATTACK: Screaming skull prefers to stay put!
Outside Bettiscombe Manor in Dorset, England, a
human skull rests atop a white picket fence. Some
believe removing it from the house results in a
blood-curdling scream of anguish. *A common side effect
of holding a human skull.*

> H. G. Carlson, *Mysteries of
> the Unexplained* (Contemporary
> Books, 1994), p. 58.

FACT ATTACK: Ship vanishes into thin air! On October 23,
1948, the U.S. Navy allegedly conducted an experiment that transported a destroyer, the USS *Eldridge*,
from Philadelphia, PA, to Norfolk, VA, and back
again. Dubbed Project Rainbow (or the Philadelphia
Experiment), the government denies that such an
experiment ever took place. *I just teleported this book to Zim-
babwe and back again. It just happened too fast for you to notice.*

> "Philadelphia Experiment," *The Skeptic's Dictionary, www.skepdic.com.*

FACT ATTACK: Wandering stones baffle scientists! The salt
flats in California's Death Valley are home to wandering stones. Rocks ranging in size from small peb-
bles to half-ton boulders appear to move across the
wasteland, sometimes as far as 860 feet in one year.
No one has witnessed one moving, and scientists are
baffled as to what causes the phenomenon. *The explanation lies in the documentary* The Neverending Story.

> H. G. Carlson, *Mysteries of
> the Unexplained* (Contemporary
> Books, 1994), p. 115.

FACT ATTACK: Disgruntled ghost offers free tutoring!
Students at the University of California at Berkeley believe the ghost of a former student haunts the school's Sather Tower. Legend has it that struggling academics can call on the apparition for help during finals, as the ghost has a grudge against the university. *We just used CliffsNotes.*

> Bill McLain, *Do Fish Drink Water? Puzzling and Improbable Questions and Answers* (William Morrow, 1999), p. 275.

FACT ATTACK: Investigators to commune with *Titanic* victims!
A group of paranormal investigators plan to ride out to the site of the *Titanic* sinking to conjure up the ghosts of the 1,500 victims. The group will bring along a dummy dressed in period costume outfitted with microphones and cameras to record signs from the afterlife. *Because the best way to attract ghosts is to patronize them.*

> Robert Nolin, "Coral Springs Man To Join Titanic Ghost-Hunting Trip," *Florida Sun Sentinel*, October 30, 2010, *www.sun-sentinel.com*.

FACT ATTACK: Pope John Paul II performs miracle from the grave!
After an armed assailant shot Cleveland resident Jory Aebly at point-blank range in the head, doctors informed his family that his wounds were not survivable. Shortly after, a local priest visited the unresponsive Aebly and bestowed upon him a rosary blessed by the late Pope John Paul II. From then on, Aebly stunned doctors and continued to improve until he eventually left the hospital on his own two feet. *How come nobody ever attributes their recovery to the blessed surgeon's scalpel or the sacred respirator?*

> Dan Harris, Jen Pereira, and Lee Ferran, "Vatican Investigates 'Miracle' Recovery of Man Shot in Head," ABC News, April 2, 2009, *http://abcnews.go.com*.

FACT ATTACK: Artificial intelligence fools judges!

The Loebner Prize is a $3,000 award given to anyone who can program a computer to convince judges it is, in fact, human. The judges converse with both a human and the computer simultaneously and must decide which they feel is a more believable human. *My condolences to the people who lose to the machine.*

❭ MacGregor Campbell, "Prize-winning Chatbot Steers the Conversation," New Scientist, October 27, 2010, *www.newscientist.com.*

FACT ATTACK: Ghosts offering free room and board!

According to a *USA Today* poll, more than half of respondents would share their home with a ghost in exchange for free rent. Twenty-seven percent would do so for half rent. *A ghost roommate is still better than a human one.*

❭ "USA Today Snapshots," *www.usatoday.com.*

FACT ATTACK: Jesus's burial cloth stumps scientists!

Since 1578 a cloth with the image of a man alleged to be Jesus Christ has resided at the Turin Cathedral. Scientists have analyzed thread fibers and attempted to recreate the Shroud of Turin, but no one has been able to determine how old the alleged burial shroud is, or been able to recreate it manually. *It's probably advanced technology sent down by aliens to mess with us.*

❭ Elisabetta Proveledo, "A Faded Relic of Christendom Reappears," *New York Times*, May 3, 2010, *www.nytimes.com.*

FACT ATTACK: Massive ship vanishes into thin air!

The largest U.S. naval vessel to ever disappear without a trace was the USS *Cyclops*. The 19,360-ton collier vanished in March of 1918 on a return voyage from Brazil. No wreckage was ever recovered. *Probably got their first look at Brazilian women, sank the boat, and never looked back.*

❭ Varla Ventura, *Beyond Bizarre: Frightening Facts and Blood-Curdling True Tales* (Weiser Books, 2010).

FACT ATTACK: Ghost halts work on tourist trap! In 2009, work on a tourist attraction at the Warwick Castle in Warwickshire, England, came to a halt when several contractors complained of encounters with ghosts. A tall, thin man wearing a tunic and trousers appeared to one of the workers on several occasions, and mediums who visited the site in the past reported a hovering female specter near where the contractors were working. *Ghosts are always popping up in old castles, but you never see one floating around a Long John Silver's or a Target.*

> Emma McKinney, "Work Halted on Warwick Castle Over Haunting Scare," *Birmingham News*, March 16, 2009, *www.birminghammail.net.*

FACT ATTACK: Devil marks witches with moles! In Colonial America, birthmarks were considered a sure sign that an individual was a witch. *And if she floated when you threw her in the water she was made of wood, and therefore was a witch. Because wood burns. And so do witches.*

> Barbara Seuling, *Your Skin Weighs More Than Your Brain: and Other Freaky Facts About Your Skin, Skeleton, and Other Body Parts* (Picture Window Books, 2007).

FACT ATTACK: Witchcraft goes out with a hang! The last woman to be executed in Europe for witchcraft was Anna Goddi, who was hanged in Switzerland in 1782. *Sure, they weren't all witches, but better safe than sorry.*

> Jennifer Uglow, *The Northeastern Dictionary of Women's Biography* (Northeast University Press, 1999), p. 473.

FACT ATTACK: Human bodies burn without fire!
Dubbed spontaneous human combustion, the phenomenon whereby a human body engulfs itself in flames has only been documented in roughly 200 cases. *I'm convinced that this only occurs if someone consumes a Cinnabon immediately after eating at Taco Bell.*

❯ Nathan Robert Brown, *The Complete Idiot's Guide to the Paranormal* (Alpha, 2010), p. 238.

FACT ATTACK: **It's not hot in here, it's just you!** A person who succumbs to spontaneous human combustion experiences temperatures between 1,700 and 3,000°F before the body reduces to ashes in a matter of seconds. *At least it's over before the unfathomable pain sets in.*

❯ Nathan Robert Brown, *The Complete Idiot's Guide to the Paranormal* (Alpha, 2010), p. 238.

FACT ATTACK: Strange hum harmless, but wildly irritating! Since the early '90s, residents of Taos, New Mexico, have complained of a maddening humming sound permeating the town. Not all of the residents experience the constant irritation, which has some speculating that the noise is a low-frequency vibration that only those with sensitive ears can detect. *It wouldn't be so bad except it's humming the Mario Bros. tune.*

❯ Nathan Robert Brown, *The Complete Idiot's Guide to the Paranormal* (Alpha, 2010), p. 238.

FACT ATTACK: **Telekinetic woman baffles scientists!**
A woman named Felicia Parise came forward in the 1970s claiming she had telekinetic abilities. While the feat left her physically exhausted, she was able to manipulate small pillboxes and similar items without touching them. She performed the feat for researchers on several occasions, but no one was ever able to explain how she did it. *One word: farts.*

❯ Nathan Robert Brown, *The Complete Idiot's Guide to the Paranormal* (Alpha, 2010), p. 222.

FACT ATTACK: **Rabies spells the beginning of the end!** Experts warn that with a few modifications, the virus that causes rabies could mutate to spawn a zombie apocalypse. Currently, the virus is transmitted through saliva; however, if it became airborne, the consequences would be disastrous. *Remember kids, remove the head or destroy the brain.*

❯ Ker Than, "'Zombie Virus' Possible via Rabies-Flu Hybrid?" National Geographic News, October 27, 2010, *http://news .nationalgeographic.com.*

FACT ATTACK: **Mathematicians solve zombie outbreak problem!**
According to a mathematical study, if a zombie infestation breaks out in a city of 500,000 people, the zombies will outnumber survivors in three days. The authors of the study insist that the only effective method for containing the outbreak is immediate and systematic eradication of the infected. *If anyone needs me, I'll be at the Winchester waiting for this whole thing to blow over.*

❯ Betsy Mason, "Mathematical Model for Surviving a Zombie Attack," *Wired*, August 14, 2009, *www.wired.com.*

FACT ATTACK: Voodoo zombie powder is real! Do voodoo witch doctors have the power to enslave victims in a zombie-like trance? The witch doctors use a powder which scientists have discovered contains tetrodotoxin, the same neurotoxin found in puffer fish. At the right dosage, the toxin creates a state of suspended animation in the victim, but the wrong dosage can be fatal. *So pray your local witch doctor is good at measuring.*

❯ Nathan Robert Brown, *The Complete Idiot's Guide to the Paranormal* (Alpha, 2010), p. 170.

FACT ATTACK: Witch doctor magically removes money from woman's wallet! After Guadalupe Fernandez Andrade cursed Jennifer Madrigal to be hit by a car, Madrigal turned to the only person she could think of to help her—a local witch doctor. Madrigal later filed a complaint against Andrade arguing that she should be responsible for the witch doctor's $800 fee he charged to reverse the spell. *Some people should not be allowed to handle money.*

❯ Mary Richards, "Woman Hires Witch Doctor, Files Complaint Over Curse," KSL.com, April 15, 2009, *www.ksl.com*.

FACT ATTACK: Russia goes up in flames! In June 1908, a ball of fire exploded near the Tunguska River in Russia, leveling 770 square miles of forest. The blast unleashed 15 megatons of energy, 1,000 times more powerful than the Hiroshima bomb. Scientists speculate that it was a meteor, but others insist it was a UFO crash landing. *Because if you were an alien, your first stop would naturally be a remote forest in Russia.*

❯ "5 Natural Events That Science Can't Explain," Mother Nature Network, *www.mnn.com*.

FACT ATTACK: **The town that danced itself to death!**

In July of 1518, a lone woman started dancing in a street in Strasbourg, France. Several days later, thirty-four dancers had joined her. Within a month the number of manic dancers had swelled to 400, and dozens had died from heart attacks, strokes, and exhaustion. Nobody knows what caused the "dance epidemic." *Perhaps they should have tried turning off the music.*

> Jennifer Viegas, "'Dancing Plague' and Other Odd Afflictions Explained," Discovery News, August 1, 2008, http://dsc.discovery.com.

FACT ATTACK: **Stonehenge actually an ancient cemetery!**

A new study conducted on human remains uncovered at Stonehenge found that the site was used as a burial ground from 3,000 B.C. until after the first large stones were raised around 2,500 B.C. An estimated 240 individuals are buried at the site. *And how many of them were aliens, exactly?*

> James Owen, "Stonehenge Was Cemetery First and Foremost, Study Says," National Geographic News, May 29, 2008, http://news.national geographic.com.

FACT ATTACK: **Researchers name weird phenomenon!**

The term "extra sensory perception" (ESP) was coined by a researcher at Duke University named J. B. Rhine, who used it to refer to clairvoyance, precognition, and telepathy when he began researching strange phenomena in 1927. *I always thought it stood for "exceptionally stupid person."*

> Robert Todd Carroll, *The Skeptic's Dictionary: A Collection of Strange Beliefs, Amusing Deceptions, and Dangerous Delusions* (John Wiley and Sons, 2003), p. 124.

FACT ATTACK: **Special caskets provide vampire insurance!**

At one point in European history, hysteria surrounding vampires became so severe that undertakers started designing caskets with failsafes to ensure the dead did not rise again. These included sharp stakes affixed to the lid to impale the heart, and blades positioned near the neck to decapitate the body. *Better safe than sorry.*

> Nathan Robert Brown, *The Complete Idiot's Guide to the Paranormal* (Alpha, 2010), p. 152.

FACT ATTACK: Jilted Japanese lovers return as ghosts!
When a woman dies in a violent manner or due to an act of betrayal, the Japanese believe she will come back as an Onryo or "angry ghost." Usually the ghosts of murdered wives, these apparitions seek vengeance against their husbands and won't stop until they have paid for their crimes with their lives. *Still unclear as to what sets them apart from regular women.*

> Nathan Robert Brown, *The Complete Idiot's Guide to the Paranormal* (Alpha, 2010), p. 32.

FACT ATTACK: "Possessed" girl exorcised to death!
When Anniliese Michel experienced thrashing fits in the 1970s, doctors insisted she had multiple mental disorders. However, her parents implored the church to perform an exorcism. A group of priests agreed, and on July 30, 1976 Anneliese died of starvation from being deprived food as part of the exorcism rites. *Sure got rid of that pesky demon, though.*

> Nathan Robert Brown, *The Complete Idiot's Guide to the Paranormal* (Alpha, 2010), p. 99–101.

FACT ATTACK: Humans can't hear ghosts, but we can feel them!
Humans can't hear the low tone of 19 megahertz, but we can feel the vibration. Many hauntings have been linked to this frequency. *So if you hear anything, you can rest assured it's not a ghost. Probably just a murderer or something.*

> "Trapped Souls," National Geographic, *Haunted Prison,* http://channel.national geographic.com/episode/ haunted-prison-4571/Facts.

FACT ATTACK: Al Capone plagued by ghosts!
Philadelphia's Eastern State Penitentiary is believed to be one of the most haunted places in America and has been closed since 1971. Its most famous ghost story involved inmate Al Capone, who claimed to be haunted by the spirit of one of his victims. *Even if I were already in prison, not sure I'd want to admit I had "victims."*

> "Trapped Souls," National Geographic, *Haunted Prison,* http://channel.national geographic.com/episode/ haunted-prison-4571/Facts.

FACT ATTACK: Germany burns witches by the thousands!
In Germany, upwards of 100,000 people accused of witchcraft were burned between the fifteenth and eighteenth centuries. In the United States and England, hanging was the preferred method of execution for suspected witches. *If they weren't witches, then how come they burned like they were made of wood?*

❯ Russell Ash, *Firefly's World of Facts* (Firefly Books, 2007).

FACT ATTACK: **Ghost sightings increased by belief!** People who believe in ghosts are more likely to report paranormal encounters. *You don't say.*

❯ "Trapped Souls," National Geographic, *Haunted Prison, http://channel.nationalgeographic.com/episode/haunted-prison-4571/Facts.*

FACT ATTACK: Planes vanish into thin air! The Bermuda Triangle first garnered attention in 1945 when five U.S. bomber planes disappeared in the area. The recovery plane sent to locate the missing pilots also vanished. *Of all the places to go missing, the middle of the Caribbean ain't too bad.*

❯ Russell Ash, *Firefly's World of Facts* (Firefly Books, 2007).

FACT ATTACK: **Bermuda Triangle claims 100 victims!** Since the first planes went missing in the Bermuda Triangle, as many as 100 other boats and aircraft have disappeared there. *Clearly there is an awesome party going on there that we are not invited to.*

❯ Russell Ash, *Firefly's World of Facts* (Firefly Books, 2007).

FACT ATTACK: **Saint levitates in front of pope!** Saint Joseph of Copertino, also known as the "Flying Friar," is said to have first levitated in 1630 and would often hover over the congregation during religious services. He is credited with more than 100 flights, one of which was performed in front of Pope Urban VIII. *Great, next we'll have to canonize David Blaine.*

❯ Russell Ash, *Firefly's World of Facts* (Firefly Books, 2007).

FACT ATTACK: **Salvaged body parts perform miracles!** During the Middle Ages, holy relics—often consisting of bone fragments, appendages, and other physical specimens taken from the bodies of saints—attracted visitors from all of Christendom. They believed they had special powers to cure the sick and perform miracles. *If only believing something made it true.*

❯ Christopher Shay, "Top 10 Famous Stolen Body Parts," *Time*, May 12, 2010. *www.time.com.*

FACT ATTACK: Italians steal Santa Claus's bones! To liberate holy relics, towns would often hire thieves to steal them from their neighbors. In one famous example, in 1087 the Italian town of Bari hired men to relocate the bones of Saint Nicholas, which were rumored to exude myrrh, from their home in Myra in what is now present-day Turkey. Today the citizens of Bari celebrate the theft annually with a parade and fireworks display. *See kids, Santa Claus is real—he's just dead.*

> Christopher Shay, "Top 10 Famous Stolen Body Parts," *Time*, May 12, 2010. *www.time.com.*

FACT ATTACK: Ghost's body found in fireplace! Patrons of King's Tavern in Natchez, Mississippi, have reported a female apparition frequenting the bar since the late 1700s. The specter appears before patrons, staring angrily with her hands on her hips. In the 1930s, excavators discovered a skeleton of the owner's mistress with a dagger in her chest sealed within a brick fireplace. *No wonder she looked so pissed.*

> Varla Ventura, *Book of the Bizarre: Freaky Facts and Strange Stories* (Red Wheel, 2008), p. 13.

FACT ATTACK: Moses story kinda sorta true! The story of the parting of the Red Sea could be based in fact. Scientist speculate that an overnight wind could have swept water off a bend adjacent to an ancient river that merged with the Mediterranean Sea. If the conditions were perfect, the result would have been a temporary land bridge. *If conditions were perfect, I'd be emperor of the world. That doesn't make it true.*

> Brett Israel, "Parting of Red Sea Jibes with Natural Laws," Live Science, September 21, 2010. *www.livescience.com.*

FACT ATTACK: Cursed phone number claims new victim! The Bulgarian mobile phone company Mobitel retired the phone number 0888-888-888 after all three of the owners of the number died suddenly. The first died of cancer, the second was murdered while out on a date, and the third was shot while eating lunch. *I'd say the creepiest bit is that they reassign phone numbers when you die.*

> "0888 888 888: The Cursed Phone Number That Killed Its Owners," Gizmodo, May 27, 2010. *www.gizmodo.com.*

FACT ATTACK: **First vampire never drank blood!** There is no evidence that Vlad the Impaler ever drank blood. *He just bathed in it.*

> Nathan Robert Brown, *The Complete Idiot's Guide to the Paranormal* (Alpha, 2010).

FACT ATTACK: World's first vampire impaled victims! The real-life inspiration for the Dracula myth dates back to fifteenth-century Romania in the form of Vlad Tepes III, or "Vlad the Impaler." Vlad was a ruthless ruler who kept his subjects in check by routinely impaling thousands of them on wooden stakes surrounding his castle. *He wasn't evil. Just misunderstood.*

> Nathan Robert Brown, *The Complete Idiot's Guide to the Paranormal* (Alpha, 2010).

ALIENS AND UFOS

WHERE THEY ARE HIDING
AND WHY WE SHOULD
PROBABLY STOP LOOKING
FOR THEM

FACT ATTACK: Alien bacteria make it rain blood! In 2001, blood-red rain fell from the skies above Kerala, India. Scientists are uncertain as to what caused the phenomenon, but some speculate alien bacteria could have been released into the atmosphere when a meteor exploded over the area. *Obviously.*

❯ Jebediah Reed, "Mysterious Red Cells Might Be Aliens," CNN, June 2, 2006, *www.cnn.com.*

FACT ATTACK: **Aliens don't want to be pen pals!** In forty years of experiments, SETI—the Search for Extraterrestrial Intelligence—has not yielded a single confirmed alien signal. *Except that one time, but it turned out to be astronauts messing with them.*

❯ Joel Achenbach, "Life Beyond Earth," National Geographic, *http://science.nationalgeographic.com.*

FACT ATTACK: Aliens might not need light! In the early 1990s researchers discovered microbial life in basaltic rock deep beneath Washington State, proving that life could exist totally cut off from the photosynthetic world. *But they'll still have two arms, two legs, two eyes, a nose, and a mouth, and speak English, right?*

❯ Joel Achenbach, "Life Beyond Earth," National Geographic, *http://science .nationalgeographic.com.*

FACT ATTACK: If aliens won't come to us, we'll go to them! Currently NASA is in plans to develop a craft dubbed "The Hundred Years Starship," which would allow for interstellar space travel. The hope is to explore and colonize other worlds outside our solar system. *To boldly go . . . you know the rest.*

> Tim Carmody, "NASA Developing Tech to Reach and Colonize Other Worlds," *Wired*, October 19, 2010, *www.wired.com.*

FACT ATTACK: Mission to Mars (not) worth the cost! As of 2010, the cost to send a single human on a one-way trip to Mars was estimated at $10 billion. *How far will $10 and a stick of gum get me?*

> Tim Carmody, "NASA Developing Tech to Reach and Colonize Other Worlds," *Wired*, October 19, 2010, *www.wired.com.*

FACT ATTACK: Green goo defies nature! In 2010, residents of Stonefield Beach noticed a green tidal pool in their remote area of Oregon. The water has the mysterious ability to support stones that would sink under normal circumstances. Scientists have determined that the cause of the discoloration is not algae, and locals insist it is the work of aliens. *Keep reading. The aliens have better things to do with their time.*

> Dave Masko, "UFOs and Aliens Reaching Out With 'Signs,' Say Paranormal Experts," Huliq.com, October 19, 2010, *www.huliq.com.*

FACT ATTACK: Fancy new science gets fancy new name! In 1996, an unknown NASA official coined the term "astrobiology" to refer to the search for extraterrestrial life. This quickly replaced the less catchy term "planetary sciences" that members of the field used previously. *Or "Star Trek nerds with tele-scopes," if you prefer.*

> Gary Bates, *Alien Intrusion* (Creation Book Publishers, 2010).

FACT ATTACK: Government insists aliens are not real! To determine the validity of UFO reports pouring in during the 1950s and '60s, the United States government created "Project Bluebook." After reviewing thousands of cases, the team concluded there was no reason to believe contact with aliens had ever occurred. *Using similar logic, and after reading thousands of fact books, I have concluded that this is the only one worth buying.*

> "The Secret of Project Blue Book," ABC News, February 24, 2005, *http://abcnews.go.com.*

FACT ATTACK: Astronaut spots UFO! Astronaut Gordon Cooper reported a greenish, glowing object ahead of his capsule in his final orbit of earth during a *Mercury* mission in 1963. When he reported the incident, a tracking station in Australia confirmed the sighting on their radar. *Well, obviously a weather balloon managed to escape the earth's atmosphere. Pesky little buggers, those weather balloons.*

> Gary Bates, *Alien Intrusion* (Creation Book Publishers, 2010).

FACT ATTACK: American skies crawling with UFOs! As many as 20 million Americans claim to have seen a UFO. *If roughly the same number claimed to see the Flying Spaghetti Monster, would you believe them?*

> Gary Bates, *Alien Intrusion* (Creation Book Publishers, 2010).

FACT ATTACK: Science fiction novel broadcast as fact! On October 30, 1938, Orson Welles adapted *War of the Worlds*, a novel depicting an alien invasion of earth, for his radio program *The Mercury Theatre on the Air*. Those who tuned in late believed the show was an actual news broadcast foreshadowing the end of the world. *Their ancestors can be seen watching old episodes of* Gilligan's Island *and wondering why nobody has rescued them yet.*

> Sam Abramson, "October 30, 1938: The 'War of the Worlds' Radio Show Is Broadcast," Howstuffworks.com, *http://entertainment.howstuff works.com.*

FACT ATTACK: Police bombarded by hysterical listeners! The New York City Police Department fielded 2,000 emergency calls within the first fifteen minutes of Welles's broadcast of *War of the Worlds*. *I wonder if they had fun with anybody and told them to head for the hills.*

❯ Stephen J. Spignesi, *The UFO Book of Lists* (Citadel, 2000).

FACT ATTACK: **Radio hoax frightens millions!** Of the 6 million individuals who heard the CBS broadcast of *War of the Worlds*, nearly one-third believed it to be true. *Fewer than .1 percent are still in hiding.*

❯ Richard J. Hand, *Terror on the Air!: Horror Radio in America, 1931–1952* (McFarland & Company, 2006).

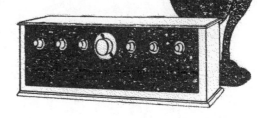

FACT ATTACK: UFO sighted by entire city! In July of 1860, nearly the entire city of Wilmington, Delaware, was lit up by a pale blue light. Residents looked up to discover a 200-foot-long object flying just 100 feet above their heads. The UFO sighting came to a sudden conclusion when the object took off bearing east. *Clearly a scientist carrying a weather balloon had traveled back in time and accidentally released it over the city.*

❯ Stephen J. Spignesi, *The UFO Book of Lists* (Citadel, 2000).

FACT ATTACK: Alien encounters fall into three categories! There are three types of close encounters. A close encounter of the first kind indicates the subject spotted a UFO at close range. The second kind involves the discovery of physical evidence left behind by an alien or alien craft. The third kind requires actual physical contact with an alien being. *If you have sex with the alien, well, best to keep that to yourself.*

> Isaac Asimov and Richard Hantula, *UFOs (Isaac Asimov's 21st Century Library of the Universe)* (Gareth Stevens Publishing, 2004).

FACT ATTACK: Cultists catch ride on alien spaceship! In 1997, members of the Heaven's Gate group committed mass suicide with the belief that they could then board an alien spacecraft following Comet Hale-Bopp. The thirty-nine dead individuals marked the largest mass suicide in U.S. history. *Balls, I missed it. I'll just catch the next one.*

> Elizabeth Gleick, Cathy Booth, and James Willwerth, "The Marker We've Been Waiting For," *Time*, April 7, 1997, www.time.com.

FACT ATTACK: **Aliens big on brand recognition!** All of the Heaven's Gate members wore matching black Nike sneakers when they committed suicide by imbibing phenobarbital, a deadly poison, mixed with applesauce or pudding. *Because aliens are nothing if not fashion-forward.*

> Elizabeth Gleick, Cathy Booth, and James Willwerth, "The Marker We've Been Waiting For," *Time*, April 7, 1997, www.time.com.

FACT ATTACK: Did aliens visit our ancestors?! UFO sightings are by no means a modern phenomenon. Ancient Egyptians reported "circles of fire" and "flaming chariots" in the skies, and Native Americans had legends of "flying canoes" and "great silvery airships." Nearly every culture has similar myths of flaming objects descending from the sky. *This would certainly explain a lot.*

> J. Allan Danelek, *UFOs: The Great Debate: An Objective Look at Extraterrestrials, Government Cover-Ups, and the Prospect of First Contact* (Llewellyn Publications, 2008).

FACT ATTACK: UFO toys with fighter jets! In the late evening of March 30, 1990, two F-16 fighter jets engaged an unidentified flying object over the town of Wavre in Belgium. Just before the fighters locked on to the target, the UFO accelerated to more than 1,120 miles an hour—without creating a sonic boom—and engaged in a series of evasive maneuvers for an hour before accelerating out of sight. *If aliens are going to come to our planet, they could at least have the courtesy to follow our rules of physics.*

> J. Allan Danelek, *UFOs: The Great Debate: An Objective Look at Extraterrestrials, Government Cover-Ups, and the Prospect of First Contact* (Llewellyn Publications, 2008).

FACT ATTACK: Aliens come from earth! Ufologists speculate that interactions with extraterrestrials are not alien encounters at all. Instead, they believe that a technologically advanced race of humans evolved cut off from society below the surface of the earth. Possibly the ancestors of the lost city of Atlantis, these "aliens" often appear human to those who encounter them. *But can ufologists repeat that with a straight face?*

> J. Allan Danelek, *UFOs: The Great Debate: An Objective Look at Extraterrestrials, Government Cover-Ups, and the Prospect of First Contact* (Llewellyn Publications, 2008).

FACT ATTACK: **Barking aliens perform weird sex experiment!**
In 1957, a Brazilian farmer reported that barking aliens abducted him, covered him in gel, and mated with him. *Actually they were furries.*

> Jason Stahl, "20 Things You Didn't Know About . . . Aliens," *Discover*, January 2007, *www.discovermagazine.com.*

FACT ATTACK: **French transmit first alien soap opera!** On September 30, 2006, the French Center for National Space Studies beamed a TV program aimed at extraterrestrials called *Cosmic Connexion* out into space. Their target was a sunlike star called Errai located 45 light-years from Earth. The video will not reach its destination until 2051. *This is still only the 457th weirdest thing the French have done.*

> Jason Stahl, "20 Things You Didn't Know About . . . Aliens," *Discover*, January 2007, *www.discovermagazine.com.*

FACT ATTACK: **Aliens get jiggy with humans!** Harvard researchers questioned a group of ten self-proclaimed abductees while under hypnosis during a 2003 study. Seven out of the ten subjects stated that their alien abductors used them for sexual experimentation and mating. *If an alien wants to have sex with you, do it. You may never get another chance.*

> Jason Stahl, "20 Things You Didn't Know About . . . Aliens," *Discover*, January 2007, *www.discovermagazine.com.*

FACT ATTACK: **Men in Black not just a movie!** Individuals who encounter UFOs often complain of subsequent hostile encounters with government officials dressed in dark suits. Dubbed the Men In Black, these men tend to have knowledge of the individual and often appear before the incident has even been reported. Some speculate that they are actually aliens themselves. *Will Smith is definitely an alien.*

> H. G. Carlson, *Mysteries of the Unexplained* (Contemporary Books, 1994), p.23.

FACT ATTACK: Former president sees UFO! Former President Jimmy Carter sighted a UFO in the winter of 1969 while in the company of several other witnesses while he was governor of Georgia. Many speculate that this led to an investigation into whether the government possessed alien spacecraft as well as the bodies of crash-landed alien beings. *Probably shouldn't trust the guy who pardoned the draft dodgers.*

❯ H. G. Carlson, *Mysteries of the Unexplained* (Contemporary Books, 1994), p. 9.

FACT ATTACK: Aliens invade the Bible!

In the book of Ezekiel, the prophet describes encountering four-winged creatures stepping forth from a whirlwind. Many believe this is evidence that biblical figures encountered aliens. *Or did drugs. Or both.*

❯ H. G. Carlson, *Mysteries of the Unexplained* (Contemporary Books, 1994), p. 9.

FACT ATTACK: NASA on the hunt for alien planets! NASA plans to launch an orbiting observatory dubbed the Terrestrial Planet Finder that will search for planets orbiting nearby stars. The organization hopes to uncover planets that might be hospitable for life. *Let's get to Mars first, and then worry about what else is out there. Baby steps, NASA.*

❯ Brandon Griggs, "Probing the Cosmos: Is Anybody Out There?" CNN, November 26, 2008, *http://edition.cnn.com.*

FACT ATTACK: Pope's astronomer wants to baptize aliens! When faced with the question of whether he would baptize an alien, one of the pope's chief astronomers insisted he would be delighted to, but only if it asked him. *I imagine he'd be happy to do a number of things to the alien if it asked.*

❯ Alok Jha, "Pope's Astronomer Says He Would Baptise an Alien If It Asked Him," *The Guardian*, September 17, 2010, *www.guardian.co.uk*.

FACT ATTACK: Papacy keen on science! The Political Academy of Sciences, of which the renowned theoretical physicist Stephen Hawking is a member, keeps senior cardinals and even the pope abreast of all scientific developments, including the search for life on other planets. *Because when I think Vatican, I think science.*

❯ Alok Jha, "Pope's Astrongmer Says He Would Baptise an Alien If It Asked Him," *The Guardian*, September 17, 2010, *www.guardian.co.uk*.

FACT ATTACK: Scientists 100 percent certain new planet contains life! Astronomers recently discovered planet Gliese 581g orbiting a nearby star in what scientists call the "Goldilocks zone," as the planet's surface temperature is neither too hot nor too cold to harbor life. One astronomer calculated the probability that life exists on the planet at 100 percent. *Nice to know we'll have somewhere to go once we're done ruining this planet.*

❯ Jeanna Bryner, "Odds of Life on Newfound Earth-Size Planet '100 percent,' Astronomer Says," Space.com, September 29, 2010, *www.space.com*.

FACT ATTACK: Gliesiens sent messages to earth!
Several years before the discovery of Gliese 581g, an astronomer in Australia picked up an unusual transmission from the area in space we now know belongs to the earth-like planet. *Let's hope they like hugs and hate lasers.*

❯ "Did Astronomer Receive An Alien Signal From Gliese?" *Digital Journal,* www.digitaljournal.com.

FACT ATTACK: Scientists hunt for aliens with balloons! British researchers from Cranfield University launched a balloon in October of 2010 to search for microbial extraterrestrial life in the earth's atmosphere. If successful, they hope to shed light on the possibility that life on Earth may have originated on another planet. *So it's the plot to Pixar's* Up! *with a little bit from the classic "film"* Red Planet *thrown in for good measure.*

❯ Lee Speigel, "Britain to Search for Alien Life in Earth's Atmosphere," AOL News, October 5, 2010, www.aolnews.com.

FACT ATTACK: **Is U.S. government hiding aliens?** Eighty percent of American citizens believe the government is hiding information about extraterrestrials from the public. *The other 20 percent is the government.*

❯ Robert Todd Carroll, *The Skeptic's Dictionary: A Collection of Strange Beliefs, Amusing Deceptions, and Dangerous Delusions* (John Wiley and Sons, 2003), p. 10.

FACT ATTACK: Alien abduction just a trick of the mind! Sleep paralysis is a condition where sufferers wake up in bed unable to move, with the sense that a menacing presence is with them in their bedroom. They often experience feelings of levitating outside of their body, and witness hallucinations similar to those described by victims of alien abduction. *So aliens didn't really kidnap me and make me their leader? Balls.*

❯ Nicholas D. Kristof, "Alien Abduction? Science Calls It Sleep Paralysis," *New York Times*, July 6, 1999, www.nytimes.com.

FACT ATTACK: **Abduction disorder afflicts billions!** Once assumed to be a rare condition, sleep paralysis affects as much as 60 percent of the world population at least once in their lives. *Good to know I'm not alone.*

❯ Nicholas D. Kristof, "Alien Abduction? Science Calls It Sleep Paralysis," *New York Times*, July 6, 1999, www.nytimes.com.

FACT ATTACK: Area 51 employees never see daylight! Buildings at Area 51 lack windows, to prevent employees from seeing anything other than the projects they are specifically working on. When researchers conduct tests on new aircraft, employees are instructed to remain indoors until the test is complete and the aircraft is back in its hangar. *My cube doesn't have windows either, but you don't see me complaining.*

❯ Jonathan Strickland, "How Area 51 Works," How Stuff Works, http://science .howstuffworks.com.

FACT ATTACK: Clinton confirms Area 51 (sort of)! In 1995, President Clinton signed an executive order exempting Area 51 from environmental regulation. The order referred to the site as "the Air Force's operating location near Groom Lake, Nevada," which is the closest the government has come to acknowledging the existence of Area 51. *In other news, that president who had an affair with some intern who will remain nameless is exempt from all wrongdoing.*

> Jonathan Strickland, "How Area 51 Works," How Stuff Works, *http://science.howstuffworks.com.*

FACT ATTACK: Civilian first to give UFOs a proper name! On June 24, 1947, a civilian pilot reported nine glowing objects flying in a V-shaped formation at speeds he estimated to be 1,700 miles per hour. He described their motion as similar to "a saucer if you skip it across water," giving rise to the popular term "flying saucer." *I wasn't aware that skipping plates across the water was a common pastime in the 1940s.*

> "UFOs and Alien Invasions in Film," The History Channel, *UFO Hunters, www.history.com.*

FACT ATTACK: Our solar system could have 900 planets! Some scientists speculate that there could be as many as 900 planets in our solar system, instead of the paltry eight (*RIP Pluto*) previously believed to exist. These planets likely reside far beyond the orbit of Neptune and would be frozen wastelands unsuitable for life. *Well, clearly we're really good at discovering where aliens aren't.*

> Jeremy Hsu, "Earth-Sized World Could Lurk in Outer Solar System," Space.com, January 4, 2010, *www.space.com.*

FACT ATTACK: Crop circle hoax revealed! In 2000, British artist John Lundberg was arrested for creating a crop circle in a wheat field. Scientists and researchers of the phenomenon had posed explanations ranging from alien landing sites to magnetic fields; however, Lundberg created the extravagant works of art with nothing but a plank of wood and carefully drawn plans. *Nice try aliens, we know it's really you.*

> Stephanie Watson, "How Crop Circles Work," Howstuffworks.com, *www.howstuffworks.com.*

> Cahal Milmo, "Police Unravel Mystery of the Crop Circle," *The Independent,* November 4, 2000, *www.independent.co.uk.*

FACT ATTACK: Galaxy at risk! Intelligent life in short supply! In 1961, astronomer Frank Drake estimated the number of probable intelligent civilizations inhabiting our galaxy. Using conservative numbers, that estimate came to 10,000. *Unfortunately, we are not included in that total.*

> Steve Ford, "What is the Drake Equation?" Seti League, *www.setileague.org.*

FACT ATTACK: Expectations of alien life contradict current evidence of existence! Realizing that the presence of intelligent life within our galaxy was almost certain, famed astronomer Enrico Fermi posed the obvious question of "where is everybody?" His question became known as the Fermi Paradox, which highlights the contradiction between the high probability that we are surrounded by intelligent life forms, and the fact that we lack any evidence that they exist. *If you were an alien, would you want to meet us?*

> Seth Shostak, "Our Galaxy Should Be Teeming With Civilizations, But Where Are They?" Space.com, October 25, 2001, *www.space.com.*

FACT ATTACK: Gods bless every planet, except earth! Earth is the only planet not named after a Roman god or goddess. *Also the only planet that believes in gods or goddesses.*

❯ Abby Cessna, "Mythology of the Planets," Universe Today, August 10, 2009, www.universetoday.com.

FACT ATTACK: Aliens make first contact! Run like hell! World-renowned theoretical physicist Stephen Hawking believes that the existence of intelligent life in the cosmos is an inevitability; however, he thinks we should do everything in our power to avoid drawing their attention. "If aliens ever visit us, I think the outcome would be much as when Christopher Columbus first landed in America, which didn't turn out very well for the Native Americans." *Just what we need, aliens with lasers and a concept of manifest destiny.*

❯ Jonathan Leake, "Don't Talk to Aliens, Warns Stephen Hawking," *The Sunday Times*, April 25, 2010, www.timesonline.co.uk

FACT ATTACK: Arizona logger abducted by aliens! Logger Travis Walton alleges that he was abducted by aliens in 1975. Walton encountered a UFO with several friends who fled the scene. Searches of the area turned up no trace of Walton, who reappeared five days later, haggard, thin, and muttering about alien beings with huge eyes. *I think aliens are like fisherman and hicks are like sunnies. They always get thrown back.*

❯ Peter Knight, *Conspiracy Theories in American History: An Encyclopedia (Volume 1)* (ABC-CLIO, 2003).

FACT ATTACK: **Redneck cashes in on abduction story!** After he was abducted by aliens, Travis Walton authored a book about his experiences that was later adapted into the Hollywood film *Fire in the Sky*. *A small consolation for repeated anal probing.*

> Peter Knight, *Conspiracy Theories in American History: An Encyclopedia (Volume 1)*, (ABC-CLIO, 2003).

FACT ATTACK: **World War II bomber intercepted by UFO!** During World War II, a British bomber was returning from a photographic mission when it encountered an unidentified flying object that matched speed with it for a time before accelerating away. When the situation was brought to the attention of Winston Churchill, he insisted it be covered up to avoid a mass panic. *Pics or it didn't happen.*

> Michael Sheridan, "Winston Churchill, Dwight Eisenhower Covered up UFO sighting in England, Letter Claims," *New York Daily News*, August 5 2010, www.nydailynews.com.

FACT ATTACK: **Aliens attack New Jersey motorists!** On January 11, 1966, near the Wanaque Reservoir in Wanaque, New Jersey, several motorists as well as Mayor Warren Hagstrom and the chief of police observed an unidentified flying object. The craft shot a beam of light down towards the ground before flying off a half hour later. *Clearly they had traveled back in time to kill Snookie's mom and prevent* The Jersey Shore.

> Mark Sceurman, and Mark Moran, *Weird New Jersey: Your Travel Guide to New York's Local Legends and Best Kept Secrets* (Sterling Publishing Company, 2003).

FACT ATTACK: **Frozen moon of Jupiter contains life!** The surface of Jupiter's moon Europa is a frigid wasteland. Sixty miles beneath the icy surface, scientists now believe lies a vast body of water twice the size of all the Earth's oceans combined. Many theorize life may congregate around hydrothermal vents similar to those found on Earth. *And surely they'll welcome us with open arms when we drill a hole into their home.*

> Jeffrey S. Kargel, Jonathan Z. Kaye, James W. Head, III, et al. "Europa's Crust and Ocean: Origin, Composition, and the Prospects for Life" (Brown University, 2000). http://planetary .brown.edu.

FACT ATTACK: **Pulsars mimic alien transmissions!**
When the first pulsar was discovered in the 1960s it was nicknamed "LGM-1" or "Little Green Men." Scientists assumed messages from space would pulsate to conserve energy, and pulsars resembled alien transmission according to this model. *If scientists spent half as much time looking for aliens as they did thinking of cute nicknames for things, I'd have my own ET by now.*

❯ Ray Villard, "Are We Overlooking Alien Beacons?" Discovery News, June 21, 2010, *http://news.discovery.com.*

FACT ATTACK: **Little green men from Mars!** Use of the term "little green men" to describe extraterrestrials stems from Edgar Rice Burroughs's book *The Princess of Mars* (1917), which references "green men of Mars." The moniker didn't become popular until the 1950s. *I call shenanigans. All the Martians I've met were fuchsia.*

❯ "Roswell Conspiracy," National Geographic, *The Real Roswell.* http://channel .nationalgeographic.com/ episode/the-real-roswell.

FACT ATTACK: **Aliens invade Wisconsin, make terrible pancakes!** In 1961, a Wisconsin farmer claimed he saw three creatures resting by a flying saucer wearing turtleneck sweaters and knit helmets. The creatures were allegedly cooking pancakes that tasted like cardboard. *Sounds more like time–traveling hipsters than aliens.*

❯ "Roswell Conspiracy," National Geographic, *The Real Roswell.* http://channel.nationalgeographic.com/episode/ the-real-roswell.

FACT ATTACK: **Alien autopsy a hoax!** In 1995 British TV producer Ray Santilli released a black and white video titled *Alien Autopsy*. The silent film showed an autopsy carried out on one of the aliens alleged to have been recovered at Roswell in 1947. Santilli has since admitted the film was staged. However, he insists that it is a recreation of a real video he viewed in the early '90s. *My brother and I once recreated the Ninja Turtles movie. That doesn't make it real.*

❯ "Roswell Conspiracy," National Geographic, *The Real Roswell. http://channel.nationalgeographic.com/episode/ the-real-roswell.*

❯ Ray Santilli, "My Story," V-J Enterprises. *www.v-j-enterprises.com.*

FACT ATTACK: **Insurance covers alien abduction!** For the bargain price of $150, you can purchase alien-abduction insurance. The policy covers up to $1.5 million in damages if the claimant can prove he or she was actually abducted. *Good luck with that one.*

❯ Kimberly Lankford, "Weird Insurance," CBS, October, 1998. *http://moneywatch.bnet.com.*

FACT ATTACK: **Green balls of light circle New Mexico!** From 1948 through 1955, scientists, civilians, military officials, and amateur astronomers observed green balls of fire streaking across the skies of New Mexico. Due to their flight patterns and lack of trailing debris, experts determined the UFOs could not have been meteors. To this day, nobody knows the cause of the phenomenon. *Aliens playing tennis.*

❯ Seth Foreman, "5 UFO Sightings That Even Non-Crazy People Find Creepy," Cracked.com, August 9, 2010, *www.cracked.com.*

FACT ATTACK: Aliens all around us! One in five adults believe aliens are hiding out on earth disguised as humans. *I believe they're disguised as lemurs. Poorly.*

❯ "One in Five Adults Believe Aliens are on Earth, Disguised as Humans," *The Telegraph*, April 9, 2010, *www.telegraph.co.uk.*

FACT ATTACK: Men more open to the supernatural! Men are more likely to believe in extraterrestrial life than women. One study found 22 percent of men believed aliens walk among us, with only 17 percent of women. *Maybe that's because we're the ones always getting probes shoved up our asses.*

❯ "One in Five Adults Believe Aliens Are on Earth, Disguised as Humans," *The Telegraph*, April 9, 2010, *www.telegraph.co.uk.*

FACT ATTACK: Alien life may resemble humans! In 2003 Professor Seth Shostak and Alex Barnett created a cartoon creature they dubbed "Jo-Alien" that had two eyes, two hands, and shared many other characteristics with humans. Their creature was based on the assumption that every creature on earth that lives in light has developed eyes, and that the cost/benefit ratio for developing multiple eyes and appendages is impractical for an intelligent life form. *Must be nice when nobody can prove you wrong.*

❯ Rebecca Wood, "Aliens Are Out There, Say Scientists," *The Guardian*, October 22, 2003, *www.guardian.co.uk.*

❯ Hillary Mayell, "Alien Life? Astronomers Predict Contact by 2025," National Geographic News, November 14, 2003, *http://news.nationalgeographic.com.*

FACT ATTACK: UFO murders Australian pilot! In 1978, Australian pilot Frederick Valentich radioed Melbourne Air Traffic Control to report a strange craft flying too close to his plane. Valentich's final communication indicated that the craft was hovering above him, followed by seventeen seconds of a violent metallic scraping sound. Neither Valentich nor his craft were seen again. *Aliens are real, and they can't drive for shit.*

> Seth Foreman, "5 UFO Sightings That Even Non-Crazy People Find Creepy," Cracked.com, August 9, 2010, *www.cracked.com.*

FACT ATTACK: Aliens hijack Voyager probe! In May of 2010, the *Voyager* spaceprobe launched in 1977 began transmitting data in an unknown format back to earth. Scientists were baffled by the transition and some speculate that aliens hijacked the probe to send messages back to Earth. Engineers instructed the probe to only transmit data regarding its own status until they could determine the cause of the malfunction. *Because if it's aliens, maybe they'll go away if we ignore them.*

> "Have Aliens Hijacked Voyager 2 Spacecraft?" *The Daily Telegraph,* May 12, 2010, *www.dailytelegraph.com.au.*

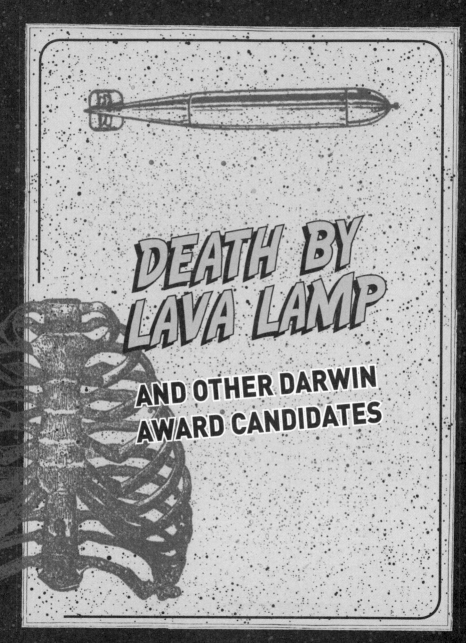

DEATH BY LAVA LAMP

AND OTHER DARWIN AWARD CANDIDATES

FACT ATTACK: Man killed by lack of foresight! A twenty-two-year-old fast-food worker died in July of 1997 when he constructed his own bungee cord and jumped from a railroad trestle. He had the foresight to fashion the cord several feet shorter than the ground, but neglected to account for the elasticity of his homemade rope. *Based on the information at hand, he wouldn't have lasted much longer anyhow.*

❯ Wendy Northcutt, *The Darwin Awards: Evolution in Action* (Dutton, 2000), p. 148.

FACT ATTACK: Man survives until millennium! Around midnight on January 1, 2000, Tod Surmon climbed a light pole on the Las Vegas strip to celebrate the new year. Shortly after, he lost his balance, caught hold of a live electrical wire, and became one of the first people to die in the new millennium. *What else is a light pole for, if not for getting drunk and climbing up?*

❯ Mark Shapiro, "Midlands Winner Surmon Dies In Fall On Las Vegas Strip," *Chicago Tribune*, January 3, 2000, www.chicagotribune.com.

FACT ATTACK: Suicidal chicken outwits six humans! In 1998, six people died while trying to rescue a chicken that had fallen down a well. The chicken survived. *And the world was a better place.*

❯ Wendy Northcutt, *The Darwin Awards: Evolution in Action* (Dutton, 2000), p. 57.

FACT ATTACK: Jogging enthusiast dies doing what he loved! James Fixx, the man who popularized jogging in America, died of a heart attack while running. *See, running isn't good for you. I'll be on the couch.*

❯ Barbara Seuling, *You Blink Twelve Times a Minute: And Other Freaky Facts About the Human Body* (Picture Window Books, 2008).

FACT ATTACK: **London loses train of the dead!** Beneath the streets of London exists a train station specifically designed to convey dead bodies. Known as the Necropolis Railway Station, the line stopped running during World War I after it was hit by a bomb. *That's just what they want you to think.*

> Jamie Frater, *Listverse.com's Ultimate Book of Bizarre Lists: Fascinating Facts and Shocking Trivia on Movies, Music, Crime, Celebrities, History, and More* (Ulysses Press, 2010).

FACT ATTACK: **Radioactive ghosts walk among us!** The term "walking ghost" refers to the period of time shortly after an individual is exposed to toxic radiation where the victim appears perfectly healthy. Radiation poisoning takes a few days to set in, during which time the patient may not exhibit any symptoms. *Offering the victim a unique opportunity to dabble in hedonism.*

> Jamie Frater, *Listverse.com's Ultimate Book of Bizarre Lists: Fascinating Facts and Shocking Trivia on Movies, Music, Crime, Celebrities, History, and More* (Ulysses Press, 2010).

FACT ATTACK: **Lack of human decency kills homeless man!** While driving home, a Texas woman struck homeless man Gregory Biggs who then became lodged in her windshield. Instead of driving him to the hospital, she continued home and left him in her garage. Although she checked on him during the night, he died several hours later. *I'm sure his biggest regret was that she never came within strangling radius.*

> Jamie Frater, *Listverse.com's Ultimate Book of Bizarre Lists: Fascinating Facts and Shocking Trivia on Movies, Music, Crime, Celebrities, History, and More* (Ulysses Press, 2010).

FACT ATTACK: Flasher exposes self one last time! A Dallas man who had been flashing passing traffic leapt to his death trying to avoid police in December of 1997. He was aiming for a concrete support below a railroad crossing, but missed and fell thirty-five feet. *Let's hope he had time to button up first.*

> Wendy Northcutt, *The Darwin Awards: Evolution in Action* (Dutton, 2000), p. 218.

FACT ATTACK: **Recycling center claims third victim!** In 1996 three people died at a transfer and recycling center in Brooklyn. Three years later, a severed human head showed up on a conveyor belt at the same facility. *That could have belonged to anybody.*

> Elizabeth Royte, "20 Things You Didn't Know About . . . Garbage," *Discover*, June 2006, *www.discovermagazine.com*.

FACT ATTACK: Hurricane crashes own party! The vast majority of Alabama residents evacuated their homes when Hurricane Camille hit the area in 1969. However, a small group stayed behind to throw a "hurricane party" to welcome the storm. The party didn't last long, as a twenty-five foot wave slammed into the apartment, killing most of the attendees. *You have Camille to thank that none of them grew up to reproduce.*

> Wendy Northcutt, *The Darwin Awards: Evolution in Action* (Dutton, 2000), p. 232.

FACT ATTACK: **Real life Dr. Dolittle communes with animals!** Vladimir Durov alleges he can communicate with animals using telepathy. To test his claims, researchers gave him a random series of tasks and asked him to convey them to his dog. Sure enough, Durov stared into the eyes of his fox terrier, Pikki, who immediately performed all of the tasks. He then repeated the experiment blindfolded with the same result. *Hopefully he uses his powers for good. But if there is one thing I am not scared of, it's an army of fox terriers.*

> "The REAL X-Men," About.com, *http://paranormal.about.com.*

FACT ATTACK: **Human lightning rod can't survive himself!** During his thirty-six year career as a forest ranger, lightning struck Roy Cleveland Sullivan on seven separate occasions, but he always walked away with minor injuries. Despite his ability to cheat death, he took his own life in 1983. *If you want something done right, do it yourself.*

> "The REAL X-Men," About.com, *http://paranormal.about.com.*

FACT ATTACK: **Boy dies trying to mask own smell!** In 1998, a sixteen-year-old British youth died from a heart attack caused by inhaling too much deodorant spray. Although he was not inhaling it recreationally, the boy was so self-conscious about his smell that he sprayed his entire body with the substance twice a day. *To be fair, nobody wants to be the smelly kid in class.*

> Charles W. Bryant, "10 Bizarre Ways To Die," Howstuffworks.com, *http://health.howstuffworks.com.*

FACT ATTACK: **Creepy sex act claims hundreds!**

Autoerotic asphyxiation, the practice of cutting off one's air supply to enhance orgasm, claims 500 lives in the United States annually. *Almost 501, but luckily I'm terrible with knots.*

> ❯ "Ten Weird Human Sex Facts," Divine Caroline, *www.divinecaroline.com.*

FACT ATTACK: **Grand Canyon claims another victim!**

In October 2010, forty-two-year-old Andrew Stires died while visiting the Grand Canyon. Witnesses claim he was jumping from outcropping to outcropping before he slipped and fell to his death. *Tragically he took the rules of "suicidal hopscotch" with him to his grave.*

> ❯ "Fall to Death in Grand Canyon: Andrew Stires, 42—Two Others Survive Lightning Strikes," *The Tucson Citizen,* October 4, 2010, *www.tucsoncitizen.com.*

FACT ATTACK: **Gopher outwits human captors!**

A janitor and two maintenance workers at the Carroll Fowler Elementary school in California nearly lost their lives while disposing of a gopher they trapped in a supply closet. When spraying cleaning solvent on the animal did nothing to harm it, one of the janitors lit a cigarette while they contemplated their next move. The resulting blast nearly killed the three men and injured fourteen students, but the gopher remained unharmed. *If Hollywood has taught me one thing, it's that gophers are invincible.*

> ❯ Wendy Northcutt, *The Darwin Awards: Evolution in Action* (Dutton, 2000), p. 42.

FACT ATTACK: Don't shine your shoes and drink martinis! When nitrobenzene, a common chemical in shoe polish, interacts with alcohol, the combination can be deadly. The U.S. Environmental Protection Agency recorded the story of a man who suffered from nitrobenzene poisoning and slipped into a deadly coma six weeks later after drinking a single beer. *Good thing I can't afford shoes. Let alone polish.*

❯ Judith Freeman Clark and Stephen Long, *Weird Facts to Blow Your Mind* (Price Stern Sloan, 1993), p. 13.

❯ David Adam, "Kitchen Confidential," *The Guardian*, May 22, 2004, www.guardian.co.uk.

FACT ATTACK: Philosopher releases god from fleshy prison! The ancient philosopher Empedocles believed he was not human, but was actually a Greek god. To prove this fact to skeptics, he vowed to jump into a volcano and return unscathed. He made good on the first half of his promise, but never followed up with the latter. *The truth hurts sometimes. A lot.*

❯ John Bayne, "7 'Eccentric' Geniuses Who Were Clearly Just Insane," Cracked.com, August 18, 2008, www.cracked.com.

FACT ATTACK: Dead man walking! Indian officials declared Lal Bahri legally dead in 1976, despite his repeated insistence he was still very much alive. It took him eighteen years to convince them otherwise, during which time he founded the Association of the Dead for individuals with similar problems. *He should have embraced his new zombie life and started eating the officials.*

❯ Michael Fathers Azamgarh, "Plight of the Living Dead," *Time*, July 19, 1999, www.time.com.

FACT ATTACK: Company offers eternal burial at sea! For a small sum, the company Eternal Reefs in Sarasota, Florida, will take a customer's ashes and incorporate them into a coral reef off the coast of Florida. *However they won't affix your body in the waving position and lash it to the reef. Trust me, I've asked.*

❯ Varla Ventura, *Beyond Bizarre: Frightening Facts and Blood-Curdling True Tales* (Weiser Books, 2010).

FACT ATTACK: Degenerate park-goer gets last free ride! In 1980, a twenty-six-year-old man hid in a roller coaster car hoping to ride a second time for free. Not realizing he was there, the operator switched the rails and diverted the train into a service area, where the young man was crushed between the back seat and a low beam. *Be careful what you wish for.*

❯ Varla Ventura, *Beyond Bizarre: Frightening Facts and Blood-Curdling True Tales* (Weiser Books, 2010).

FACT ATTACK: Travel itinerary kills photographer! Wildlife photographer Carl McCunn killed himself to avoid starvation after being stranded in the Alaskan wilderness. He had chartered a flight to take him there, but neglected to arrange for anyone to pick him up. *The devil is in the details.*

❯ Larry Boa, "Top 10: Stupid Deaths," Askmen.com, *www.askmen.com.*

FACT ATTACK: Man's misplaced faith costs him his life! To test his faith, Ohtaj Humbat Ohli Makhmudov climbed into a lion exhibit at Ukraine's Kiev Zoo, insisting that God would protect him. Moments later, a lioness seized his throat and severed his carotid artery. *God did protect him. From reproducing.*

❯ Larry Boa, "Top 10: Stupid Deaths, Askmen.com, *www.askmen.com.*

FACT ATTACK: Horse loves man to death! Kenneth Pinyan of Seattle, WA, died from injuries sustained after receiving anal intercourse from a horse. *RIP Mr. Hands.*

❯ "Top 25 Craziest Deaths," 2Spare.com, March 23, 2006, *www.2spare.com.*

FACT ATTACK: **Beard turns on its master!** The owner of the world's longest beard tripped over it and broke his neck while running to escape a fire. *Perhaps the beard became self-aware and just wanted it all to end.*

> "30 Strangest Deaths in History," Neatorama.com, March 12, 2007, *www.neatorama.com.*

FACT ATTACK: **Gamer gets real-life kill screen!** A South Korean man dropped dead in an Internet cafe after playing the popular computer game Starcraft for fifty hours straight. *He required more vespene gas.*

> "S. Korean Dies After Games Session," BBC News, August 10, 2005, *http://news.bbc.co.uk.*

FACT ATTACK: Man drowns to prove partiers wrong!
To celebrate their first season without a drowning victim, the New Orleans recreational department threw a pool party in the summer of 1985. After the party ended, lifeguards discovered the body of Jerome Moody at the bottom of the pool, a guest who had drowned during the festivities. *Well, there's always next summer.*

❯ "30 Strangest Deaths in History," Neatorama.com, March 12, 2007, *www.neatorama.com.*

FACT ATTACK: **Whiskey man undone by own temper!** Tennessee whiskey distiller Jack Daniel once kicked his safe in frustration because he couldn't remember the combination. He injured his toe, which developed an infection and killed him. *If only he'd had access to some form of delicious disinfectant. . . .*

❯ "30 Strangest Deaths in History," Neatorama.com, March 12, 2007, *www.neatorama.com.*

FACT ATTACK: Nature enthusiast killed by nature!
"Grizzly Man" Timothy Treadwel communed with Alaskan brown bears while filming his adventures. Although Treadwel had no formal training, he was able to get closer to the bears than many skilled biologists. So close, in fact, that he was mauled to death by one of his furry companions. *If only somebody had warned him that* Winnie the Pooh *was not a documentary.*

❯ "Top 25 Craziest Deaths," 2Spare.com, March 23, 2006, *www.2spare.com.*

FACT ATTACK: **Fickle finger of fate kills singer!**
Richard Versalle suffered a heart attack at the New York Metropolitan Opera after delivering the line "Too bad you can only live so long." *Proof that God exists, and that he's kind of a dick.*

❯ "Top 25 Craziest Deaths," 2Spare.com, March 23, 2006, *www.2spare.com.*

FACT ATTACK: **Dog kills Napoleon's distant heir!** Jérôme Napoleon Bonaparte, the last member of the infamous family, died in 1945 from injuries he sustained after tripping over his dog's leash. *His great-great-great uncle would be so proud.*

❯ Glen Vecchione, Joel Harris, and Sharon Harris, *The Little Giant Book of Animal Facts* (Sterling Publishing, 2004).

FACT ATTACK: **Dead woman mistaken for decoration!**
In 2005, a Delaware woman hung herself from a tree in the early hours of the morning and went unnoticed for hours as numerous people drove by and walked right past her without batting an eye. It was almost Halloween, and passersby assumed she was a decoration. *And some were just really in a hurry.*

❯ Associated Press, "Corpse Mistaken for Halloween Decoration," MSNBC, October 27, 2005, *www.msnbc.msn.com.*

FACT ATTACK: **Company sends greeting cards from the grave!** In the early '90s, Donald Mir started a company called Cards from Beyond that would send post-mortem greeting cards to a customer's loved ones after the customer passed away. The customer needed to simply supply a name and address, the date to send the card, and $25—in advance, of course. *"Happy Birthday Billy! Death sucks. Wish you were here!"*

❯ Ray Recchi, "Happy Birthday to You, In Advance," *The Sun Sentinel*, August 17, 1992, *www.sun-sentinel.com.*

FACT ATTACK: **Dead jockey wins final race!** A horse named Sweet Kiss once won a race at Belmont Park in New York, moments after his jockey Frank Hayes died in the saddle. *Shows how unimportant the jockey really is.*

> ❯ Julie Mooney, *Ripley's Believe It or Not Encyclopedia of the Bizarre* (Black Dog & Leventhal, 2002).

FACT ATTACK: **Man contracts deadly virus proving safety of drinking water!** British novelist Arnold Bennett died from typhoid fever that he contracted while demonstrating that the water in Paris was safe to drink. *Serves him right for not hiring an assistant.*

> ❯ Julie Mooney, *Ripley's Believe It or Not Encyclopedia of the Bizarre* (Black Dog & Leventhal, 2002).

FACT ATTACK: **Money does buy happiness!** Wealthy people comprise only 8 percent of suicides in the United States. *I tried to think of a problem money couldn't solve. I failed.*

> ❯ Julie Mooney, *Ripley's Believe It or Not Encyclopedia of the Bizarre* (Black Dog & Leventhal, 2002).

FACT ATTACK: **Thrill-seeker done in by banana peel!** Several months after he survived a trip down Niagara Falls in a wooden barrel, Bobby Leech slipped on a banana peel and died. *Actually, it wasn't the banana peel so much as the lightning bolt and red turtle shell that hit him moments later.*

> ❯ Julie Mooney, *Ripley's Believe It or Not Encyclopedia of the Bizarre* (Black Dog & Leventhal, 2002).

FACT ATTACK: **Backseat drivers fight back!** "Give Me a Brake" is a device marketed toward nervous automobile passengers. When the driver becomes reckless, passengers can place the device at their feet and step on an actuator to activate a sound of screeching tires and give the driver a not-so-subtle hint to slow down. *I prefer to just close my eyes and hope for the best.*

❯ Julie Mooney, *Ripley's Believe It or Not Encyclopedia of the Bizarre* (Black Dog & Leventhal, 2002).

FACT ATTACK: **Deceased husband gets last laugh!** German Poet Heinrich Heine left his entire estate to his wife as long as she agreed to remarry. His reason: "So that there will be at least one man to regret my death." *Something tells me she didn't regret it.*

❯ Mitchell Symons, *That Book: . . . of Perfectly Useless Information* (HarperCollins, 2004).

FACT ATTACK: **Theater troupe uses human skull as prop!** After his death in 1955, Juan Potomachi left his local theater more than $37,500 on the condition that they use his skull when performing *Hamlet*. *I have a similar offer for those guys who do* Puppetry of the Penis.

❯ Mitchell Symons, *That Book: . . . of Perfectly Useless Information* (HarperCollins, 2004).

FACT ATTACK: **Killer lava lamp still at large!** In 2004, while attempting to heat up a lava lamp on his stove, twenty-four-year-old Phillip Quinn was killed by a glass shard that pierced his heart when the lamp inevitably exploded. *There are no stupid inventions, just stupid people.*

> Kevin Reece, "Kent Man Killed By Exploding Lava Lamp," *Komo News*, August 31, 2006, *www.komonews.com*.

FACT ATTACK: **Experienced skydiver jumps without parachute!** In 1988, Ivan Lester McGuire, an experienced skydiver with more than 800 jumps under his belt, died filming an instructional skydive in North Carolina. While preparing to film the event he neglected to strap on a parachute before jumping out of the plane to his imminent death. McGuire only realized his mistake after he finished filming and went to pull a nonexistent ripcord. *Sad that he spent the last minute of freefall hating himself.*

> United Press International, "Police Say Excited Sky Diver Forgot to Put on His Parachute," *Orlando Sentinel*, April 5, 1988, *www.orlandosentinel.com*.

FACT ATTACK: Unbreakable glass fails, kills overconfident lawyer! Garry Hoy, a lawyer working in the Toronto Dominion Bank Tower, crashed through a pane of glass and plunged 24 stories to his death while demonstrating the strength of the windows to a crowd of onlookers. *If you were there, you'd have laughed. Admit it.*

❯ "True and Untrue Legends," ABC News. *http://abcnews .go.com.*

FACT ATTACK: GPS fails floating priest! While attempting to beat the world flight record for cluster ballooning, priest Adelir Antonio was lost at sea on April 20, 2008. He took numerous precautions including packing a parachute, helmet, safety suit, GPS, and several days worth of food and water; however, he neglected to learn how to operate the GPS device before his voyage. *Always RTFM.*

❯ "Flying Priest's Balloons Found," BBC News, April 23, 2008, *http://news.bbc.co.uk.*

❯ Associated Press, "Priest On Party Balloon Flight Missing," CBS News, April 22, 2008, *www.cbsnews.com.*

FACT ATTACK: Robber killed by clever disguise! In South Carolina in 2009, two men entered a Sprint PCS store and robbed customers and employees at gunpoint. One of the men, Thomas James, spray-painted his face in an attempt to conceal his identity. As a result, he had trouble breathing and died shortly after the robbery. *Kids: Spraypaint is very dangerous. But not nearly as dangerous as being a dumbass.*

❯ "Robbery suspect spray-paints face for disguise, dies," Wistv, August 21, 2009. *www.wistv.com.*

FACT ATTACK: Hubris kills woman with help from concrete! On May 30, 2009, twenty-two-year-old Tamera Batiste was stuck in traffic with her boyfriend when she complained about how slowly he was driving and joked that she could get to work faster if she walked. She then opened the door of the moving pickup truck, stuck out her foot, and fell to her death. *I'm sure the boyfriend was sad. But he must have chuckled just a little.*

❯ "Woman Killed on I-12 Was Joking with Boyfriend When She Opened Door and Fell from Pickup," Nola.com, June 24, 2009, *www.nola.com.*

FACT ATTACK: Stoic philosopher dies laughing!
Chrysippus, an ancient Greek stoic living in 207 B.C., is said to have died from a laughing fit caused by a drunken donkey trying to eat figs. *Not much of a stoic, was he.*

❯ John William Donaldson and Karl Otfried Müller, *A History of the Literature of Ancient Greece* (John W. Parker and Son, 1858), p. 27.

FACT ATTACK: Parasitic fish kills king! King Henry I of England died from overindulging on lampreys, a parasitic fish and one of his favorite foods. *Who sees a lamprey and thinks, "Mmm, lunch!"?*

❯ "The Prehistoric Visitors," BBC, September 18, 2007, *www.bbc.co.uk.*

FACT ATTACK: Commander killed with prosthetic limb! In 1649, Sir Arthur Aston was beaten to death with his own wooden leg during the Siege of Drogheda in Ireland. The opposing soldiers believed it concealed golden coins. *There were other ways to get the coins out, but they weren't nearly as fun.*

❯ "Sir Arthur Aston," British Civil Wars. *www.british-civil-wars-co.uk.*

FACT ATTACK: Explorer killed during botched ceremonial salute! John Kendrick, an American explorer, was killed in 1794 near the Hawaiian Islands when a British ship fired a salute to his vessel. Instead of a ceremonial plume of smoke, the ship inadvertently fired a loaded shell. *There had to be a less dangerous way to say "Hi."*

❯ "Kendrick (Kenwick, Kenwrick), John," Dictionary of Canadian Biography Online. *www.biographi.ca.*

FACT ATTACK: **Death by 200,000 quarters!** Hrand Araklein was crushed by $50,000 worth of quarters that fell from his armored truck. *There's a special place in hell for whoever asked him to make change.*

> Noel Botham, *The Book of Useless Information* (Perigee, 2006).

FACT ATTACK: **Nine dead following beer tsunami!** Nine people were killed during the infamous London Beer Flood of 1814 when 323,000 gallons of beer from the Meux and Company Brewery gushed out into the streets. The noise of the explosion was heard five miles away. *There are worse ways to go.*

> "The London Beer Flood of 1814," BBC, October 24, 2008, *www.bbc.co.uk*.

FACT ATTACK: **Man cheats death, dies moments later!** While Vittorio Luise was driving in Naples, Italy, in 1980, a gust of wind blew his car into a nearby river. He managed to break the window and swim to safety, but was killed by a falling tree when he reached the shore. *That'll show him to try and cheat death.*

> Noel Botham, *The Book of Useless Information* (Perigee, 2006).

FACT ATTACK: **Tailor invents overcoat parachute, initial test disappointing!** Franz Reichelt, an Austrian tailor and creator of the overcoat parachute, tested his invention on February 4, 1912. He jumped from the top of the Eiffel Tower and plummeted 986 feet to his death. *He should have invented the test dummy first.*

❯ Alan Bellows, "The Intrepid, Ill-Fated Parachutist," *Damn Interesting*, January 4, 2006. www.damninteresting.com.

FACT ATTACK: **Submarine sunk by AWOL torpedo!** Seventy-four men were killed when the USS *Tang* was hit by a torpedo near the coast of Taiwan in 1944. The torpedo had been fired from the vessel itself, but immediately turned around and slammed into the submarine. *Cute, it just missed its mommy.*

❯ Richard O'Kane, *Clear the Bridge!: The War Patrols of the U.S.S. Tang* (Presidio Press, 1989).

FACT ATTACK: **Burial at sea sparks murder investigation!** When Daniel Scott Lasky died of Lou Gehrig's disease in 2010, his dying wish was to be buried at sea. Twenty-four hours later, a fisherman spotted the floating body and called the Coast Guard. A murder investigation ensued until authorities discovered his family merely neglected to weigh down the body. *My dying wish will probably be not to die.*

❯ Diana Moskovitz, "Man's Sea Burial Goes Awry," *Miami Herald*, September 14, 2010, www.miamiherald.com.

FACT ATTACK: Robot turns on human masters!
In 1979, Robert Williams became the first human to be killed by a robot when a hydraulic arm slammed into him at a Michigan Ford Motor Company factory. *I assure you, he won't be the last.*

> David Kravets, "Jan. 25, 1979: Robot Kills Human, " Wired.com, January 25, 2010, *www.wired.com.*

FACT ATTACK: Singer murdered twice! Mexican singer Sergio Vega was shot dead mere hours after he called an interview to dispel rumors he had already been murdered. *"No, no. I promise you, my death isn't scheduled for a few hours yet."*

> Thuenis Bates, "Mexican Singer Killed Hours After Denying He'd Died," AOL News. *www.aolnews.com.*

FACT ATTACK: Invincible homeless man cheats death! In 1933, a group of men dubbed the Murder Trust set out to kill notorious drunk Michael Malloy and collect on several life insurance policies amounting to $3,500 (which equates to about $60,000 today). The gang tried everything from feeding Malloy various poisons, to dousing him with water and leaving him in a snowbank, to running him over with a car, but Malloy always survived. They eventually did succeed in their plot by shoving a gas pipe down his throat, but the group were all convicted for murder when they couldn't keep their mouths shut about their invincible nemesis. *Clearly, they should have tried kryptonite.*

> Brian O'Connor, "The Durable Mike Malloy," *New York Daily News*, October 14, 2007, *www.nydailynews.com.*

FACT ATTACK: Wife cures hiccups, murdered for her efforts! Beatriz Robeldo was stabbed to death by her frightened husband when, in an attempt to cure his hiccups, she snuck up on him wearing a carnival mask. *Bet his hiccups went away, though.*

❭ Paul Simmons, Ian Stevenson, and Val Sievking, *Strange Deaths: More Than 375 Freakish Fatalities* (Barnes & Noble, 2000).

FACT ATTACK: Automatic carwash kills worker! When business was slow at his Melbourne carwash, Reggie Peabody would frequently hang onto the large mechanical brushes and ride through the automated system. That is until something went horribly wrong during one of his joyrides and coworkers found him dead, still clinging to the brush. *At least he was clean.*

❭ Paul Simmons, Ian Stevenson, and Val Sievking, *Strange Deaths: More Than 375 Freakish Fatalities* (Barnes & Noble, 2000).

FACT ATTACK: Mysterious mass-death solved! In 1942, a British officer discovered around 300 skeletons near a lake in Roopkund, India, and was baffled by how so many people could have perished simultaneously. The mass-death remained a mystery until a 2004 expedition noticed that nearly all of the victims possessed injuries to the head and shoulders and determined that they were victims of a massive hailstorm. *Did nobody think to use human shields?*

❭ "Roopkund—The Mystery of the Skeleton Lake," Hottnez.com. *www.hottnez.com.*

FACT ATTACK: Sentient car murders creator! Vitoria Cavaletti, the owner of the security firm responsible for the armored car, was killed by his creation after a heavy door slammed shut on his neck. Moments earlier the door had jammed open, so Caveletti had kicked it to jar it loose. *Mission accomplished.*

❯ Paul Simmons, Ian Stevenson, and Val Sievking, *Strange Deaths: More Than 375 Freakish Fatalities* (Barnes & Noble, 2000).

FACT ATTACK: Turtle kills ancient Greek! Aeschylus, the father of Greek tragedy, died when a passing eagle mistook his head for a rock and hurtled a tortoise at him in an attempt to break the shell. *Tragically.*

❯ Ned Resnikoff, and Peter Hildebrand, "The 5 Historical Figures Who Died the Weirdest Deaths," Cracked.com, April 17, 2008, *www.cracked.com.*

FACT ATTACK: President dies mid-coitis! On February 16, 1899, French president Félix Faure died while in the company of his mistress Marguerite Steinheil. He suffered a stroke shortly after both parties achieved orgasm. *Félix Faure, you died an honorable death.*

❯ Ned Resnikoff, and Peter Hildebrand, "The 5 Historical Figures Who Died the Weirdest Deaths," Cracked.com, April 17, 2008, *www.cracked.com.*

FACT ATTACK: King Herod's junk rots off! Herod the Great died of Fournier Gangrene, a disease which causes gangrene of the genitals as well as intestinal pain and convulsions. *This is why God invented mercy killings.*

❯ Ned Resnikoff, and Peter Hildebrand, "The 5 Historical Figures Who Died The Weirdest Deaths," Cracked.com, April 17, 2008, *www.cracked.com.*

FACT ATTACK: Student falls out of bed, never wakes up! In 2008, University of Miami student Aaron Miller died when he fell out of bed. He was sleeping just six feet off the ground. *Guess the homemade loft wasn't so cool after all.*

> David Schoetz, "Fatal Fraternity Bunk Tumble a Mystery," ABC News, May 21, 2008, http://abcnews.go.com.

FACT ATTACK: Military jet dive-bombs skiers! Twenty vacationers skiing on Mount Cermis in Italy were killed when a low-flying U.S. military jet clipped the cable holding their gondola with its wing. The pilot and passengers were unharmed. *God is not without a sense of humor.*

> John Tagliabue and Matthew L. Wald, "Death in the Alps: A Special Report; How Wayward U.S. Pilot Killed 20 on Ski Lift," *New York Times*, February 18, 1998, www.nytimes.com.

FACT ATTACK: Lawyer dies re-enacting a murder! To demonstrate to a jury that it was possible that an alleged murder victim had actually shot himself, Clement Valladigham mortally wounded himself when he used a loaded pistol he believed to be empty. He died several days later, but his demonstration was not in vain—the defendant was acquitted. *Now that's dedication.*

> Lorraine Firmin, "Strange, Weird, Odd and Funny Deaths," Associated Content, June 29, 2009, www.associatedcontent.com.

FACT ATTACK: Bottled water kills! Jennifer Strange died following a 2007 radio contest dubbed "Hold your Wee for a Wii." In the hopes of winning a Nintendo Wii video game system, contestants drank large amounts of water and competed to see who could go the longest without going to the bathroom. Strange died of acute water intoxication several hours after the contest. *She probably played it and died of disappointment.*

> Associated Press, "Woman Dies After Water-Drinking Contest," MSNBC, January 13, 2007, www.msnbc.msn.com.

LET'S SEE WHAT HAPPENS

STRANGE FAILED EXPERIMENTS AND THE EVEN WEIRDER ONES THAT ACTUALLY SUCCEEDED

FACT ATTACK: Astronauts get busy in space! In his book *The Last Mission*, French astronomer Pierre Kohler alleges that NASA studied the feasibility of various sex positions in zero gravity during a 1996 space shuttle mission. NASA vehemently denies the allegation. *Anything in the name of science.*

❯ Robert Lamb, "Top 5 Crazy Government Experiments," Howstuffworks.com, *http://science.howstuffworks.com.*

FACT ATTACK: Man risks life in name of science! Jose Delgado was convinced that he could control the actions of animals by implanting electrical stimuli into their brains. To test his theory, he outfitted a bull with electrodes and stood in the center of a bull ring holding a remote control. His assistants let the bull loose, which immediately charged at Delgado. Just before it reached him he pressed a button on the remote, activated the electrodes, and the bull stopped mid-charge and sauntered off. *Shame this couldn't have gone in the chapter about Darwin Awards.*

❯ "Top 10 Bizarre Science Experiments," Toptenz.com, *www.toptenz.com.*

FACT ATTACK: All men look at porn! In an effort to study the viewpoints of men in their twenties in regards to pornographic imagery, researchers at the University of Montreal began a nationwide search for men who had never looked at porn. The study came to an immediate halt when they couldn't find a single candidate. *And they never will.*

❯ Jonathan Liew, "All Men Watch Porn, Scientists Find," *The Telegraph*, December 2, 2009, *www.telegraph.co.uk.*

FACT ATTACK: **Male turkeys are shameless!** Martin Schein and Edgar Hale were fascinated by the mating habits of turkeys, and in the 1960s they tried to determine what features male turkeys found attractive. They created a dummy turkey and slowly removed portions of it to see if the males would lose interest. Even when presented with a turkey head, the males still attempted to mate with the dummy. *How hot was the head though?*

❯ "Top 10 Bizarre Science Experiments," Toptenz.com, *www.toptenz.com.*

FACT ATTACK: **Government pulls fast one on pilots!** In the 1960s, the government sent several pilots up in planes to test the effects of near-death experiences on judgment. Shortly into the flight, researchers informed the pilots that the plane was malfunctioning and would need to crash into the ocean. They then presented the terrified men with forms waiving the government of any responsibility for what was about to happen. Sure enough, the men made more mistakes on the forms than those that were not presented with the news of their imminent death. *JK, OMG, ROFL, BOHICA!*

❯ "Top 10 Bizarre Science Experiments," Toptenz.com, *www.toptenz.com.*

FACT ATTACK: **Inmate proves death is scary!** In 1938, death row inmate John Deering agreed to wear a heart-rate monitor during his execution by firing squad. Despite his bold demeanor, when he heard the order to fire Deering's heart rate shot up from a panicked 120 beats per minute to a terrified 180 beats per minute. *So scary things make your heart race. Intriguing.*

❯ "Top 10 Bizarre Science Experiments," Toptenz.com, *www.toptenz.com.*

FACT ATTACK: **Prison study gets out of hand!** In 1971, psychology professor Philip Zimbardo set up a mock prison at Stanford University. He randomly assigned the volunteers roles as either guards or prisoners. The guards soon lost sight of the experiment and began to torture and abuse the "inmates" mercilessly. Zimbardo shut down the planned two-week study after just six days. *Just when it was starting to get good, too.*

❯ Ryan Dilley, "Is It In Anyone To Abuse a Captive?" BBC News, May 5, 2004, *http://news.bbc.co.uk.*

FACT ATTACK: **Doctor raises chimp like one of his family!** When children raised by animals return to normal society, they often continue to exhibit animal-like behavior. To determine if the reverse was true, psychologist Winthrop Kellogg took a seven-month-old chimpanzee into his home and raised it as a human alongside his ten-month-old son. The experiment came to an abrupt end when Kellogg realized the presence of a simian playmate was retarding the development of his natural child. *Translation: The chimp was smarter.*

❯ "The Top 20 Most Bizarre Experiments of All Time," The Museum of Hoaxes, *www.museumofhoaxes.com.*

FACT ATTACK: **Lunatic doctor cheats death!** To prove his theory that yellow fever was not a contagious disease, Stubbins Ffirth tried desperately to infect himself. He poured vomit from infected patients onto open wounds; smeared his body with blood, urine, and saliva tainted with the disease; and even drank a cup of vomit from a patient, but he never fell ill. It seemed as if his theory was true; however, the doctor was lucky to be alive. Had he tried directly injecting himself with the blood of an infected patient, he would have discovered the disease to be highly contagious. *Isn't that why they have lab rats?*

> "The Top 20 Most Bizarre Experiments of All Time," The Museum of Hoaxes, *www.museumofhoaxes.com.*

FACT ATTACK: **People will kill if you ask them to!** During Stanley Milgram's famous obedience study, he discovered that subjects would willingly deliver a painful shock to a partner if an authority figure demanded it of them. Most disturbingly, two-thirds of subjects continued to shock the victim beyond levels they believed to be lethal. *In their defense, it looks really fun.*

> "The Top 20 Most Bizarre Experiments of All Time," The Museum of Hoaxes, *www.museumofhoaxes.com.*

FACT ATTACK: **Puppy endures shocks in the name of science!** Shortly after Milgram reported his findings, two skeptical researchers repeated the experiment with a live puppy to ensure that the subjects had not realized Milgram's ruse and simply played along. Much to their horror, twenty of the twenty-six test subjects shocked the puppy up to the maximum voltage. *In their defense, it was a really menacing-looking puppy.*

> "The Top 20 Most Bizarre Experiments of All Time," The Museum of Hoaxes, *www.museumofhoaxes.com.*

FACT ATTACK: **Men say no to animal abuse!** All of the subjects who refused to shock the puppy were men. Every woman in the experiment agreed to deliver the shocks. *Fairer sex indeed.*

> "The Top 20 Most Bizarre Experiments of All Time," The Museum of Hoaxes, *www.museumofhoaxes.com.*

FACT ATTACK: **Minnesota chamber quietest place on earth!** The title for quietest place on earth belongs to the Anechoic Test Chamber at Orfield Laboratories in Minneapolis, MN. The background noise in the room measured in at -9.4 dBA (decibels A-weighted). The low range of human hearing is around 0 dBA, with the sound of a pin drop falling in at around 15 dBA. *Second place: Martha Stewart's vagina.*

> Neil Middlemiss, "*The Quietest Place on Earth,*" Audio Junkies, December 18, 2007, *www.audiojunkies.com.*

FACT ATTACK: **Scores of bodies found at University of Tennessee!** An area of the University of Tennessee is sectioned off by the Anthropological Research Facility to study the decomposition of bodies, and is referred to as the "body farm." Unlike cadavers used for medical research, the bodies of the deceased are not returned to families. *When I read "body farm" I was hoping for something completely different.*

> "FAQ," The University of Tennessee, Forensic Anthropology Center, *http://web.utk.edu.*

FACT ATTACK: **Cyborg filmmaker fulfills dream!** Canadian filmmaker Rob Spence lost his eye in a childhood accident, but turned the traumatic experience to his advantage by having a camera inserted into the empty socket. Spence fulfilled his dream in 2010 when doctors outfitted him with a tiny camera that streamed video wirelessly to a computer. *Trust me, you don't want to document everything you see.*

> Simon Leo Brown, "Eyeborg—Part Man, Part Webcam," ABC News, August 25, 2010, *www.abc.net.au.*

> Eyeborg Blog, *www.eyeborgblog.com.*

FACT ATTACK: Facial expression experiment turns gruesome! In 1924, Carney Landis gathered a group of students so he could catalogue human facial expressions. He exposed them to stimuli ranging from smelling ammonia to viewing pornography and monitored their reactions. The final task was to decapitate a mouse, with a shocking two-thirds complying without hesitation. *"But the guy in the lab coat said it was okay."*

> "The Top 20 Most Bizarre Experiments of All Time," The Museum of Hoaxes, *www.museumofhoaxes.com.*

FACT ATTACK: Plants can think! In 2010, scientists shone light on a single leaf of *Arabidopsis thaliana* and discovered that not only did the entire plant react, but it continued to do so after they removed the light, implying that the plant remembered the experience. *Or it didn't notice the light had left. But their explanation sounds cooler.*

> Rebecca Boyle, "Can Plants Think?" Popsci.com, July 15, 2010, *www.popsci.com.*

FACT ATTACK: Exercise can't beat a cold! In 1998, researchers injected fifty students with rhinovirus, the cause of the common cold, to determine what effect exercise might have on the duration of symptoms. One group ran, climbed stairs, and bicycled for forty minutes each day, while the other remained sedentary. There was no difference between the two groups. *Although group A was slightly more miserable.*

> Anahad O'Connor, *Never Shower in a Thunderstorm: Surprising Facts and Misleading Myths About Our Health and the World We Live In* (Times Books, 2007).

FACT ATTACK: Man becomes world's first cyborg! In the hopes of becoming the world's first cyborg, British scientist Kevin Warwick implanted a small chip in his arm that allowed him to perform mundane tasks around his house such as turning on lights and opening doors. He later embedded a more advanced chip linked to his nervous system through which he could control a robotic arm. *I feel as if I've seen this movie.*

❯ Ian Fortey, "The 10 Craziest Scientific Experiments Ever Conducted," Cracked.com, March 31, 2008, *www.cracked.com*.

FACT ATTACK: **Scientist discovers weight of a soul!** Duncan MacDougall weighed individuals immediately before and after death and determined that the human soul weighs 21 grams. He also weighed dogs in his experiment and determined they do not have souls, as their weights did not change. *I finally get that movie.*

❯ Sanjeev Garg, *501 Astonishing Facts* (Pustak Mahal, 2010).

❯ Ian Fortey, "The 10 Craziest Scientific Experiments Ever Conducted," Cracked.com, March 31, 2008, *www.cracked.com*.

FACT ATTACK: Evil inventor dies, but not soon enough! Thomas Midgley Jr., the inventor of both leaded gasoline and chlorinated fluorocarbons (CFCs), suffered from polio. The disease didn't kill him directly, but he did accidentally strangle himself to death with an elaborate pulley system he used to help himself in and out of bed. *Too little, too late.*

❯ Ian Fortey, "The 10 Craziest Scientific Experiments Ever Conducted," Cracked.com, March 31, 2008, *www.cracked.com*.

FACT ATTACK: **Women do it for love! Men, not so much!** U.S. researchers discovered 237 distinct reasons why human beings choose to have sex. The top ten are mostly the same for both sexes with one notable exception: "I realized I was in love" ranks number nine for women, but number seventeen for men. *If your man tells you he loves you, and you haven't had sex, he's lying.*

❯ Wing Sze, "10 Things You Didn't Know About Sex," *Fashion,* www.fashionmagazine.com.

FACT ATTACK: **Kamikaze bats never saw action!** During World War II, the U.S. government rounded up more than 2 million bats with the hope of outfitting them with tiny bombs. Despite several million dollars in investments, scientists were never able to perfect the weapon. *Until a young Adam West stopped by the lab . . . and the rest is history.*

❯ Judith Freeman Clark and Stephen Long, *Weird Facts To Blow Your Mind* (Price Stern Sloan, 1993), p. 29.

FACT ATTACK: **All paranormal phenomenon solved!** By outfitting volunteers in a specially designed helmet that emitted a magnetic field, neuroscience researcher Michael Persinger may have found an explanation for many paranormal phenomenon. More than 80 percent of participants reported feeling an ethereal presence in the room that they believed to be either God or a deceased loved one. He theorized that magnetic fields could account for everything from UFO sightings to near-death experiences. *God then disappeared in a puff of logic.*

❯ Ian Fortey, "The 10 Craziest Scientific Experiments Ever Conducted," Cracked.com, March 31, 2008, www.cracked.com.

FACT ATTACK: Two heads are better than one! In 1954, soviet surgeon Vladimir Demikhov successfully attached the head of a puppy to the neck of an adult German shepherd. Both animals died shortly after. *Most elaborate means of euthanasia ever.*

❯ "Top 10 Mad Scientists in History," Oddee.com, Ocotober 13, 2008, *www.oddee.com.*

FACT ATTACK: **Nineteen two-headed dogs are better than one!** Vladimir Demikhov created nineteen more similar specimens during the next fifteen years. *After two-headed dog number four, I can't imagine anybody was too impressed.*

❯ "Top 10 Mad Scientists in History," Oddee.com, Ocotober 13, 2008, *www.oddee.com.*

FACT ATTACK: Scientists create life in a tube! While trying to recreate the origins of life on Earth, scientists Stanley Miller and Harold Urey passed an electrical current through a cocktail of compounds they believed were present in the seas of early Earth. The result was the creation of amino acids, the building blocks of life. *Nonsense. Everyone knows life started when the Great Green Arkleseizure sneezed the universe out of his nose.*

❯ Reader's Digest, *Facts At Your Fingertips* (Reader's Digest, 2003).

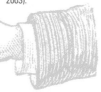

FACT ATTACK: **What doesn't kill you makes you immortal!**

To test the possibility of slowing down the dying process, researcher Mark Roth started exposing insects and rats to doses of hydrogen sulfide. Instead of killing the animals, the substance negated the effects of oxygen loss inherent to the dying process and actually prevented cell death. Though tests with larger mammals were disappointing, Roth is confident the technique will someday allow medical professionals to gain more time to help critically injured patients. *So kind of like* Inception, *but without dreams, and without DiCaprio.*

> Caleb Hellerman, "Scientists Hope Work with Poison Gas Can Be a Lifesaver," CNN, October 15, 2009, *www.cnn.com.*

FACT ATTACK: **Flatworms ingest memories!** In the

1960s, James McConnell conducted an experiment where he flashed a light on flatworms and gave them a shock. Once the worms came to expect the shock, McConnell ground them up and fed them to a new group of flatworms. When he repeated the experiment with the new group, they recoiled after the flash without conditioning. *Perhaps group B was just smarter.*

> Nathan Robert Brown, *The Complete Idiot's Guide to the Paranormal* (Alpha, 2010), p. 215.

FACT ATTACK: **Gay bomb stays in closet!** Air Force

researchers tried to develop a weapon in the mid-'90s that when unleashed on enemy troops would transform them into temporary homosexuals, turning them away from combat and into each other's arms. They soon abandoned the research when they discovered they could not create such an aphrodisiac. *Sounds like a high idea that somebody took way too far.*

> Alan Bellows, *Alien Hand Syndrome and Other Too-Weird-To-Be-True Stories* (Workman Publishing, 2009), p. 285.

FACT ATTACK: **Eye contact sows seeds of love!** In 1992, psychologist Arthur Arun instructed pairs of heterosexual men and women who had never met to talk openly about their lives for thirty minutes, and then stare into one another's eyes for a period of four minutes. A disproportionate number of the pairs confessed they felt strong feelings for their partner, and one randomly assigned couple wound up getting married. *If Steve Buscemi listened to you drone on for a half hour and then gazed deeply into your eyes, you'd probably feel butterflies, too.*

❯ Alan Bellows, *Alien Hand Syndrome and Other Too-Weird-To-Be-True Stories* (Workman Publishing, 2009), p. 107.

FACT ATTACK: **Russians drill tunnel to nowhere!** In the 1960s, Russian geologists began drilling a hole in the Earth's crust to reach where the crust and mantle met. Thirty years later they had drilled to a staggering depth of seven miles, but had to stop when temperatures around 360°F made it impossible to drill farther with their current technology. *I've seen* Journey to the Center of the Earth. *Probably best they didn't make it.*

❯ Alan Bellows, *Alien Hand Syndrome and Other Too-Weird-To-Be-True Stories* (Workman Publishing, 2009), p. 128.

FACT ATTACK: **Giant hole still exists!** Known as the Kola Superdeep Borehole, the Russian's massive tunnel still exists today. They made no attempt to cave it in after they abandoned the project. *So be careful when you walk around Russia.*

❯ Alan Bellows, *Alien Hand Syndrome and Other Too-Weird-To-Be-True Stories* (Workman Publishing, 2009), p. 128.

FACT ATTACK: CIA develops cutest espionage tool ever! During the Cold War, CIA scientists created a biological weapon that outfitted a house cat with advanced bugging equipment to eavesdrop on Russian officials. Operation Acoustic Kitty (its actual name) came to a halt when during the cat's first test run, it hopped out of the surveillance van and a taxi cab ran over it before it reached its target. *So close.*

❭ Alan Bellows, *Alien Hand Syndrome and Other Too-Weird-To-Be-True Stories* (Workman Publishing, 2009), p. 54.

FACT ATTACK: Kitty roadkill cost government millions! The total cost of producing Operation Acoustic Kitty's bionic cat came to $15 million. *But the lesson they learned was priceless.*

❭ Alan Bellows, *Alien Hand Syndrome and Other Too-Weird-To-Be-True Stories* (Workman Publishing, 2009), p. 54.

FACT ATTACK: Syphilis sufferers denied treatment! In conjunction with the Tuskegee Institute in Alabama, the Public Health Service studied 400 poor black men suffering from syphilis in 1932. Doctors told participants that they were treating them, but in reality they provided no care of any kind and were documenting the effects of syphilis. *Which is why you should never trust a doctor willing to treat you for free.*

❭ "Remembering Tuskegee," NPR, July 25, 2002, *www.npr.org.*

FACT ATTACK: Tuskegee subjects could have been cured! The Tuskegee experiment went on for forty years, during which time dozens of the participants died, despite the discovery of penicillin as a reliable treatment for the disease in 1947. *Being Punk'd was way less funny back then.*

> "Remembering Tuskegee," NPR, July 25, 2002, *www.npr.org.*

FACT ATTACK: President apologizes for cruel experiment! In May of 1997, President Bill Clinton officially apologized for the Tuskegee experiment. *That and $1 will get you a cup of coffee.*

> "Clinton Apologizes To Tuskegee Survivors," CNN, May 16, 1997, *www.cnn.com.*

FACT ATTACK: Mad scientist castrates inmates! Dr. Leo Stanley was the chief surgeon at San Quentin Penitentiary from 1913 to 1951. He became obsessed with the notion that by removing his patients' testicles and replacing them with those of executed prisoners he could cure his patients of their criminal nature. *Prisoner: "Doc, I can't even move anymore, it hurts so much. All I want to do is crawl into bed and never leave my cell." Doctor: "You're cured!"*

> Ethan Blue, "The Strange Career of Leo Stanley: Remaking Manhood and Medicine at San Quentin State Penitentiary, 1913–1951," Caliber, May 2009, *http://caliber.ucpress.net.*

FACT ATTACK: Government infects own citizens! Following a botched CIA biowarfare test in 1955 involving the bacteria that caused whooping cough, the area of Tampa, Florida, experienced a sharp rise in cases of the disease, twelve of which resulted in death. *Could have been a coincidence, like that time I ran over my girlfriend's cat and its heart spontaneously stopped six seconds later.*

> Tom Burghardt, "Biological Warfare and the National Security State," Global Research, August 9, 2009, *www.globalresearch.ca.*

FACT ATTACK: Government used LCD to modify behavior! In the 1940s, doctors at Stateville Penitentiary in Illinois infected nearly 400 inmates with malaria in the hopes of discovering a cure. Inmates endured mosquito bites, hallucinations, raging fevers, and endless untested "potions" in exchange for leniency and reduced sentences. *In the hierarchy of prison maladies, malaria will always be better than shower rapings.*

❯ Allen M. Hornblum, "They Were Cheap and Available: Prisoners as Research Subjects in Twentieth Century America," *British Medical Journal*, November 29, 1997, *www.bmj.com.*

❯ Larry Bernard, "Historian Examines U.S. Ethics in Nuremberg Medical Trial Tactics," *Cornell Chronicle*, December 5, 1996, *www.news.cornell.edu.*

FACT ATTACK: Doctors inject prisoners with cancer! The Ohio state prison system once allowed researchers from the Sloan-Kettering Institute for Cancer Research to inject more than 100 inmates with live cancer cells. Inmates were told they faced no real danger, and any cancer they contracted would spread slowly and be easy to remove. *"Don't worry guys, you should be okay as long as you aren't allergic to cancer."*

❯ Allen M. Hornblum, "They Were Cheap and Available: Prisoners as Research Subjects in Twentieth Century America," *British Medical Journal*, November 29, 1997, *www.bmj.com.*

FACT ATTACK: Project Bluebird has nothing to do with ornithology! The CIA's first behavior modification program, code-named Project Bluebird, sought to develop methods to control human behavior through hypnosis, sleep induction, and chemical means. The program eventually morphed into the infamous Project MKULTRA, a branch of the CIA that experimented with drug therapy to solicit compliance in its subjects. *You don't even want to know what Project Blue-Footed Booby was.*

❯ Fred Burks, "CIA Behavior Modification: Project Bluebird," *The Examiner*, July 4, 2009, *www.examiner.com.*

❯ Tim Weiner, *Legacy of Ashes: The History of the CIA* (Doubleday, 2007).

FACT ATTACK: **U.S. Army puts 1,000,000 citizens at risk!** In 1966, the U.S. Army conducted an experiment in New York City that exposed more than a million people to *Bacillus subtilis variant Niger*, a bacterium they determined to be harmless. Scientists dropped light bulbs filled with a combination of the bacteria and charcoal through vents into the subway system to determine if an attack with a more dangerous substance was feasible. The NYC Transit Authority was not made aware of the experiment. *Initial reaction: shocked and appalled. After a few seconds: yeah, sounds about right.*

> "What Were They Really Up To?" National Geographic, *CIA Secret Experiments*, http://channel.national geographic.com/series/cia-secret-experiments.

FACT ATTACK: **Decapitated heads still conscious!** During the French Revolution, when beheading via the guillotine was a popular means of execution, scientists would ask the condemned to blink for as long as possible after the blade dropped to help measure post-decapitation awareness. Many actually succeeded; blinking and even responding to their own name minutes after head and body became two. *"Blink twice if you were innocent."*

> Alan Bellows, *Alien Hand Syndrome and Other Too-Weird-To-Be-True Stories* (Workman Publishing, 2009), p. 23.

FACT ATTACK: CIA provides prisoners with free acid!
In the 1960s, the CIA began testing the effects of LSD on prison volunteers, searching for ways to manipulate and control human behavior. In one experiment, the prisoners were put on increasing doses of LSD for seventy-seven straight days. *It was actually only three days; it just felt like seventy-seven.*

> ❯ "What Were They Really Up To?" National Geographic, *CIA Secret Experiments*. http://channel.nationalgeographic.com/series/cia-secret-experiments.

FACT ATTACK: **Scientists develop remote-controlled beetle!** In 2009, the Pentagon funded a project at UC Berkeley in which scientists successfully grafted electrodes and tiny radio antennae to flying beetles, turning the bugs into remote-controlled cyborgs. Scientists implanted the electrodes when the beetles were in the pupal stage so they could control them remotely when they matured. *Want!*

> ❯ Stephen Ornes, "The Pentagon's Beetle Borgs," *Discover*, May 2009. www.discovermagazine.com.

FACT ATTACK: Jacket made from living cells! Scientists have developed a material grown from a combination of human and mouse bone cells that they hope will somebody replace natural leather. The scientists harvest immortal cells (those that keep multiplying indefinitely once removed), and apply them to a biodegradable polymer base. *But a jacket is way cooler when you know a creature died to make it.*

> ❯ "Tissue Culture's 'Victimless'," Treehugger.com, November 10, 2004, www.treehugger.com.

FACT ATTACK: Scientist creates zombie kitten! In the 1800s, scientist Karl Weinhold reanimated a dead kitten. He removed the kitten's head and replaced the contents of the spinal column with silver and zinc. This created a makeshift battery which jump-started the kitten's heart and allowed it to walk around for several minutes. *I sure hope he removed the head again when he was done. Everyone knows that's the only way to kill a zombie.*

> Alex Boese, *Elephants on Acid: And Other Bizarre Experiments* (Harcourt, 2007), p. 7.

FACT ATTACK: **Scientist keeps brain alive outside body!** On January 17, 1962, American scientist Robert White successfully removed the brain from a monkey and proved it could survive independently of its body. *Unfortunately, the monkey could not survive independently of its brain.*

> Alex Boese, *Elephants on Acid: And Other Bizarre Experiments* (Harcourt, 2007), p. 25.

FACT ATTACK: Scientist performs first head transplant! Eight years after his initial experiment, Robert White performed the first documented head transplant, connecting the head of one monkey to the body of another. *The sixties was a great time to be a mad scientist.*

> Alex Boese, *Elephants on Acid: And Other Bizarre Experiments* (Harcourt, 2007). p. 25.

FACT ATTACK: LSD kills elephant! On August 3, 1962, Tusko, a fourteen-year-old Indian elephant residing at the Oklahoma City Zoo, became the first elephant to consume LSD. Scientists were uncertain what the required dosage would be, so they gave him 297 milligrams, or nearly 3,000 times the human dosage. Several minutes later, Tusko died. *But those were probably an awesome few minutes.*

> Alex Boese, *Elephants on Acid: And Other Bizarre Experiments* (Harcourt, 2007), p. 116.

FACT ATTACK: Study reveals men easier than women! At Florida State University in 1978, attractive young male and female students approached members of the opposite sex and propositioned them for sex as part of an experiment. Seventy-five percent of men were happy to oblige, but not a single woman accepted the offer. *Really, only 75 percent?*

> Alex Boese, *Elephants on Acid: And Other Bizarre Experiments* (Harcourt, 2007), p. 154.

FACT ATTACK: Scientists test world's first gaydar! In the late 1950s, scientists at Stanford University developed a device to measure men's homosexual tendencies. One hundred men tested the alleged gay detector while viewing images of other men in various stages of undress. As the experiment progressed, the subjects watched in horror as the dial bounced around confirming their latent homosexuality. In reality, the experimenters were manipulating the dials themselves to determine the reactions of 1950s men to discovering they were homosexual. *Most hilarious experiment ever.*

> Alex Boese, *Elephants on Acid: And Other Bizarre Experiments* (Harcourt, 2007), p. 143.

FACT ATTACK: Artificial skin gives robots sense of touch! Scientists at Stanford and Berkeley have developed sensitive artificial skin that could revolutionize robotics and lead to more lifelike artificial limbs. Sensors in the skin make it possible for a device grafted with the substance to perform delicate tasks like unloading a dishwasher without breaking any glasses. *Might want to wait for version 2.0 before you try those out.*

> Tim Carmody, "Pyramids, Nanowires Show Two Futures for Artificial Skin," Wired.com, September 13, 2010, *www.wired.com.*

FACT ATTACK: Goats produce milk laced with spider silk! In an attempt to produce spider silk for commercial purposes, Canadian scientists have successfully isolated the silk-producing gene of spiders to inject into goats. They hope to harvest the silk from the goat's milk to produce everything from artificial tendons and ligaments to biodegradable fishing line. *I knew goats were good for something.*

> Bijal P. Trivedi, "Lab Spins Artificial Spider Silk, Paving the Way to New Materials," National Geographic News, January 17, 2002, *http://news .nationalgeographic.com.*

FACT ATTACK: Scientists create mouse/newt hybrid! By incorporating amphibian DNA into mammalian cells, Stanford scientists believe they may be able to coax limbs to regenerate in mice and possibly even humans. Normal mammalian cells restrict the regeneration process to reduce the likelihood of cancerous growths. However, the amphibian DNA would bypass this natural roadblock. *Bring on the cancer, Daddy needs a new toe!*

> "Newts' Ability to Regenerate Tissue Replicated in Mouse Cells," Science Daily, August 6, 2010, *www.sciencedaily.com.*

FACT ATTACK: Princeton researchers discover mind meld! Researchers at Princeton discovered that the brain patterns of people listening to a story actually mirror those of the storyteller, albeit a few seconds behind. In some instances, however, the brain patterns of the listener were actually ahead of the storyteller. *Yeah, but they'd already heard the story, like, a thousand times.*

> Andy Coghlan, "We Humans Can Mind-Meld Too," New Scientist, July 26, 2010. *www.newscientist.com.*

FACT ATTACK: **Keep on smiling!** It takes 200,000 frowns to produce a wrinkle. *And only one Botox injection to fix it!*

> Barbara Seuling, *Your Skin Weighs More Than Your Brain: and Other Freaky Facts About Your Skin, Skeleton, and Other Body Parts* (Picture Window Books, 2007).

FACT ATTACK: Fingerprints develop in utero! A three-month-old fetus has identifiable fingerprints. *Makes it easy to identify when it escapes and commits a crime.*

> Barbara Seuling, *Your Skin Weighs More Than Your Brain: and Other Freaky Facts About Your Skin, Skeleton, and Other Body Parts* (Picture Window Books, 2007).

FACT ATTACK: **Gaming nerds can control dreams!** A 2006 study found that people who play video games may be able to control their dreams. The concept, dubbed lucid dreaming, was reported by a disproportionate number of gamers in relation to those that did not play video games. *However, they are ten times less likely to have friends to talk to about said dreams.*

> Andy Coghlan, "We Humans Can Mind-Meld Too," Live Science, July 26, 2010, *www.livescience.com.*

FACT ATTACK: **Video games protect dreamers!** Another study found that video gamers are also less likely to experience threatening dreams and often reversed potentially dangerous dream scenarios to put themselves in the dominant position. *Which is all well and good until they can't tell the difference between Grandma and a Nazi soldier.*

> Andy Coghlan, "We Humans Can Mind-Meld Too," Live Science, July 26, 2010, *www.livescience.com.*

WEIRD WORLDWIDE CUSTOMS

WHEN IN ROME . . .

FACT ATTACK: Spanish ban fake facial hair! In the 1300s it was very fashionable for Spanish men to wear false beards. Unfortunately, this made it very easy for criminals to commit crimes, as everyone looked fairly similar. As a result, King Peter stepped in and banned them from Spain. *Merkins were still okay though.*

> Francesca Gould, *Why You Shouldn't Eat Your Boogers and Other Useless or Gross Information About Your Body* (Tarcher, 2008).

FACT ATTACK: Old habits die hard! In some areas of Italy, it is still customary to sprinkle salt around a newborn baby's bed to ward off evil spirits. *It also seasons them, just in case things don't turn out well.*

> H. G. Carlson, *Mysteries of the Unexplained* (Contemporary Books, 1994), p.143.

FACT ATTACK: White people immune to Brazilian executions! When European colonists passed a law in Brazil exempting white people from execution, authorities found a loophole. They dyed condemned Europeans blue before executing them. *A moment of silence for all of the innocent Smurfs that were killed in the resulting confusion.*

> Erin Barrett, *Dracula Was a Lawyer* (Conari Press, 2002).

FACT ATTACK: Japanese never voted off the island! In seventeenth-century Japan, immigration into the country was strictly prohibited, and it was also illegal for citizens to leave. *But why would they ever want to leave such a welcoming place?*

> Erin Barrett, *Dracula Was a Lawyer* (Conari Press, 2002).

FACT ATTACK: **Polar bear hunts illegal, mostly!** Only Alaskan natives such as the Inuit are permitted to hunt polar bears. It is illegal for anyone else to participate. *The polar bear will not extend you the same courtesy.*

> Bill McLain, *Do Fish Drink Water? Puzzling and Improbable Questions and Answers* (William Morrow, 1999), p. 139.

FACT ATTACK: **Japanese tourists should never visit Paris!** Japanese tourists are prone to a disorder called "Paris syndrome." Afflicted individuals are so overwhelmed by the disparity between their idealization of the city and the actual experience of being there that they suffer a nervous breakdown. *No matter how incapacitated they are, I'm sure they still take pictures.*

> Sergiu Vidican, "Strange Mental Disorders," Metrolic.com, September 18th, 2010, *www.metrolic.com.*

FACT ATTACK: **Mayan parents long for cross-eyed babies!** Believing crossed eyes to be a sign of beauty, Mayan parents hung reflective objects between the eyes of their children to induce the condition. *Almost as sick as forcing little girls to wear makeup and dress like prostitutes for beauty pageants. Almost.*

> Eric Elfman, *Almanac of the Gross, Disgusting, & Totally Repulsive, a Compendium of Fulsome Facts* (RGA Publishing Group, 1994), p. 73

FACT ATTACK: **African women purposely lengthen their lips!** Women of the Sara tribe in central Africa gradually lengthen their mouths by cutting a slit in the lips and inserting rings of increasing width until the lower lip protrudes up to seven inches. *That might be weird, but I no longer have a barometer to gauge that.*

> Eric Elfman, *Almanac of the Gross, Disgusting, & Totally Repulsive, a Compendium of Fulsome Facts* (RGA Publishing Group, 1994), p. 73.

FACT ATTACK: **Bornean jars contain dead relatives!** Until recently, families in Bornea kept the bodies of deceased family members in jars in their homes. They inserted bamboo tubes into the jar to remove excess liquids until one year after the death, when they buried what was left of the body in a lavish ceremony. *Only mildly creepier than keeping Grandma's ashes on the mantle.*

> Eric Elfman, *Almanac of the Gross, Disgusting, & Totally Repulsive, a Compendium of Fulsome Facts* (RGA Publishing Group, 1994), p. 29.

FACT ATTACK: **Aztecs appease gods with human sacrifice!** Ancient Aztecs believed that the only respectable offering for the sun god was the still-beating heart of a human sacrifice. The victim walked up the steps of a massive pyramid to a stone altar where the high priest removed his or her heart with a special knife and held it up to the sun. *So dumb. Everyone knows gods prefer macaroni pictures.*

> Eric Elfman, *Almanac of the Gross, Disgusting, & Totally Repulsive, a Compendium of Fulsome Facts* (RGA Publishing Group, 1994), p. 11.

FACT ATTACK: **Jainists love animals, hate fun!**
Adherents to the Jainist religion in India follow a strict code of nonviolence toward all living creatures. Jains are strict vegetarians who even try to minimize the suffering of insects when engaging in farming. While sexual activity is permitted between two married individuals, it is advised that they cease after the birth of a son. *Wouldn't want to kill any sperm needlessly.*

> "Jainism," BBC, *www.bbc.co.uk.*

FACT ATTACK: **Mummy brains leak out their noses!**
When mummifying corpses, ancient Egyptians removed the brain with a small spoon inserted into the nose. They extracted the gray matter bit by bit and later fed it to stray animals, as they did not believe the brain to be an important organ. *Or they were trying to prevent the zombie apocalypse.*

> Joy Masoff, *Oh Yuck! The Encyclopedia of Everything Nasty* (Workman Publishing, 2000).

FACT ATTACK: **Beaver balls eliminate unwanted pregnancies!** North Americans once believed beaver testicles could produce a spontaneous abortion. *This might work, assuming the fetus was self-aware and would choose self-termination over being born to somebody who would believe something so stupid.*

> William Hartston, *Mr. Hartston's Most Excellent Encyclopedia of Useless Information: The Supreme Miscellany of Fantastic Facts* (John Blake, 2006).

FACT ATTACK: **Aboriginels stab one another as punishment!** In several Aboriginal tribes the punishment for manslaughter was to be stabbed in the thigh by a tribal elder. *The secret was to pick the oldest, most feeble elder to do the honor.*

> William Hartston, *Mr. Hartston's Most Excellent Encyclopedia of Useless Information: The Supreme Miscellany of Fantastic Facts* (John Blake, 2006).

FACT ATTACK: Ancient birth control still better than rhythm method! Ancient Greeks practiced a primitive and assumedly ineffective form of birth control by having the woman hold her breath, squat, and sneeze. *It might work if she did this in front of her partner immediately before they were supposed to have sex.*

❯ Shane Mooney, *Useless Sexual Trivia* (Simon & Schuster, 2000).

FACT ATTACK: **Commercials, the ultimate time suck!** The average American spends about a year and a half of his or her life watching commercials on television. *And then God created Tivo, and He saw that it was good.*

❯ Erin Barret and Jack Mingo, *Random Acts of Factness: 1001 (or so) Absolutely True Tidbits About Everything* (Conari Press, 2005).

FACT ATTACK: Victorian women shunned monthly! In the Victorian age, menstruating women were forced to retreat to "sick beds" to rest, as it was assumed the ordeal would wear on them. *In general, men know more about the surface of Mercury than we do about a woman's menstrual cycle.*

❯ Shane Mooney, *Useless Sexual Trivia* (Simon & Schuster, 2000).

FACT ATTACK: **Women are easier down under!** Australian women are the most likely to have sex on the first date. *Already booked my tickets.*

> Shane Mooney, *Useless Sexual Trivia* (Simon & Schuster, 2000).

FACT ATTACK: **Leader's emergence births star!** According to official North Korean accounts, the birth of the country's dictator Kim Jong-Il was culminated by the appearance of a new star in the night sky, as well as a double rainbow. *The Great Leader also discovered Australia, was the first man to walk on the moon, and invented fingernails.*

> "Profile: Kim Jong-Il," BBC News, June 9, 2000, *http://news.bbc.co.uk.*

FACT ATTACK: **Lucky hare feet not so lucky for rabbits!** Europeans once believed that the feet of hares held magical properties and were lucky. Since they frequently mistook the common rabbit for the hare, we now also consider rabbits' feet as good-luck charms. *Somehow when I was a kid I completely overlooked the morbid fact that I was carrying around the dried-up appendage of a defenseless bunny.*

> Charles Panati, *Extraordinary Origins of Everyday Things* (Harper, 1989).

FACT ATTACK: **Silly names save pirate families!** Pirates used nicknames to prevent government officials from persecuting their families on land. *And because Captain Robert Francis Howard wasn't especially scary.*

> Varla Ventura, *Beyond Bizarre: Frightening Facts and Blood-Curdling True Tales* (Weiser Books, 2010).

FACT ATTACK: **Bowing more prestigious than a handshake!**
In many Asian cultures, rather than shaking hands
to greet one another, individuals fold their hands
together and bow, performing a "wai." How high one
holds his or her hands depends on the importance of
the person to whom the bow is made. If two individuals are on equal footing, they hold their hands at nose
level. *Which explains why everyone kept their hands in their pockets
last time I visited Thailand.*

❯ "Culture and Society: Customs Around the World," essortment.com, *www.essortment.com.*

FACT ATTACK: **Poop travels farther in Australia!** In
general, the water in an Australian toilet rests nine
to ten inches from the rim of the bowl. In contrast,
a North American toilet has the water no more than
three to four inches from the top. *Congratulations, you
are actually dumber now that you know that.*

❯ "Culture and Society:
Customs Around the World,"
essortment.com,
www.essortment.com.

FACT ATTACK: **Vegetables sacrificed in record numbers!** The majority of people in Orissa, India, still
sacrifice animals to appease their mother goddess,
despite the complaints of animal rights activists.
Some have transitioned to the more humane practice of sacrificing gourds and cucumbers. *And there
was much rejoicing.*

❯ Clifford Sawhney, *Strange
But True Facts* (Pustak Mahal,
2004), p. 13.

FACT ATTACK: India boasts world's best delivery boys! Every day, a group of food service workers called dabbawalas organize the delivery of 200,000 warm lunches throughout the city of Mumbai. Despite the monumental task, the dabbawalas only lose one lunch out of every 16 million. *Yet somehow Domino's can't figure out the difference between extra cheese and pepperoni.*

❯ Clifford Sawhney, *Strange But True Facts* (Pustak Mahal, 2004), p. 23.

❯ Dean Irvine, "Mumbai's Dabbawalas Still Serving Up Lessons in Lunch," CNN, November 11, 2008, *www.cnn.com.*

FACT ATTACK: Japanese live forever! Botswanans, not so much! The average Japanese woman will live to age eighty-four, while the average Botswanan will only live to thirty-nine. *Things go downhill after forty anyway.*

❯ Jessica Williams, *50 Facts That Should Change the World* (The Disinformation Company, 2004), p. 3.

FACT ATTACK: Kenyan families bribed into destitution! In Kenya, one-third of the average household income is spent on bribery payments. *We have that in the United States, they just don't call it a bribe. They call it Social Security.*

❯ Jessica Williams, *50 Facts That Should Change the World* (The Disinformation Company, 2004), p. 137.

FACT ATTACK: Homosexuality punishable by death!
Same-sex relationships are illegal in more than seventy countries around the world, and in nine of those the crime is punishable by death. *My solution: a disinformation campaign stating that killing a homosexual makes you catch gay.*

> Jessica Williams, *50 Facts That Should Change the World* (The Disinformation Company, 2004), p. 53.

FACT ATTACK: Smile, or else! Employees of Japan's Keihin Electric Express Railway undergo daily "smile checks" conducted by computer software that analyzes their facial expression to ensure they remain upbeat. *You'll be happy and you'll like it!*

> Dan Fletcher, "The 50 Worst Inventions," *Time*, May 27, 2010, *www.time.com*.

FACT ATTACK: Medieval architects torture animals for good luck! In medieval England, it was customary to bury a live cat in the wall of a newly constructed building. The deed supposedly brought good luck and assured the structural integrity of the building. *Good luck for everyone, unless you like cats.*

> Glen Vecchione, Joel Harris, and Sharon Harris, *The Little Giant Book of Animal Facts* (Sterling Publishing, 2004).

FACT ATTACK: Shaman bodies don't burn! The Tlingit tribe of Alaska cremated all of their dead except for the bodies of shamans. They believed they would not burn, so instead they embalmed the bodies and placed them in primitive shelters with a slave to serve them in the afterlife. *Only one?*

> Julie Mooney, *Ripley's Believe It or Not Encyclopedia of the Bizarre* (Black Dog & Leventhal Publishers, 2002).

FACT ATTACK: **English try to look even uglier, most unsuccessful!** In English slang, a "gurn" is a grotesque facial expression, and the English have celebrated this pastime since the thirteenth century. At the World Gurning Championship in Egremont, England, competitors don a horse collar and compete to see who can make the most grotesque face imaginable. *I thought I was at this competition once. Turned out I was just out at a pub on an ordinary night in London.*

> Stuart Inamura, "Top 10: Unusual Traditions Around the World," Totally Top 10, July 27, 2010, *www.totallytop10.com.*

FACT ATTACK: **Turkish gather to be sprayed with camel spit!** In Turkey, spectators flock to watch camel wrestling, a sport where two specially bred male camels are led to a ring where they proceed to fight one another for the amusement of the crowd. Serious injuries are rare, but spectators are often sprayed with milky, frothy saliva. *And sometimes the camels spit on them, too.*

> Stuart Inamura, "Top 10: Unusual Traditions Around the World," Totally Top 10, July 27, 2010, *www.totallytop10.com.*

FACT ATTACK: **Japanese masseuses couldn't see what they were doing!** Traveling masseuses in ancient Japan were required by law to be blind. *"How many fingers am I holding up?" "Two." "You're fired."*

> Julie Mooney, *Ripley's Believe It or Not Encyclopedia of the Bizarre* (Black Dog & Leventhal Publishers, 2002).

FACT ATTACK: **Kayan "Giraffe Women" actually have normal necks!**

Despite popular belief, the extravagant rings worn by the Kayan women of Southeast Asia do not elongate their necks. Instead, they gradually push down the collarbone and give the appearance of a long, swan-like neck. *I feel somehow cheated.*

> Richard Lloyd Parry, "Kayan 'Giraffe Women' Trapped in Thailand by Tourist Trade," *The Sunday Times*, April 8, 2008, *www.timesonline.co.uk.*

FACT ATTACK: **British annually celebrate anarchy!**
Every November 5, people throughout England gather together to celebrate Bonfire Night by building raging infernos and setting off fireworks to commemorate the day that a British radical named Guy Fawkes tried (and failed) to blow up Parliament. *"Remember, remember the fifth of November."*

> Ferne Arfin, "The Best of Britain's Weird and Wacky Folk Traditions," About.com, *http://gouk.about.com.*

FACT ATTACK: **Spitting shows respect in Africa!**
The Masai tribe of Kenya and Tanzania greet one another by spitting. When greeting elders, it is customary for a tribesman to spit in his palm before shaking hands, which is a sign of respect. *Don't try this unless you are 100 percent certain the person is a Masai.*

> "10 Extremely Weird Traditions from Around the World," Infozooms.com, July 24, 2010, *www.infozooms.com.*

FACT ATTACK: American Indian code wins World War II!

During World War II, the United States Government turned to Navajo American Indians to transmit sensitive information to troops. The Navajo language has no alphabet or symbols and is only spoken by the Navajo people. It remains the only unbroken code in modern military history. *I sincerely hope we apologized for that manifest destiny misunderstanding first.*

> Paul Niemann, *Invention Mysteries (Invention Mysteries Series)* (Horsefeathers Publishing, 2004), p. 25.

FACT ATTACK: Samurai never taken prisoner!

Seppuku, a form of ritual suicide, was a common practice among samurai warriors. To avoid being taken prisoner, the warrior would plunge a knife into his abdomen and have his attendant cut his neck, leaving just a small band of flesh attaching the head to the body. *Or you could, you know, run.*

> "10 Extremely Weird Traditions From Around the World," Infozooms.com, July 24, 2010, *www.infozooms.com.*

FACT ATTACK: Buddhist monks mummify themselves!

The Sokushinbutsu were a group of Buddhist monks who underwent the painful process of self-mummification. To achieve the effect, the monks drank a poisonous tea, which caused violent vomiting and eliminated much of the body's fluids. It also killed off anything that might later cause the body to decompose. The monk then sealed himself in a tomb with nothing but an air hole and a bell to alert the others he was still alive. When the bell stopped ringing, the monks would seal the tomb. *I have lost all respect for other non–mummifying monks.*

> Jamie Frater, "Top 10 Bizarre Traditions," Listverse.com, August 12, 2007, *www.listverse.com.*

FACT ATTACK: Saint Bernard feeds China! In China, breeders of St. Bernards have popped up en masse, but they are not selling the animals as pets. Because the dogs are large and fast-growing, they make for a good source of protein and are sold for slaughter and consumption. *Watch* Cujo *and tell me if you still feel bad for them.*

> Elizabeth Blunt, "Swiss SOS for St. Bernards," BBC News, February 6, 2001, *http://news.bbc.co.uk.*

FACT ATTACK: Mysterious coffins hang from cliffs! Rather than bury their dead in the ground, the ancient Bo people of China constructed simple wooden coffins and hung them on the sides of cliffs on wooden stakes or nestled in caves. *Smart thinking. If they turned out to be vampires, they'd at least be stranded vampires.*

> "Mysterious Hanging Coffins of the Bo," China.org, *www.china.org.*

FACT ATTACK: **Chinese considered tiny feet the pinnacle of beauty!** Mothers would break the bones in the feet of their daughters in an attempt to produce miniature "golden lotus" feet that would ensure they could find a suitable husband. The government banned the practice of footbinding in 1912, but many women continued to disfigure their feet in secret. *Because nothing's hotter than a club foot.*

> Louisa Lim, "Painful Memories for China's Footbinding Survivors," NPR, March 19, 2007, *www.npr.org.*

FACT ATTACK: **Indian hijras blur gender lines!**
Traditionally hired by kings to watch over their harem, Indian hijras are born physiologically male but take on a feminine gender identity. Ridiculed and shunned by other members of society, hijras frequently turn to the sex industry to support themselves or are forced to beg on the streets. *Don't worry. The people who make fun of them will be reincarnated as silkworms.*

> Meenakshi Ganguly, "In From the Outside," *Time Asia,* September 18, 2000, *www.time .com/time/magazine/asia/.*

FACT ATTACK: **Young boys beaten to test manhood!** When young men of the Fulani tribe of Nigeria are interested in taking a wife, they participate in a traditional competition known as sharo. The hopeful contestants strike one another with sticks and do their best to avoid crying out in pain or showing any outward signs that the opponent is causing them any discomfort. Individuals who take the beatings in stride get their pick of potential brides. *Makes sense. If you can't take abuse, you are ill-suited for married life.*

> "The Marriage Method The Hausa - Fulani in Nigeria," World News Vine, November, 2009, *www.worldnewsvine.com.*

FACT ATTACK: **New brides prostituted for money!** In Poland, the bride's first dance is auctioned off to the highest bidder, with the proceeds going toward the newly married couple's honeymoon. *Which traditionally takes place in a submarine with a screen door.*

> Andra Picincu, "The Most Weird Wedding Traditions in the World," Associated Content, March 23, 2009, *www.associatedcontent.com.*

FACT ATTACK: Wife worth her weight in beer! The practice of "wife-carrying," a competition where men carry their wives around a course, started in Finland in the 1800s to honor Vikings who kidnapped women and later married them. The tradition has spread to other countries including the United States, where a victor in Maine wins his wife's weight in beer. *Hard decision. Marry a skinny wife, or get more beer.*

❯ "6 Weirdest Traditions Still Respected Nowadays," Weird-worm.com, April 21, 2010, *www.weirdworm.com.*

FACT ATTACK: World's largest food fight! Every year, residents of the Spanish town of Bunol gather in the town square and pelt one another with tomatoes for exactly one hour. No one is sure how the event, known as La Tomatina, started, but the townspeople have been chucking produce since 1945. *"Look at all this food, should we donate it to needy families?" "Hell, no! Let's throw it at each other!"*

❯ "La Tomatina: The World's Largest Food Fight," *Life*, *www.life.com.*

FACT ATTACK: Babies launched from fifty-foot tower! Villagers in Solapur, India, gather every year to drop screaming babies from a fifty-foot-tall temple tower to a group of men on the ground below, holding a bed sheet to catch them. The event is said to bring good luck to the infants, and in the 500 years the tradition has existed, participants claim to have never lost a single child. *Except for that one time.*

❯ "Villagers Throw Babies from Temple Roof," CNN, May 1, 2008, *http://edition.cnn.com.*

FACT ATTACK: Polygamy comes with a price tag! Zulu men may have as many wives as they can afford *Financially, or mentally?*

❯ Elizabeth Diffin, "How Do Zulus Explain Polygamy?" BBC News, March 4, 2010, *http://news.bbc.co.uk.*

FACT ATTACK: **Hands off our vaginas!** Popular in Indonesia and many other African countries, the practice of female circumcision—often referred to as genital mutilation—has been banned in many countries. The process is performed by traditional circumcisers who remove part or all of the clitoris as a rite of passage, as well as a means to curb the sex drive of the girl so that she will remain faithful to her husband. *You know what might make her more faithful? Not slicing up her vag.*

> Sara Corbett, "A Cutting Tradition," *New York Times*, January 20, 2008, *www.nyimes.com*.

FACT ATTACK: **Santa's devil partner beats bad children!** In Austria, a devilish horned creature called Krampus accompanies St. Nikolaus as he makes his Christmas season rounds. While Santa doles out presents to all the good little boys and girls, Krampus beats the bad children with a stick or whip. *Corporal punishment is a way better incentive to be good than empty threats of coal in your stocking.*

> Lisa Chapman, "Krampus and Nikolaus to Visit Austria This Weekend," *Austrian Times*, December 4, 2009, *www.austriantimes.at*.

FACT ATTACK: **Ancient civilization buys children to sacrifice!** The ancient Carthaginians of North Africa are best known for their penchant for sacrifice, specifically the practice of killing small children and infants. To avoid the nasty business of sacrificing their own children, wealthier families would often purchase children from others to sacrifice. *Should have just cut out the middleman and burned the money.*

> Malcolm W. Browne, "Relics of Carthage Show Brutality Amid the Good Life," *New York Times*, September 1, 1987, *www.nytimes.com*.
> "Cultures that Practiced Human Sacrifice," Discovery Channel, *http://science.discovery.com*.

FACT ATTACK: **Sympathetic tribal warriors shun death!** Warriors of the Toltec tribe used wooden swords in battle to avoid killing their enemies. *They didn't win very often, but everyone still got a trophy.*

> "320 Useless Facts that You Most Likely Didn't Know and Most Likely Won't Need to Know," UK Coalition, *www.ukcoalition.org.*

FACT ATTACK: **Tribal men marry infants!** The women of the Tiwi tribe in the South Pacific are married at birth. *If the husbands are also babies, I'm strangely okay with this.*

> Laura Schaefer, "25 Fascinating Love Facts," MSN.com, *http://lifestyle.msn.com.*

FACT ATTACK: **Nudists flock to Spain!** There are no laws against nudity in Spain, so technically one can walk around in the buff wherever one chooses. *Public nudity is awesome, until you realize the types of people who take advantage of it.*

> Damian Corrigan, "Is Nudism Legal in Spain and Where Can You Go Nude in the Country?" About.com, *http://gospain.about.com.*

FACT ATTACK: **Mountain men use cigarettes to tell time!** In the Andes, people often measure time by how long it takes to smoke a cigarette. *They briefly tried switching to marijuana, but nothing ever got done.*

> Mitchell Symons, *This Book: . . . of More Perfectly Useless Information* (HarperCollins, 2005).

FACT ATTACK: Man weds woman, receives unlimited booze! In some cultures it was common practice for the father of the bride to provide the husband with a large supply of mead (honey wine) during the month after the wedding. It is from this tradition that we get the common term of "honeymoon." *Replace mead with bourbon and sign me up.*

> Robert Gayre, *Wassail! In Mazers of Mead* (Brewers Publications, 1986), p. 22.

FACT ATTACK: Natives resort to vampirism to survive! In many parts of Kenya where meat is hard to come by, natives will often drink cow's blood mixed with milk as a renewable source of protein. The process does not injure the cow, and the natives get protein without the need to slaughter the animal. *Everybody wins! Except the cow.*

> Arkady Leokum and K. R. Hobbie, *The Little Giant Book of Weird & Wacky Facts* (Sterling Publishing, 2005).

FACT ATTACK: Men protect women from flying sewage! In sixteenth-century Europe, it was customary for men to walk closest to the street when traveling with a woman. This made him more likely to be hit with sewage that residents routinely tossed into the streets. *Wondering what killed chivalry? There's your answer.*

> Russell Ash, *Firefly's World of Facts* (Firefly Books, 2007).

FACT ATTACK: **Whipping a common punishment in United States!** Flogging, more commonly referred to as whipping, was an acceptable form of punishment in the United States until 1972, when Delaware became the last state to outlaw the practice. *Way to cave to peer pressure, Delaware.*

❯ Russell Ash, *Firefly's World of Facts* (Firefly Books, 2007).

FACT ATTACK: **Lions banned from West Virginia!** A law in Alderson, West Virginia, states that "No lions shall be allowed to run wild on the streets." *But what if they run nonchalantly?*

❯ Russell Ash, *Firefly's World of Facts* (Firefly Books, 2007).

FACT ATTACK: **France censors pig names!**

In France, it is illegal to name a pig Napoleon. *When visiting France, leave your copy of* Animal Farm *at home.*

❯ Russell Ash, *Firefly's World of Facts* (Firefly Books, 2007).

FACT ATTACK: Nose plugs protect tribal women from outsiders! Women of the Apatani tribe in Arunachal Pradesh, India, still wear plugs in their nostrils to make themselves appear ugly and undesirable to invaders. *I've seen pictures, the nose plugs aren't necessary.*

> Clifford Sawhney, *Strange But True Facts* (Pustak Mahal, 2004), p. 37.

FACT ATTACK: Women give birth in trees! When women in the Dumka district of Jharkhand, India, begin to feel labor pains, instead of going to the hospital they head to the nearest tree and start climbing. They give birth in trees to avoid rogue elephants which plague the area. *Suddenly Northern New Jersey ain't looking so bad.*

> Clifford Sawhney, *Strange But True Facts* (Pustak Mahal, 2004), p. 58.

FACT ATTACK: Jews more likely to jaywalk! An Israeli survey reported in *New Scientist* revealed that Orthodox Jews were three times more likely to jaywalk than other people. The researcher speculated it could be because religious people have less fear of death. *Or they are just better at dodging cars.*

> "100 Things We Didn't Know This Time Last Year," BBC News, December 30, 2005, *http://news.bbc.co.uk.*

FACT ATTACK: Little girls getting married! Nepal has one of the highest percentages of child marriage. More than 60 percent of Nepalese girls tie the knot before age eighteen, while 7 percent get married before age ten. *Not sure I'm prepared to make a joke about pedophilia.*

> "It's Complicated," National Geographic, *Taboo.* *http://channel.national geographic.com/series/taboo.*

FACT ATTACK: **Women sacrificed to stop volcano!** The people of Nicaragua once believed that the best way to stop a volcano from erupting was to throw beautiful young women into it. *Did they even try ugly ones first?*

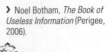

> Noel Botham, *The Book of Useless Information* (Perigee, 2006).

FACT ATTACK: **Romans invent biological dildo!**
Ancient Roman women reportedly inserted live snakes and fish into their vaginas to help them reach orgasm as the animals tried to wiggle their way out. *People still do that, but nowadays they pretend they tripped and fell on them when they wind up in the hospital.*

> Greta Garbage, *That's Disgusting!: An Adult Guide to What's Gross, Tasteless, Rude, Crude, and Lewd* (Ten Speed Press, 1999), p. 16.

FACT ATTACK: **World's laziest society revealed!** The Kalapalo tribe of Brazil are arguably the most relaxed society known to man. They spend more than half of their lives resting in hammocks. Adults sleep for an average of twelve hours a night and take several naps during the heat of the day. *Moving to Brazil. Who's coming with me?*

> Bruce Felton and Mark Fowler, *The Best, Worst, & Most Unusual: Noteworthy Achievements, Events, Feats & Blunders of Every Conceivable Kind* (Galahad, 1994).

EVEN CRAZIER PHENOMENA

THE WEIRDEST FACTS THE UNIVERSE HAS TO OFFER

FACT ATTACK: Tiny tot murders helpless woman! In 2010 a judge ruled that a four-year-old girl could be sued for negligence for striking an eighty-seven-year-old woman with her bicycle. The woman suffered a fractured hip and died several weeks later. *Not like she had much longer, anyway.*

> Alan Feuer, "Court: Girl, 4, Can Be Sued for Negligence," MSNBC, October 29, 2010, *www.msnbc.com.*

FACT ATTACK: Hairball prevents arsenic poisoning! Animal bezoars, condensed balls of hair, food, mucus, and vegetable fiber, can effectively prevent arsenic poisoning if dropped into a drink the individual believes may be poisoned. *Mostly because you won't drink it afterwards.*

> Francesca Gould, *Why You Shouldn't Eat Your Boogers and Other Useless or Gross Information About Your Body* (Tarcher, 2008).

FACT ATTACK: Incas bathe in pee! Before European colonization spread to Peru, the Incas washed their hair with urine to cure head lice. *It's not really a "cure" if it's worse than the malady.*

> The Sanders Family, *Gross News: Gross (but Clean) Stories from Around the World* (Andrews McMeel, 2006).

FACT ATTACK: Rotting corpses wash up in Big Easy! After the Hurricane Katrina disaster, the city of New Orleans became inundated with coffins. More than 130 above-ground coffins had been washed away by rising waters, with some winding up hanging in trees or washed up on the front lawns of residents. *If everyone agreed to be shot into space, we wouldn't have this problem. Aliens would.*

> The Sanders Family, *Gross News: Gross (but Clean) Stories from Around the World* (Andrews McMeel, 2006).

FACT ATTACK: **Burgler convicted because he couldn't hold it in!** A burgler in Elko, Nevada, was once convicted based on DNA evidence secured from urine he deposited on the snowy roof of the restaurant he was robbing. *That could have been anybody's.*

❯ The Sanders Family, *Gross News: Gross (but Clean) Stories from Around the World* (Andrews McMeel, 2006).

FACT ATTACK: **Royal government sets human body cap!** In the early days of human dissection, the British College of Surgeons was limited to six bodies per year. *They didn't say anything about conjoined twins. Wink!*

❯ The Sanders Family, *Gross News: Gross (but Clean) Stories from Around the World* (Andrews McMeel, 2006).

FACT ATTACK: **Doctor says it's okay to go nose mining!** Some doctors recommend eating one's own boogers. The dry residue found in the nose collects bacteria which, when ingested, can bolster the immune system. *Gross kid from first grade, I owe you an apology.*

❯ The Sanders Family, *Gross News: Gross (but Clean) Stories from Around the World* (Andrews McMeel, 2006).

FACT ATTACK: **Church adorns its walls with corpses!** The walls and pillars of the chapel at the St. Francis Monastery in Portugal are lined with human skulls and bones. *Everyone knows dead bodies make great insulation.*

> Sanjeev Garg, *501 Astonishing Facts* (Pustak Mahal, 2010).

FACT ATTACK: **Russian bears find morbid food supply!** When their food supplies dwindle, Russian bears have been known to dig up and eat human bodies buried in cemeteries. *In Russia, bear eats you!*

> Luke Harding, "Russian Bears Treat Graveyards As 'Giant Refrigerators,'" *The Guardian*, October 26, 2010, *www.guardian.co.uk.*

FACT ATTACK: **Inventor becomes his invention!** When the inventor of the modern Frisbee died, his ashes were molded into his trademark flying discs. *Well, this book has ruined yet another childhood pastime.*

> Barbara Seuling, *You Blink Twelve Times a Minute: and Other Freaky Facts About the Human Body* (Picture Window Books, 2008).

FACT ATTACK: Pope stages penis crusade! To protect sixteenth-century Catholics from wanton sexual imagery, Pope Paul IV affixed marble fig leaves over the genitalia of various statues within the Vatican. Later popes would continue this tradition, with some even going so far as to remove the genitalia entirely. *Which means that somewhere in the Vatican rests a box full of dicks.*

❭ Robin O'Lachian, "7 Priceless Works of Art Ruined by Staggering Acts of Idiocy," Cracked.com, September 30, 2010, *www.cracked.com.*

FACT ATTACK: Druids discover mystical plant! The Druids believed that mistletoe was a magical plant that could ward off evil spirits. *If by "spirits" they meant "pretty girls at parties," they were absolutely right.*

❭ H. G. Carlson, *Mysteries of the Unexplained* (Contemporary Books, 1994), p. 115.

FACT ATTACK: Singer worth more dead than alive! Several years after the singer's death, the wife of Sammy Davis Jr. faced bankruptcy. To track down some extra money, she exhumed the singer's body and recovered $70,000 worth of jewelry buried with him. *Which is why we should just bury people in newspaper.*

❭ Jamie Frater, *Listverse.com's Ultimate Book of Bizarre Lists: Fascinating Facts and Shocking Trivia on Movies, Music, Crime, Celebrities, History, and More* (Ulysses Press, 2010).

FACT ATTACK: Mistletoe origins anything but romantic! Mistletoe is an Anglo-Saxon word, which translates to "dung on a twig." *Which is how you feel when the ruse fails.*

❭ Bill McLain, *Do Fish Drink Water? Puzzling and Improbable Questions and Answers* (William Morrow, 1999), p. 95.

FACT ATTACK: **Assassins never settle for second best!** No one has ever assassinated an American vice president. *That's only because McCain lost.*

> Bill McLain, *Do Fish Drink Water? Puzzling and Improbable Questions and Answers* (William Morrow, 1999), p. 79.

FACT ATTACK: **Dead men can still vote!** If you vote by absentee ballet but die before election day, your vote still counts. *I feel as if it should count twice, because that would give rise to a new sport undertaken by the nominees: absentee hunting.*

> Erin Barret and Jack Mingo, *Random Acts of Factness: 1001 (or so) Absolutely True Tidbits About Everything* (Conari Press, 2005).

FACT ATTACK: **Sci-fi geeks mourn loss of ultimate weapon!** It is physically impossible to develop a lightsaber akin to those wielded by the characters in the popular *Star Wars* films. Light cannot be condensed into a physical form. *Maybe not here, but in a galaxy far, far away. . . .*

> Sherry Seethaler, *Curious Folks Ask: 162 Real Answers on Amazing Inventions, Fascinating Products, and Medical Mysteries* (FT Press, 2010).

FACT ATTACK: Vegas death ray attacks tourists!
Because of a flaw in the building's design, the Vdara Hotel in Las Vegas reflects light onto a section of its pool area in such a way that it melts plastic and has even burned several guests. The phenomenon can increase temperatures in the "death ray zone" by as much as twenty degrees Fahrenheit. *If that's the worst thing that happens to you in Vegas, consider yourself lucky.*

❯ Scott Mayerowitz, "Vegas Hotel Pool 'Death Ray" Burns Tourists," ABC News, September 28, 2010, http://abcnews.go.com.

FACT ATTACK: Philosopher's body still at large!
No one knows the location of Voltaire's body. It was stolen in the 1800s and has never been recovered. *It's definitely not buried underneath a tool shed in Somerville, MA.*

❯ Noel Botham, *The Book of Useless Information* (Perigee, 2006).

FACT ATTACK: **In space, nothing goes to waste!** When astronauts use the bathroom in space, solid waste is dried and dumped into the abyss. The water that's left over is saved. *I'd rather not know what for.*

❯ John Farndon, *1001 Facts on Space* (Miles Kelly Publishing, 2001).

FACT ATTACK: Criminal bribes his way to freedom!
While on trial for charges of bank robbery, Bert Winkler slipped the jury a note stating he would pay them each $1,000 if they acquitted him. He made good on his promise and awarded the judge $5,000, the bailiff $250, and gave $5 to each individual who attended his trial. The prosecuting attorney received a nickel for his troubles. *I'd have acquitted him for $50.*

❯ Sheryl Lindsell-Roberts, K. R. Hobbie, Ted LeValliant, and Marcel Theroux, *Wacky Laws, Weird Decisions, & Strange Statutes* (Sterling Publishing, 2004), p. 191.

FACT ATTACK: Freak occurrence claims two brothers!
In 1974, while seventen-year-old Neville Ebbin was riding his moped on a Bermuda street, a taxi struck and killed him. The following year, the same taxi carrying the same passenger struck and killed his seventeen-year-old brother on the same street, while he drove the same moped. *Bitch-slapped by the cold, uncaring backhand of fate.*

❯ Jacopo Della Quercia, "The 5 Most Mind-Blowing Coincidences of All Time," Cracked.com, October 11, 2010, *www.cracked.com.*

FACT ATTACK: Space rock hits woman!
Ann Elizabeth Hodges is the only human in recorded history to be struck by a meteorite. The cantaloupe-sized ball of space rock crashed through her home and struck her on the hand and hip. She suffered bruises from the impact, but was otherwise unharmed. *When I die, I hope it's caused by several meteorite-related wounds. That way my obituary can read, "Local Man Killed By Spaceballs."*

❯ Alan Bellows, *Alien Hand Syndrome and Other Too-Weird-To-Be-True Stories* (Workman Publishing, 2009), p. 112.

FACT ATTACK: Youth group defiles ancient art!
Mistaking ancient cave drawings for graffiti, a youth group in southern France did what any self-respecting cleanup crew would do—they attacked it with steel wool. They soon realized the mistake, but not before ruining 15,000-year-old art. *Because most graffiti looks just like ancient drawings of buffalo.*

❯ "French Youths Clean a Cave and Damage Prehistoric Art," *New York Times*, March 22, 1992, *www.nytimes.com.*

❯ Robin O'Lachian, "7 Priceless Works of Art Ruined by Staggering Acts of Idiocy," Cracked.com, September 30, 2010, *www.cracked.com.*

FACT ATTACK: **Artist destroys paintings in fit of rage!**

Impressionist painter Claude Monet was most well-known for his multiple paintings of water lilies. The plants in his art started out a natural green hue but transitioned to red as his eyes worsened. When he had surgery to correct his vision and realized the mistake, he destroyed the majority of his red lilies in a fit of rage. Luckily friends and family saved some of the paintings, which today remain some of his most famous. *Good thing he never realized they were also blurry.*

❯ Robin O'Lachian, "7 Priceless Works of Art Ruined by Staggering Acts of Idiocy," Cracked.com, September 30, 2010, *www.cracked.com.*

FACT ATTACK: **Governator spent time in prison!**

Arnold Schwarzenegger spent seven days in jail in the 1960s for going AWOL from the Austrian army. He left to compete in (and win) a bodybuilding contest. *Can we just elect him emperor of the universe already?*

❯ Dane Sherwood, Sandy Wood, and Kara Kovalchik, *The Pocket Idiot's Guide to Not So Useless Facts* (Penguin Group, 2006), p. 8.

FACT ATTACK: **Presidential assassination timed with script!**

Before he shot and killed President Lincoln, John Wilkes Booth waited in the shadows for an actor to deliver the line, "You sockdologizing old man-trap!" He knew this would cause the audience to roar with laughter, providing him with the cover he needed. *Can't wait to use that one on somebody.*

❯ Dane Sherwood, Sandy Wood, and Kara Kovalchik, *The Pocket Idiot's Guide to Not So Useless Facts* (Penguin Group, 2006), p. 10.

FACT ATTACK: Earthquake interrupts flow of Mother Nature! In 1812 an earthquake felt near the New Madrid Fault Line in Missouri was so strong that it caused parts of the Mississippi River to flow backwards. *Not sure how two parts of a river can flow in opposite directions, but I'm not a scientist.*

❯ Suzan Clarke, "Most U.S. States Have Earthquake Risk; Major Fault Lines," ABC News, January 18, 2010, *http://abcnews.go.com*.

FACT ATTACK: Business settles scores for you! For the bargain price of $20 plus shipping, the kind folks at ThePayback.com will deliver a dead fish to any unsuspecting enemies you might have. They will also send everything from dead flowers to melted chocolates. *For those times when you care enough to send the very worst.*

❯ "Dead Flowers, Fish and Other Paybacks," The Payback.com, *www.thepayback.com*.

❯ "Buck Wolf, Toilet Landing Lights . . . and Other Strange Valentine's Day Gifts," ABC News, *http://abcnews.go.com*.

FACT ATTACK: Florida home to world's most polluted beach! As of 2009, the Natural Resources Defense Council (NRDC) ranked Florida's Shired Island the most polluted beach in America. Ninety percent of samples taken failed inspection, and swimmers complain of everything from pinkeye and gastrointestinal discomfort to hepatitis and meningitis. *Somehow a "Swim at Your Own Risk" sign doesn't seem adequate.*

❯ Aefa Mulholland, "Deadliest Swim Vacations," AOL Travel News, May 18, 2010, *http://news.travel.aol.com*.

FACT ATTACK: **Airport makes travellers declare porn!** As of September 2009, visitors to Australia are required to declare any and all pornography they might have on their person upon arriving in the country. The measure is an attempt to curb the importation of illegal sexual material. *Well, looks like I'm leaving the laptop at home this summer.*

❯ "Strange Customs," The Economist, May 26, 2010, *www.economist.com.*

FACT ATTACK: **More bikes = less death!** Research has shown that tripling the number of bike riders on the street cuts motorist-bicyclist crashes in half. *I don't believe I need to point out that more bikers = less drivers = less accidents. But I will.*

❯ Mickey Z , "22 Weird & Somewhat Useful Bicycle Facts for Staying Green on 2 Wheels," Planetgreen.com, December 2, 2009, *http://planetgreen. discovery.com.*

FACT ATTACK: **Children forced to ride unicycles!** Unicycling is a mandatory subject at St. Helen's School in Newbury, OH. *I'd say it's more of a hobby than a subject.*

❯ Mickey Z , "22 Weird & Somewhat Useful Bicycle Facts for Staying Green on 2 Wheels," Planetgreen.com, December 2, 2009, *http://planetgreen. discovery.com.*

FACT ATTACK: **Adorable two-headed kitten monster ravages Ohio!** A two-faced kitten was born in Ohio in August of 2008 with two noses, two sets of eyes, and two mouths that meowed in unison. *It may have just been two kittens standing really close together though.*

❯ "Top 10 Animal Oddities," Animal Planet, *http://animal.discovery.com.*

FACT ATTACK: **Shoppers want ads in 3-D!**
Eighty percent of online shoppers claim
3-D advertisements would make them
more likely to purchase products. *Obviously
they failed to consider penis enlargement ads.*

❯ "USA Today Snapshots," *USA Today*, www.usatoday.com.

FACT ATTACK: **Drug causes yawngasms!** Some
patients who take the drug clomipramine to treat
depression experience an unusual side effect in the
form of yawn-induced orgasms. While rare, both
male and female patients experience the phenomenon. *Sounds awesome. Just never read* War and Peace *in
public.*

❯ John Schwartz, "Depression Drug's Side Effect Has Users Aroused," *The Washington Post*, November 7, 1995, www.washingtonpost.com.

FACT ATTACK: **Horse smarter than a fifth grader!** In the late
1800s, a German mathematics teacher stunned the world by
unveiling a horse named Hans that could perform complex
mathematics problems. By stamping his foot, Hans could
add, multiply, and even provide square roots. When scientists tested Hans's knowledge, they discovered that his abilities diminished the farther away the questioner stood. As it
turned out, Hans was reading the questioner's body language
and simply stopped stamping when he appeared satisfied with
his response. *For a horse, I'd say that's still pretty good.*

❯ Alan Bellows, *Alien Hand Syndrome and Other Too-Weird-To-Be-True Stories* (Workman Publishing, 2009), p. 44.

❯ Laura Schaefer, "25 Fascinating Love Facts," MSN.com, *http://lifestyle.msn.com.*

FACT ATTACK: **Dying in Parliament? Take it outside!** It is illegal to die inside the House of Parliament. *Luckily, if you break this law you will be somewhat out of their jurisdiction.*

❯ "UK Chooses 'Most Ludicrous Laws,'" BBC News, November 7 2007, *http://news.bbc.co.uk.*

FACT ATTACK: **Teen witch a math wiz!** Melissa Joan Hart, the actress who starred on *Sabrina the Teenage Witch*, can recite pi to 341 digits. *If she spent more time learning to act, and less time studying, she might still be relevant.*

❯ Kassidy Emmerson, "Little Known Facts about Melissa Joan Hart," Associated Content, October 5, 2007, *www.associatedcontent.com.*

FACT ATTACK: **Lawyer scams insurance company, self!** A North Carolina lawyer once took out an insurance policy for a box of expensive cigars to protect them in case of a fire. After consuming the box, he filed a claim stating the cigars had been lost in a series of small fires (read: he smoked them) and was awarded $15,000. Shortly after, his insurance company had him arrested for 24 counts of arson, using his own insurance policy as evidence. He was sentenced to two years in jail and a $24,000 fine. *He smart. Insurance company smarter.*

❯ Mitchell Symons, *This Book: . . . of More Perfectly Useless Information* (HarperCollins, 2005).

FACT ATTACK: **Pope has mad skillz!** In 2000, the Harlem Globetrotters basketball team made Pope John Paul II an honorary member of the squad. He was the seventh person to carry the prestigious title. *He honed his skills by passing sex-offending priests from parish to parish.*

❯ "Newest Harlem Globetrotter: The Pope," ABC News, November 30, 2000, http://abcnews.go.com.

FACT ATTACK: **Hitler's grave becomes a stage!** In 1958, actor Groucho Marx performed a two-minute Charleston on top of Hitler's grave for an audience of five. *And thus "getting served" was officially born.*

❯ "A Holocaust Survivor Dances at Auschwitz," *The Atlantic*, July 12, 2010, www.theatlantic.com.

FACT ATTACK: **Scientists solve diamond shortage with peanuts!** With the proper application of pressure, it is possible to convert peanut butter into diamonds. *The peanuts are now diamonds!*

❯ "Peanut Butter Diamonds on Display," BBC News, June 27, 2007, *http://news.bbc.co.uk.*

FACT ATTACK: **"Pond of Death" deemed harmless!** In April, 2005, reports poured in from Hamburg, Germany, of toads spontaneously exploding around the local lake, propelling their entrails up to three feet in the air. The lake was sealed off and locals dubbed it the "pond of death." Scientists later discovered the lake was harmless. The local crow population had been attacking the toads and removing their livers (the only edible portion of their anatomy). The toads filled themselves with air as a defense mechanism, but with a hole in their body and no liver, the pressure caused their blood vessels to rupture, resulting in the explosions. *I find it hard to feel bad for a creature whose best defense mechanism is to swallow air.*

❯ Francesca Gould, *Why Dogs Eat Poop & Other Useless or Gross Information About the Animal Kingdom* (Penguin Group, 2010), p. 107.

FACT ATTACK: **Prop body actually real corpse!** While shooting scenes for the popular TV show *The Six Million Dollar Man* at an amusement park in California, a production worker discovered human bones inside of a prop "hanging man" on the set. The remains were later identified as belonging to train robber Elmer McCurdy. *I guess he was [puts on sunglasses] just hanging around.*

❯ "True and Untrue Legends," ABC News. *http://abcnews.go.com.*

FACT ATTACK: Plant develops metal armor! Alpine pennycress, a plant indigenous to areas of Europe, accumulates metals in its leaves such as zinc, nickel, and cadmium from the mineral-rich soil. Scientists believe the metal armor protects it from certain bacteria. *Also handy against ninja attacks.*

> "Wildflower 'Armors' Itself Against Disease," Science Daily, September 14, 2010, *www.sciencedaily.com.*

FACT ATTACK: Farts are all around you! On average, you will inhale one liter of gas emitted from the anuses of other people every day. *I wish I could unknow that.*

> Ayami Chin, "Gross Facts You May Have Never Wanted to Know," Associated Content, May 24, 2007, *www.associatedcontent.com.*

FACT ATTACK: Soldiers only break step on bridges! Soldiers never march in step when crossing a bridge. They do this to prevent the vibrational frequency of their steps from causing the bridge to oscillate and collapse. *Even if it's not true, why risk it?*

> Clifford Sawhney, *Strange But True Facts* (Pustak Mahal, 2004), p. 77.

FACT ATTACK: Napoleon's penis worth thousands! During Napoleon's autopsy in 1821, his doctor kept the dictator's penis as a souvenir. The relic went on display in 1927 and is said to resemble a piece of leather. A New Jersey urologist purchased the penis in 1977 for $3,000 and his daughter inherited it. It could now be worth as much as $100,000. *If my penis is ever worth more than a cup of coffee, I'll be happy.*

> Christopher Shay, "Top 10 Famous Stolen Body Parts," *Time*, May 12, 2010.

FACT ATTACK: Ikea beds ideal location to conceive! It has been estimated that one in ten Europeans are conceived in an Ikea bed. *Future children, you will undoubtedly fall into this category. Good luck getting that image out of your heads.*

❯ "100 Things We Didn't Know This Time Last Year," BBC News, December 30, 2005, http://news.bbc.co.uk.

FACT ATTACK: Cat travels 1,500 miles! A two-year-old Persian cat named Sugar once traveled more than 100 miles per month for fourteen months to reach her family in Gage, Oklahoma, when they moved from Anderson, California, and left her behind. *Cue the song "The Cat Came Back."*

❯ David Wallechinsky, *The New Book of Lists: The Original Compendium of Curious Information* (Canongate U.S., 2005), p. 397.

FACT ATTACK: Men replace women with dolls! Every year, men throughout the world shell out as much as $6,500 for life-like female "real dolls" that serve as both physical and emotional companions. The concept inspired the 2007 film *Lars and the Real Girl* and also spawned an online community of so-called "iDollators," where men gather to share their experiences with their silicone companions. One of the most successful manufacturers of real dolls pulls in $2 million annually. *Yeah, but can they make you a sandwich?*

❯ "It's Complicated," National Geographic, *Taboo.* http://channel.nationalgeographic.com/series/taboo.

❯ Meghan Laslocky, "Just like a Woman," Salon.com, October 11, 2005, *www.salon.com.*

FACT ATTACK: Perfume contains whale spit! Ambergris is a foul-smelling substance created in the intestines of sperm whales. After the whale expels it, the substance floats to the surface where it ages and takes on a smell likened to tobacco, pine, or mulch. Depending on the quality, it can fetch thousands of dollars for use as an additive in perfumes. *That's right ladies, you're smearing yourselves with whale vomit.*

> Cynthia Graber, "Strange but True: Whale Waste Is Extremely Valuable," *Scientific American*, April 26, 2007, *www.scientificamerican.com.*

FACT ATTACK: **Motorcycle found in sewer!** The largest object ever removed from the Los Angeles city sewer system was a motorcycle. *Amy Winehouse was a close second.*

> Noel Botham, *The Book of Useless Information* (Perigee, 2006).

FACT ATTACK: Dinosaurs found in sewer! While working in a drainage sewer in Edmonton, Canada, workers stumbled upon a near perfectly preserved tooth belonging to an albertosauraus, a dinosaur similar to the tyrannosaurus rex. Workers also uncovered a limb bone, and continued to remove bones from the site. *A step up from their usual discoveries, I'd wager.*

> "Dinosaur Bones Found in Canadian Sewer Tunnel," BBC, August 23, 2010. *www.bbc.co.uk.*

FACT ATTACK: **Helium wells running dry!**
Experts warn that the world could run out of helium within twenty-five to thirty years at the current rate of consumption. *But how will I impress children at parties? How?!*

❯ Steve Connor, "Take a Deep Breath—Why the World Is Running out of Helium," *NZ Herald*, August 23, 2010, *www.nzherald.co.nz.*

FACT ATTACK: **Pirates beat terrorists by 200 years!** In July of 2010, construction workers discovered the remains of a thirty-foot-long wooden ship buried underneath the remains of the World Trade Center in New York City. Archaeologists estimated that the ship could have been stranded there for more than 200 years. *Pirates: the original terrorists.*

❯ David Dunlap, "18th-Century Ship Found at Trade Center Site," *New York Times*, July 14, 2010, *www.nytimes.com.*

FACT ATTACK: **Four-time lottery winner scams system?!** Joan Ginther has won the Texas Lottery on four separate occasions, winning more than $20 million during a period of seventeen years. Ginther refuses to speak about her winnings to the press, and some speculate that she may have discovered a way to beat the system. *If I figured it out, I'd keep it to myself too.*

❯ "Who Is the Lucky Four-Time Lottery Winner?" ABC News, *abcnews.go.com.*

FACT ATTACK: **Human ashes found in tattoo ink!**
When her twenty-year-old son passed away in 2007, Kim Mordue did as many mothers have before her and got a tattoo in honor of his memory. Instead of run-of-the-mill tattoo ink, however, Mordue opted for a more morbid medium—dye infused with the ashes of her deceased son. *I wonder which came first, the idea or his death.*

❯ "Mum Kim Mordue Uses Dead Son's Ashes in Tattoo," Metro.com, June 22, 2010. *www.metro.co.uk.*

FACT ATTACK: Dog sentenced to life for murder! A black Labrador retriever named Pep was sentenced to life in prison in 1924 after he killed a cat belonging to Governer Gifford Pinchot of Pennsylvania. Pinchot served as the judge in the case and there was no jury. Pep even received an inmate number: C2559. *He turned out okay though. He found Jesus, spent a lot of time lifting weights, and got the phrase "cat-killer" tattooed on his back.*

❯ Bart King and Chris Sabatino, "*The Big Book of Boy Stuff,*" (July 2004).

FACT ATTACK: Fireproof tree discovered! Redwood trees are resistant to fire. The trees rely on fire to enrich the soil which allows them to grow so tall. *I tested this fact. Let's just say I'm no longer welcome in California.*

❯ "50 Weird Science Tidbits," Science News Review. *www.sciencenewsreview.com.*

FACT ATTACK: Fear is enough to kill you! A sudden shock or a profound sense of dread can lead to heart failure or arrhythmia, literally scaring an individual to death. Scientists believe that the majority of cases involve those with pre-existing heart conditions, though the phenomenon can happen to anyone. *More reason to knock on your parent's bedroom door before entering.*

❯ Rich Maloof, "Freaky Facts About Death," MSN Health and Fitness. *health.msn.com.*

FACT ATTACK: Dead bodies spring back to life! Because of the rapid dehydration that occurs shortly after death, the mouth and eyes of the deceased will swiftly open if left unsecured—which can be very disconcerting for the living. To solve the problem, morticians close the mouth with wires stapled into the gums and seal the eyelids closed with Krazy Glue. *Which is why the dead make terrible ventriloquist dummies.*

❯ Rich Maloof, "Freaky Facts About Death," MSN Health and Fitness. *health.msn.com.*

FACT ATTACK: **Massive freight ship nearly sunk by pudding!** In August 1972, the twelve-ton Swiss freighter *Cassarate* caught fire while transporting cargo that included rubber, lumber, and 1,500 tons of tapioca pudding. The crew managed to contain the fire which smoldered for nearly a month, but they were forced to dock and unload their cargo when the tapioca started to cook and expand, stressing the steel-reinforced walls of the ship. *"Gentlemen, grab a spoon and eat like your life depends on it. Because it does!"*

> "Wishing They'd Saved Room for Dessert," *Pittsburgh Post-Gazette*, January 17, 2008. *www.post-gazette.com.*

FACT ATTACK: **King won't sit on porcelain throne alone!** King Louis the XIV preferred to have company while defecating in the royal bathrooms. The ruler was also quite fond of enemas, averaging one a day during the last year of his life. *I prefer reading on the can. And so do you, most likely.*

> Greta Garbage, *That's Disgusting!: An Adult Guide to What's Gross, Tasteless, Rude, Crude, and Lewd* (Ten Speed Press, 1999), p. 6.

FACT ATTACK: **Marilyn Monroe's corpse loses its boobs!** Shortly following the death of Marilyn Monroe, her breasts were mutilated by an unknown individual. A makeup artist created artificial breasts for her burial. *Like spitting in the face of God.*

> Greta Garbage, *That's Disgusting!: An Adult Guide to What's Gross, Tasteless, Rude, Crude, and Lewd* (Ten Speed Press, 1999), p. 23.

DAILY BENDER

Want Some More?

Hit up our humor blog, The Daily Bender, to get your fill of all things funny—be it subversive, odd, offbeat, or just plain mean. The Bender editors are there to get you through the day and on your way to happy hour. Whether we're linking to the latest video that made us laugh or calling out (or bullshit on) whatever's happening, we've got what you need for a good laugh.

If you like our book, you'll love our blog. (And if you hated it, "man up" and tell us why.) Visit The Daily Bender for a shot of humor that'll serve you until the bartender can.

Sign up for our newsletter at
www.adamsmedia.com/blog/humor
and download our Top Ten Maxims No Man Should Live Without.